Rape is always an exercise of power and control.

The RAPE OF CANOLA

Brewster Kneen

NC PRESS

Toronto, 1992

Cover Design: Tineke Jorritsma
Cover Photo: Brewster Kneen
Editing and Design: Cathleen Kneen

Canadian Cataloguing in Publication Data

Main entry under title:

The rape of canola

Includes bibliography and index.
ISBN 1-55021-066-1

1. Canola – Canada   2. Agricultural industries –
Canada – Foreign ownership.   I. Title.

SB299.R2K62 1992   332.6'73   C92-094992-4

We would like to thank the Ontario Arts Council, the Ontario Publishing
Centre, the Ontario Ministry of Culture and Communications, and the
Canada Council for their assistance in the production of this book.

New Canada Publications, a division of NC Press Limited,
Box 452, Station A, Toronto, Ontario, Canada, M5W 1H8.

Printed and bound in Canada

ACKNOWLEDGEMENTS

I have been most fortunate in the assistance I have received in the preparation of this book. If there is one person who provided critical evaluation and editing at the crucial moment, it is Rod MacRae of the Toronto Food Policy Council. As critical readers of portions of the book, I want to thank Wally Beversdorf, Bob Broeska, Keith Downey, and Frank Scott-Pearse, each of whom provided both comments and corrections. I also want to express my gratitude to the many people I interviewed in the course of researching this book. Without their generous cooperation the book would not have come to life.

I hope I have given all of these people credit where credit is due. I do not charge any of them with my own errors, biases or outlook.

A grant from the Social Sciences and Humanities Research Council helped finance the basic research. Credit for the title goes to Zack Gross of the Marquis Project in Brandon, Manitoba.

It is difficult, and inappropriate, to apportion gratitude as if it were a commodity. So I simply express my thanks to Cathleen, my partner, editor, critic, and support, for her many contributions to this book.

The Rape of Canola

The Social Construction of Canola, 1950-1992

CONTENTS

PREFACE

Unlike some social transformations, where the control of the state was siezed from the faltering hands of a dominant class, this revolution is being planned from boardrooms and government ministries. It is a revolution by and for corporate capital.   *Edward Yoxen*

Canola is the infant offspring – a mere 45 years old or so – of the ancient and complex Brassica family. Some of the more well-known, if not more illustrious, members of this family are broccoli, turnips, brussels sprouts, radishes, Chinese cabbage and the mustards. Canola's immediate forebear is oilseed rape, which itself has a known history of several millennia. Canola is, in fact, simply a variety of rapeseed with certain defined characteristics which earn it the current title of the world's healthiest vegetable oil.

Canola was developed in Canada as a means of ensuring a reliable domestic edible oilseed industry. Some of the impetus for this came from the disruptions to international trade caused by World War II, which made the Canadian edible oil refiners and manufacturers acutely aware of their dependence on imported oils and oilseeds. At the same time, western Canadian plant breeders were recognizing that Canada's extreme dependency on the production and export of wheat was unwise and were beginning to wonder about alternative crops. Farmers as well as plant breeders knew that rapeseed grew well on the Prairies, but that the crop enjoyed only a limited market, primarily as an industrial oil.

Although rapeseed oil has been in use for cooking and as lamp oil in China and India for 4000 years, its use as an edible oil in North America was questionable because of the large amount of animal and vegetable fats and oils consumed directly (as margarine, for example) or in baked goods. In addition, the meal left after crushing the seed to extract the oil was suitable only for fertilizer because it contained sulphur compounds that act as growth inhibitors, making it unsuitable for animal feed. It was this negligible value of the meal that made the oil, in the language of current ideology, "uncompetitive" with other edible oils, particularly soybean.

If rapeseed was to become an acceptable edible oil and thus a real alternative crop for Prairie agriculture, certain of its negative characteristics would have to be disposed of and other characteristics enhanced. Through scientific research and technological development, the necessary modifications were achieved and the transformed oilseed was given the name canola.

The transformation of rapeseed into canola, although an interesting and important story in itself, is also a paradigm of privatization. The very agenda of the seed – its genetic information – was transformed, re-programmed to promote private gain, not public good. This new agenda of the seed has been widely viewed by the agricultural research establishment as the result of natural evolution or technological progress rather than the deliberate project of special, sentient interests.

The development of rapeseed in the late 1950s and through the 60s and 70s was carried out almost totally in the public domain following a widely accepted model of scientific research and development. It was financed with public money and virtually all information, including genetic information in the form of the seed itself, flowed freely between participating parties, public and private. It was, by all accounts, very much a collective, public enterprise.

In the 1980s, after rapeseed had been transformed into canola, the research and development process began to undergo a metamorphosis. Research funding and the information it bought became increasingly private; canola varieties were hybridized and their characteristics and the processes used to achieve them were patented.

Concurrently, another phase in the transformation of rapeseed began, this time from a generic crop with certain characteristics into a specialty crop with specific corporate objectives programmed into the seed itself. Nature's drive to survive and reproduce was replaced, through conventional breeding and genetic engineering, by the corporate drive for marketable and profitable products.

This choice of development, and the enlistment of personnel and resources to carry it out, raise questions too little considered. But then one of the issues is precisely that this whole field has never been the subject of public debate or decision. The public has never been asked whether it wishes to continue to fund public research, or whether hybridization is to be preferred to the pursuit of diversity through open-pollinated varieties of canola. As the seed and its information have become privatized, so has the industry itself.

By 1991 the oilseed crushing industry in Canada was dominated by two foreign transnational corporations, Ferruzzi of Italy via its subsidiary Central Soya of the U.S.A., and Archer Daniels Midland (ADM) of the

U.S.A.; while the export market for the whole seed (roughly half of Canada's annual production) was controlled by five Japanese-based transnationals.

So the Cinderella Crop, as canola was affectionately nicknamed, turned from the darling of Prairie agriculture into an alternative crop with a dubious Canadian future. The public breeders who once worked for the farmers of Canada now work largely on contract for one or another transnational corporation transforming rapeseed once again, this time into a crop that can be grown wherever conditions are most favourable to those who now control the seed and its information (companies like Calgene, ICI, Senofi and Pioneer); or creating designer oils for corporations like Proctor & Gamble and Frito Lay. This is not what those early rapeseed researchers had in mind.

There are two marks of this transformation: privatization and the accumulation that marks the progress of capital. It is not that there have not been choices along the way, but that the purposes of progress and accumulation have been perceived to be best served by pursuing the course of development that is fast becoming embodied in canola.

The privatization of canola raises the question of Whose canola? and, indeed, Whose science? Who owns what we know – or can knowledge be owned? The rapid development of biotechnology and the deliberate engineering of novel life forms capable of reproducing themselves raises urgent questions about their regulation and about how we distinguish between process and product.

A few words on method

To understand what happened we need to understand the culture – the context of assumptions and outlook – out of which canola emerged. This is why I have chosen to let the story be told to a great extent in the words of the people directly involved. It is their words, and their memories, that reveal the operative culture and the context of meaning for the story of canola.

The interviews upon which much of the story is based would be better described as conversations. Just as there is a distinction between a science of discovery and a goal-directed science (or technology), there is a difference between a conversation of discovery and an interview seeking answers to pre-determined questions. The problem always is, what are the right questions? I initiated most interviews with an invitational question, such as, How did you get into this? or, When did your company start working on canola? I wanted to hear what they remembered and consider important.

I make no pretence of offering a "factual" history, since I do not believe such a thing is possible. Every event and experience in our lives – every text – has a context that shapes or delivers it and through which it is perceived. What is remembered may well be shaped by a different context, such as the one the next day or the next year, or back home.

It is also that we experience life in particular. We relate to or confront transnational corporations not in general, but in the person of our neighbour or in the name on the package we purchase – or choose not to purchase. In the same way, people reveal their assumptions, their values and their culture in the words they use as they speak about *their experience*.

Toronto
November, 1992

Chapter 1

LOADING THE PROGRAM

People have to eat, and rapeseed oil, bad as it was, was the one crop that farmers out west here could grow, so we knew we could produce the stuff. So then it was just a matter of seeing, if it was at all possible, if we could modify that oil so that it could enter the market. . .

This rapeseed thing was a gamble for quite a few years. . . At that time the division operated independently. We could work on any research we wanted to work on, as long as it was essentially directed in the agricultural line.

Burton Craig

The Seed

The story of the transformation of rapeseed into canola is an expression of a larger story about the transformation of the practice of science over the past four decades or so. It is also a story about privatization and control. What has happened to rapeseed is what has happened to agricultural research in particular and the food system in general. The rhetoric continues to refer to feeding the hungry; but feeding people has become essentially a by-product of marketing commodities for corporate profit.

The story of canola provides an unusual opportunity to study this transformation in that it has a distinct and available history: nearly everyone who was involved in the beginning of the process in the 1950s is still alive. It is within the span of their working lives that the structure and ownership of agricultural research in Canada has undergone a profound transformation from public to private, from an existential speculative or "discovery" model (a model of "tinkering" or invention) to a teleological (end-oriented) model of corporately directed product development.

This whole process could also be described as the production of uniformity (monoculture) and predictability (manageability).

One of the earliest discoveries of the people who started working on rapeseed was the tremendous variability in the seed. While it might all look identical, or might all be yellow or black, they discovered that the internal characteristics of the seed, that is, the genetic information expressed in the characteristics of the oil or the meal, varied widely, to say nothing of widely differing agronomic characteristics. A seed that might require spring seeding in one geography, for example, might also thrive as a winter crop in another place.

Initially the breeders did what they were trained to do; they concentrated their efforts on the selection of seed for specific agronomic and/or oil processing characteristics. This was essentially a laborious process of screening and testing for desired characteristics, reproducing the best examples of what was considered desirable, and then engaging in traditional crossing to further "improve" the plant.

When it turned out that there was one single variety of seed with the desired characteristics, it became the genetic base of all subsequent breeding work. This involved a process of selecting a very few seeds out of thousands, thus significantly narrowing the genetic base, and then very slowly expanding the genetic diversity on the base of those few seeds by incorporating that characteristic, through traditional crossing and backcrossing, into other varieties with other desirable characteristics. In other words, the natural diversity of the seed was replaced with uniformity around a particular characteristic, and then diversity gradually reintroduced. I describe this process as the deliberate production of monoculture.

In the ideal monoculture system, the seeds of any particular crop are uniform externally and internally. This can be achieved with both highly selected open-pollinated varieties or, more reliably, with hybrids. The seeds are planted in straight rows at uniform depth on ground as free of any plant or insect "competitors" as possible and subsequently protected from their environment and its hazards by a variety of externally obtained hydrocarbon-based "crop protection agents". As they grow, the crops are of uniform height and every plant in a single field matures on the same day. They are grown to market specifications, and their price hedged on the commodity exchange (futures market). At some point, the crop is sold at a "competitive" price regardless of the costs of its production. It is a commodity: its disposition has little or nothing to do with where it is grown or at what cost or with what effect on the land or on the people where it is grown.

Once the crop has been transformed into a commodity, it no longer has any intrinsic relationship to being a food. Its consumption is merely a disposal process to make way for more product.

Agricultural organizations in North America replicate the structure of monoculture, being composed uniformly, if not entirely, of white males of European origin. The organizations follow commodity lines, in straight rows, the most powerful being those of the highest-priced and most intensively produced crops: corn and soybeans. If a farm is growing more than one monoculture crop, then the farmer has to belong to more than one competing commodity group. Rapeseed, in becoming canola, became one of these high-priced commodities, and its status as a commodity came to be articulated by the Canola Council of Canada. The Council is responsible for the development and marketing of the crop, not for the nutritional status of the public. (See Chapter 2.)

If one looks more closely at the structure of the industry, one will find that its purpose becomes even more removed from meeting human needs, whether those of hungry people or of farmers trying to make a living. So plant breeder Kees Kennema of King Agro may have told his neighbours in 1990 that Listowell, Ontario, was going to become the canola-seed capital of North America, but unfortunately, as a result of the privatization process, it is the bottom line of Elf Aquitane that will be the final arbiter and, quite possibly, sole beneficiary. King Agro, you see, is owned by Senofi which is owned by energy giant Elf Aquitane of France. Their business is profit, not the welfare of a small piece of Ontario or the people of Canada. The seed is only a means to an end. Of course, it has always been the case, at least from a human perspective, that the seed is a means to an end; but historically that end has been the provision of food for the population growing the plants and harvesting the seed, not the year-end results reported to the corporate shareholders.

It may seem far-fetched to compare plant breeding with the development of a racing car, but when a single company is involved in both enterprises, perhaps we ought to think twice. Elf Aquitaine is working with Renault to develop a way to make fuels burn more quickly in order to provide more power in an engine of a certain size.

> When the engines in racing cars are working flat out, their speeds can be as high as 14,000 r.p.m. . . . In its pursuit of faster engine speeds to produce more power, Renault and Elf, the French oil company, have been trying to reduce combustion times in the cylinders.[1]

The effort to make a seed perform better and better within the same basic genetic context partakes of the same mentality: trying to increase production by optimizing circumstances. The problem is that production of the crop becomes an increasingly fragile, or dependent, process.

The story of the development of canola also provides a dramatic account of the privatization of information: the genetic information of the seed as well as the corporate information about the seed and the seed business itself. Control over the information of the seed, whether the internal genetic information, the external information about producing the seed, or the "ownership" of the product of that information, raises difficult questions about the distinctions made between process and product, whether for purposes of regulation or ownership itself. (I explore these issues in Chapters 11-13.)

The first phase of rapeseed breeding in Canada began in the 1940s as a search for plants, and plant populations, that exhibited desired agronomic and oil processing qualities. At that stage the meal was considered a useless byproduct, at least in Canada.

In the second phase, which began in the 60s with the discovery of the variability in the chemical composition of both oil and meal, the exercise of plant breeding science became a search for the genetic material – the genetic information – that would produce certain desired characteristics, namely low erucic acid content in the oil and low glucosinolate levels in the meal.

The quest for seed that would yield low, or no, erucic acid in its oil led first to a selection out of the *B.napus* variety Liho, a German forage rape variety. "Selection within Liho produced the first plants that had zero erucic acid. In the *B.campestris* species the low erucic acid gene was found within the landrace 'Polish' through selection and inbreeding", according to breeder Keith Downey, who believes that, "this was a unique source of the gene. All present varieties of both *B.napus* and *B.campestris* derive their low erucic genes from these two original sources."[2] No other low-erucic *B.campestris* seed source has ever been identified.

This *B.napus* seed has often been referred to as "Argentine" because, according to Downey, the seed was introduced into Canada in 1940-41 when a bag of it was found on a wharf in Argentina and brought to Canada. It was probably of European origin and never grown in Argentina.

Because of the extent of natural genetic variability in rapeseed, even among seeds from the same plant or even the same pod, it was obviously necessary to be able to select a single seed with the desired characteristics and reproduce it. But to do this, one had to be able to analyze the seed characteristics and then reproduce the same seed – an apparent impossibility, at least until Downey came up with his half-seed technique.

It is technically possible to propagate rapeseed from only one half of the embryo, or seed, because it is a dicotyledon, meaning that it has two leaf-like cotyledons each of which contain the genetic material required to produce a whole plant. The trick which Downey had to master was cutting the seed so that one cotyledon (or parts of both cotyledons) could be removed without damaging the root and growing tip. Once the seed was carefully cut in half, the oil from one half could be analyzed and the other half grown out if it seemed desirable.

Downey's scientific work, itself based on his half-seed technique (which used the simple technology of an eye-surgeon's scalpel), was dependent on a more complex technology. The analysis of a half-seed's worth of oil only became possible when the analytical technology of Gas Liquid Chromatography became available to him. Prior to this, it took two pounds of oil and two weeks, rather than one half-seed and 15 minutes, to obtain an analysis.

It was not by accident that this technological development took place concurrently with the breeding work. Because of the open environment in which the research was taking place and the cooperative culture that pervaded the public research establishment, the whole project was really a team effort, and it was another member of the team, Burton Craig, who was working on the analytical technology to complement Downey's breeding work.

In this cooperative culture, information moved freely amongst all those working on the project, including the genetic information in the form of the seed. Yet at the same time, the genetic information base itself was being reduced by selection for specific traits. When it took two pounds of seed to achieve an analysis, genetic diversity was both inevitable and protected because it took so many plants to produce the seed yielding that much oil. The new analytical technology made it possible to select just one seed as the source of a specific characteristic, reducing the genetic information base in the process.

In recent years, of course, the movement of information has itself followed this same pattern, becoming narrower and narrower as plants are bred or engineered to the tighter and tighter specifications demanded by the corporate sponsors of the research. As the information base has narrowed, so has the movement of that information, concluding with the development of hybrids on the one hand and patented varieties and genetic characteristics on the other.

In the case of canola the science of genetics was enhanced by the development of an analytical technology which was itself based on certain scientific insights and goals. The breeding could have proceeded without the technology, but its results would surely have been different since the work would have been done with whole plant populations over a much longer time period. This would have permitted the functioning of the dialectical relationship between organism – in this case plant – and environment that is characteristic of natural evolution.

Just as one can never be sure when a mutation might "spontaneously" occur and an organism veer off in an unpredicted direction, one cannot be sure that the course chosen for the development of canola was the only way to reach the stated objectives. There might well be other ways and surprising mutations, but once the enterprise has been consolidated in the hands of interests with a large amount of capital at stake, alternatives are more likely to be excluded than explored. The longer the process continues, the more certain this will be. The results are then not more scientific, just better financed, supported and disseminated – or "marketed" in current jargon. (Bruno Latour explores this issue in compelling detail in his book *Science in Action*.)

Nevertheless, today, nearly twenty years after the first double-low (low erucic acid, low glucosinolate) rapeseed began to be commercially grown as canola, one of the early co-operants in the whole enterprise is still, quite unnoticed, pursuing a different route to the same end. In a lab in Toronto a processing technology has been created which can transform the old rapeseed into a high quality edible oil and a high protein meal (or protein isolates) suitable for food and feed purposes. Although this process awaits commercial application and analysis of its economic feasibility, it does suggest that there is always more than one way to do anything.

Processing and Utilization

Oilseed processing has traditionally been referred to as crushing, a term which describes the primary process of crushing the seed, one way or another, to squeeze the oil out of the fibre, which becomes the meal.

"Processing" and "crushing" are used more or less interchangeably, though "extraction" might now be a more technically correct term. The goal in processing rapeseed and subsequently canola seed is simply to get the most oil of the highest quality from the seed.

The second stage of processing is refining, which means clarifying and stabilizing the oil by extracting what would otherwise appear as residue in the oil (oxidants). The refining process is now often integrated with the crushing, but in the early years the two processes were quite separate.

There are, of course, two products of the crushing process for any oilseed: the oil, and the meal, or cake, composed essentially of fibre and protein. Rapeseed meal has never been used for human consumption, and it has always been known to have negative effects on animal health (actually because of its negative effects on the thyroid). Consequently it has traditionally been used as a fertilizer, whereas the meal left from flax, sunflowers or soybeans can be used as a valuable protein supplement in animal feed.

The crushing industry evolved sporadically, with a number of plants scattered around the growing regions. Most of them were sustained not by the returns on crushing canola alone, but also crushing other oilseeds when possible, and by federal or provincial government support of one sort or another. Of course one of the contributing factors to the poor economics of rapeseed crushing was the worthlessness of the meal in the Prairie context.

While rapeseed meal has always been used as a fertilizer, particularly for citrus trees in Japan and China, its value depends on the crushing mill being close to where the meal can be utilized readily. Traditionally the farmer would bring his or her rapeseed to the mill for crushing and return home with the meal to be used as fertilizer and with enough oil for family use; the rest was sold in the village. Centralization of processing may create certain efficiencies, but it destroys others, and the industrial scale of Prairie oilseed production renders the use of the meal as fertilizer impractical.

The structure of the crushing industry changed very suddenly around 1990 through a series of events that had its direct parallel in what was happening in canola breeding: the industry was taken over by very large foreign-based transnational corporations. These changes in the control of the canola industry were, again, never the subject of public or political discussion, nor were there any public studies as to their economic or environmental impact to determine if this radical shift in control was desirable or beneficial, or to whom. Given the political environment of the late 1980s and early 90s, this is hardly surprising. These are the days, after all, of the invisible corporate sector and a public ideology that allows governments to become simply the agents of transnational capital.

Statistics

Canadian canola production - details on page 15

	1981	1991
area	1.40m ha	3.27m ha
yield	1320 kg/ha	1320 kg/ha
production	1.85m t	4.30m t.
crushed	1.00m t.	1.44m t.
exports(seed)	1.37m t.	1.88m t.(1.84 to Japan, about 95% of its requirements)

(Canada Grains Council, Statistical Handbook '91)

Canola oil accounts for 60% of the total Canadian domestic production of deodorized oils which accounts for
    80% of all salad oils,
    54% of shortenings, and
    40% of the margarine.

The major oilseeds produced around the world are:
soybeans	50% of world production
cottonseed	15%
rapeseed	10%
sunflower	10%
peanuts	10%

Rapeseed/canola is the world's third largest oilseed crop with 43 million acres.   *(AgBiotechnology News, 11-12/91)*

Rapeseed/canola production, 1991/2 crop year (August-July)

Country	tonnes produced	hectares used
China	7.30 million	6.13 million
India	5.80 m.	6.10 m.
Canada	4.30 m.	3.27 m.
EC-12	7.20 m.	2.42 m.
East Europe	1.65 m.	0.71 m.
USA	0.08 m.	0.06 m.
Sweden	0.25 m.	0.15 m.
world	28.09 m.	20.34 m.

(Oil World Annual Review 4/92)

China: 1981: 3.8-m ha. cultivated yielding 4-m tonnes
              1991: 5.85-m ha. cultivated yielding 7.5-m tonnes
Average yield is 1.3t/ha., with range of several hundred kg to 1.8-2.0t/ha.
Rapeseed ranks fifth after rice, wheat, maize and cotton in importance.
Edible vegetable oil consumption is 4-5 kg/person/year.

(International Development Research Centre)

USA: 1991-2 canola production: 84,000 t. canola oil, 150,000 acres

        1986-7 consumption: 83,000 t. canola oil
        1991-2 consumption: 327,000 t. canola oil   *(Oilseeds, 5/92)*

Total U.S. consumption of edible oils is approximately 13.5 billion pounds (6.14-b kg) per year, with canola oil supplying only 725 million pounds (329-m kg of the total). It is estimated that in 1991 only 90,000 acres of winter canola were planted, while it would take 975,000 acres to meet domestic demand.   *(Calgene 1992 prospectus)*

In 1982 there were just six canola cultivars grown in the world, all bred in Canada. In 1992 there are over 100 canola cultivars, bred and grown all over the world. In 1982 there were only three canola breeding programs in the world, all of them in Canada. In 1992 there are more than 50 canola breeding programs around the world. *(McVetty, 1992)*

Area, Production and Disposition of Canola/Rapeseed

Area in thousands of hectares, Production etc. in thousands of tonnes

	Area	Production	Exports	Domestic Crush
1943/44	1.3	1.0		
1944/45	4.4	2.8		
1945/46	5.1	3.8		
1946/47	9.5	5.9		
1947/48	23.6	9.9		
1948/49	32.4	29.0		
1949/50	8.1	7.7		
1950/51	.2	.1		
1951/52	2.6	2.7		
1952/53	7.5	6.3		
1953/54	11.9	11.1		
1954/55	16.1	13.1		
1955/56	55.8	35.4		
1956/57	142.4	136.0	83.1	
1957/58	249.8	196.4	144.0	
1958/59	253.3	176.0	129.7	17.3
1959/60	86.5	80.8	65.3	5.1
1960/61	308.8	252.2	70.1	21.8
1961/62	287.5	254.5	156.9	29.8
1962/63	150.2	132.9	129.5	36.6
1963/64	193.4	189.5	120.4	35.7
1964/65	320.1	300.0	210.4	48.9
1965/66	580.7	512.6	309.1	84.9
1966/67	617.1	585.1	313.3	112.5
1967/68	661.7	563.6	279.1	117.0
1968/69	427.3	441.4	324.5	157.2
1969/70	818.2	760.3	503.7	176.1
1970/71	1,648.7	1,646.5	1,061.5	194.4
1971/72	2,161.4	2,165.9	966.1	273.2
1972/73	1,342.7	1,317.7	1,226.0	353.2
1973/74	1,297.1	1,223.7	888.7	334.4
1974/75	1,278.8	1,163.5	593.0	276.0

continued next page

Area, Production and Disposition of Canola/Rapeseed

Area in thousands of hectares, Production etc. in thousands of tonnes

	Area	Production	Exports	Domestic Crush
1975/76	1,829.2	1,839.2	683.2	347.2
1976/77	719.5	836.9	1,017.9	549.7
1977/78	1,452.8	1,973.1	1,013.6	630.3
1978/79	2,824.6	3,497.1	1,720.3	725.1
1979/80	3,407.5	3,411.1	1,742.6	897.3
1980/81	2,080.1	2,483.4	1,372.1	1,003.3
1981/82	1,401.4	1,848.5	1,359.3	945.4
1982/83	1,768.5	2,218.1	1,271.3	904.1
1983/84	2,313.9	2,593.3	1,497.6	1,159.3
1984/85	3,071.3	3,411.9	1,456.0	1,290.4
1985/86	2,783.3	3,497.9	1,456.0	1,211.1
1986/87	2,640.1	3,786.4	2,126.0	1,551.6
1987/88	2,670.7	3,846.2	1,749.7	1,607.5
1988/89	3,671.8	4,288.0	1,948.6	1,361.7
1989/90	2,903.6	3,095.8	2,047.8	1,228.5
1990/91	2,581.6	3,281.1	1,887.7	1,441.2
1991/92	3,140.5	4,144.8		

Note: export statistics for the years prior to 1956/57 and crush statistics for the years prior to 1958/59 are unavailable.

(Courtesy of Canadian Oilseed Processors Association, 7/92)

1976-91: The number of growers varies widely from year to year, with a low of 20,000 in 1976 to a high of 58,000 in 1979, and 44,000 in 1991.

Chapter 2

INDUSTRY STRUCTURE: THE CANOLA COUNCIL

The Canola Council of Canada is a non-profit commercial association representing all sectors of the Canadian canola industry. The Council was established under the name of its forerunner, the Rapeseed Association of Canada, in 1967. In 1980 its name was changed to acknowledge the development and acceptance of canola varieties.[3]

It's no simple task to represent all sectors of the production process of even a single crop like canola, including researchers, growers, handlers, crushers, exporters, refiners and feed manufacturers, but at least in the beginning they were all Canadian and they all needed each other: public and private, corporate and cooperative. By the late 1980s, however, the Council began to show the effects of both the subtle and the obvious changes that have taken place as canola has been restructured, from seed to retail bottle, from farm to corporate boardroom.

The first "double-low", canola-quality rapeseed was not to come on the market until 1974, but with the establishment of the Rapeseed Association in 1967 the Federal Government had given its official public support to the industry by setting up the Rapeseed Utilization Assistance Program, funded by the Federal Department of Industry, Trade and Commerce and administered by the Council, "to foster the team approach to solutions of problems in the rapeseed industry."[4]

It is easy to forget, from the present perspective, what the context of the original Rapeseed Association was, and thus who its members logically were. Oilseed crushing was an infant industry and entirely in Canadian hands. The major player was Canada Packers, although the Saskatchewan Wheat Pool's Industrial Division in Saskatoon and Western Canadian Oilseed Processors (now Canbra Foods) at Lethbridge also worked closely with the Rapeseed Association in developing the industry. Seed breeding and production were also completely in Canadian hands at public institutions such as the Agriculture Canada lab at Saskatoon and the University of Manitoba. The only significant foreign presence was the Japanese buyers of the seed. It is not surprising, then, that there was a congruence of interests and that the Council itself could fairly represent the whole industry engaged in a common project, though with different perspectives.

Mac Runciman, the first president of the Rapeseed Association, presented his reflections on the 25th anniversary of the association: "There were a few growing pains because the group was bringing together people who had never worked together before. For the first time, crushers heard producers' laments and producers learned how the product they grew was marketed."[5]

The sectors represented in the Council now may be the same, but the interests have certainly changed, with most of the significant players being foreign corporations. Now the Council faces questions such as: How are the interests of Mitsubishi to be harmonized with those of Proctor & Gamble as represented by Allelix/Pioneer Hi-Bred? Are the interests of ICI in canola breeding and seed production really the same as those of the Agriculture Canada Research Station in Saskatoon? Does Archer Daniels Midland care what happens to the canola growers in Alberta?

When the Rapeseed Association was established in 1967, its first objective was "trade development programs. . . to ensure that Canadian rapeseed growers will have an expanding market for their crops." The second was to "encourage research work in the field of plant breeding and animal feeding and become involved in programs relating to continued improvement in the quality of rapeseed."[6] In line with this second objective, when the funds for the Rapeseed Utilization Assistance Program (RUAP) became available, "priorities for the work undertaken with these funds were established by the Research and Technical committees of the Association in consultation with scientists and researchers in government departments. The bulk of the work was carried out in universities across Canada."[7]

We have become so accustomed to hearing words like "trade development" and "improvement" that it is easy to let them slip by unnoticed. When considering the growth of an industry, however, these words, and others like them, can give us an indication of the context of that industry's development. In this case, the Council was to develop "trade", but since the kind of trade is not specified, it is probably safe to assume that it is exporting that was intended, not the satisfaction of the domestic market, since this is usually referred to as "market" or, more likely at the time, "sales." In other words, industry development was to be directed toward export.

The second objective of the Council was to encourage and support research in seed "improvement", meal utilization, and oil quality. The emphasis has been on increasing overall productivity by increasing yields, reducing disease problems, increasing the amount of land that can be used to grow canola successfully, and so on – the standard industrial agriculture agenda. In recent years the Council has also run farm-scale production trials at a variety of locations scattered around the canola-growing regions of the Prairies. The emphasis has been on production practices as well as variety comparisons, including hybrids.

While there is no reason to be overly critical of any of these objectives by themselves, one can wonder at the absence of nutritional studies, studies in ecological or sustainable production (that is, of canola production as part of a farming system), and studies in global oil production and utilization.

The priorities, as described above, to be met by the Canola Utilization Assistance Program (CUAP) are established by the Canola Research Priorities Committee. The CUAP is funded by the federal government through Agriculture Canada to the extent, in 1991-2, of $400,000, while the Canola Varietal Development Program (CVDP) and the agronomic research programs of the Canola Council are funded by the council out of its own budget. These priorities have to address and reconcile the needs of producers, processors and export customers.

As Eileen MacGregor, then on the Council staff, put it, the Canola Council is a very democratic organization which does the things everybody can agree to for the good of the entire industry, while balancing the various needs and interests as best they can. As a result, there are few areas where one little group can come in and lobby for something in particular. If a group has something in particular that it wants to have done and it can't get the support of everyone else, then it is free to do it for themselves.

While most of the Council-sponsored research has been in traditional breeding, there has been some support of work on hybrids, which, in MacGregor's view, would "have a lot greater yield and be more commercially viable." At the same time, she believed the public institutions would stick to traditional breeding. It would be the private companies that would go for the hybrids because they could get more money from them: "They are going to take a little bit of risk, but *they want a guaranteed return, and they want control.*"[emphasis added][8]

MacGregor's assumption that hybrids would be "a lot more productive" reflects the bias that has dominated both public and private plant science. Yet there have always been other opinions held, particularly by people working in the public domain. J. K. Daun, head of oilseeds chemistry at the Canadian Grain Commission, told me in 1990 that, "It is quite possible that the same level of performance could be achieved in open-pollinated varieties." Daun emphasized that there is pressure to apply a technology, like hybridization, with a specific objective in mind. "If you don't achieve that objective then you have not succeeded, which is not really science."[9] W.C. Beversdorf, of the University of Guelph, discussed this same problem with me two years later:

> Sometimes I think it is not the scientific question you ask but rather the tool you are employing that determines whether or not you get funded, which is illogical. It should be the question you are asking and maybe the approach you are taking to answer it, which may include the tools you will use, but it seems like we go through phases where you have to be using this tool if you want funding, and then two years later we go through another phase where you have to use some new tool. The tool becomes more important than the question.[10]

The Canola Council does not share Daun's or Beversdorf's scepticism. In a 1992 booklet the Canola Council accentuates a much more goal-oriented or teleological approach which, in the current ideological climate, is probably considered by some as more "competitive" and businesslike:

> Adding to the bright future of canola is biotechnology which identifies and incorporates specific plant genes into canola lines to address situations such as herbicide and insect resistance. Hybrid development is ever increasing with the assumption that canola hybrids will significantly out-yield pureline varieties and offer the possibility for specific crosses adapted to regional growing areas.[11]

Speaking about the supposed common interests of all the participants in the canola industry, Daun commented that, "it has become more factionalized in the last three years. There is a crushing faction and a farm faction, each with their own needs and ends, and they do not mesh. It is reflected in the Canola Council."[12]

There is another interpretation that can be given to the structure and functioning of the Canola Council in particular and the canola industry in general. We have noted that the rationale of the earliest work on rapeseed was the search for another crop in order to diversify Prairie agriculture. If, however, diversification was the intent, then the subsequent structuring of the industry, and of the Canola Council itself, contradicts that intent: it places canola, not within a mix of agricultural enterprises in a holistic approach to the farm, but as a single commodity in isolation. The welfare of the canola industry, from seed breeder to crusher, is then pursued in a fashion that makes it a competitor with other crops, both domestic and in the global marketplace, rather than as one aspect of an integrated ecological system of farming. (This is particularly strange when one pauses to recognize that canola requires a four-year rotation.)

Such a specialized monoculture approach was not without precedent, for canola came along at a time when agriculture was specializing and being organized along commodity lines rather than on an integrated basis. Commodity organizations were becoming the voice of the farmer to the ears of government. Commodity organizations also served the interests of capital far more effectively than general farm organizations, by creating a competitive environment between commodities that stressed a reductionist emphasis on production as measured almost exclusively by yield. This created an ideal climate for the sale of agro-toxins, fertilizers, and farm machinery. Specialization also gave a great push to increasing farm size in order to rationalize the capital investment. As commodity organizations became conveniently single-minded they added another push to the vicious circle of growing specialization, capital intensification, and size.

Commodity programs really began in the U.S. during the depression. Parity pricing, floor prices and credit programs were the New Deal response to the rising tide of agrarian radicalism. Subsequently, as rural sociologist Fred Buttel explains, "commodity programs . . . played a major role in underwriting post-war capital accumulation and technological change in agriculture in a potentially unstable milieu of excess capacity and volatile world market prices. . . "

> Commodity program legislation [in the United States] con-trib-uted to the formation of large commodity associations whose major role came to be that of advancing the cause of producers of specific commodities. . . As farm programs and technological change led to increased concentration, larger farms, and greater specialization, the role of commodity groups as the focal point of farmer representation in the political process was progressively strengthened at the expense of general farm organizations.[13]

In a 1989 article on the canola industry, *Forbes* magazine inadvertently provided an acute description of the U.S. Canola Association and the interests it represents:

> The U.S. Canola Association was born in May, 1989, with seed money from businesses like Proctor and Gamble, Archer Daniels Midland, Cargill, Central Soya and Calgene. By August the canola

people had gotten the law changed so that a farmer could plant canola on some of his wheat (or other subsidized crop) acres without shrinking his subsidized base for next year. In May Archer Daniels Midland opened a canola crushing plant and Cargill bought Canola Inc., a seed company. In August a joint venture of Central Soya and Calgene opened another crushing plant.[14]

While it may appear that the farmer achieved some planting flexibility as a result of corporate lobbying, the real result was that the processors, all very large transnational corporations, could count on a large enough supply of canola to justify their further investment in the industry. (See Chapter 7 for a closer look at the crushing industry.)

Little effort, then, goes into either research or development of the crop as one player in a balanced, diverse and integrated farming system.

Instead, the production of canola becomes one aspect of a vertically integrated production system. Integrating canola into a diversified farming system remains the challenge of the individual farmer; there are no research studies on canola as part of a sustainable or organic production pattern.

In other words, while organizations like the Canola Council may (or may not) be models of cooperation among different players in the production chain of a single crop, they are, at the same time, obstacles to the development of an ecological approach to agriculture and a diversified food system. They can also facilitate the effective control of a whole sector of the food system by a very small number of people and/or companies.

This reality is often reflected in the relationships and movements of key people, such as David Sommerville of CanAmera Foods or Dwight More. More, president of the Canola Council, moved there in 1985 from a job with Eli Lilly (Elanco), one of whose major products is Treflan, which was key to expanded canola production in western Canada. It has about 80% of market share for canola herbicides, according to More.

Treflan was introduced in Canada in 1971. Following that, acreage expansion really took off. Weed management was the major problem with canola, and Treflan was a great help. Elanco did demonstrations of yields that could be achieved – 30 bu/ac. rather than 10, for example.[15]

More's experience in the agro-toxin industry is sure to colour how he thinks about agriculture and agri-business and how he leads the Council.

_____

Outside of its own leadership, there have been, and continue to be, a variety of other strong forces influencing the Council and the canola industry. For example, More described how, in 1970, the industry was told that rapeseed-had harmful characteristics and could not be sold for human consumption, so they might as well pack it in. Although the Japanese crushers were and are not in any way members of the Council, it was the chairman of Nisshin Oils, Mr. Sakaguchi, who reassured the growers that "we will keep buying from you while you try to solve this problem."[16]

Other outside pressures came into play in the late 1980s when the small Canadian crushers of oilseeds were in trouble and became preoccupied with their survival, putting them at odds with the needs of the farmers.

As More put it, corporations in North America are very concerned with the appearance of their quarterly financial statements. Balancing the short term demands of some its members with the long-term demands of others continues to be a challenge to the Council. This leaves the Council vulnerable to outside interests, as More indicated:

> The Canola Council is, and will probably remain, more controlled by the Canadian crushers, or Continental and Cargill as exporters, who will tell us that their customers are looking for this or that in the product. . . As an example, Frito-Lay is interested in canola, but would like high-oleic, and they have an agreement with Allelix to develop those varieties, so it is Allelix that pushes us. [17]

At the time More made this comment about "Canadian" crushers, the crushing plants in Ontario were already owned by foreign transnationals and the purchase of the major western crushing plants by the same two companies was just around the corner. (See Chapter 7.)

Another factor that affects the council is proprietary interest and the desire to patent or secure information in other ways. The Council has not taken a position on patenting or Plant Breeders' Rights due to the lack of agreement among the members on these issues. This has pushed companies like Proctor & Gamble to dodge the issue and pursue another tactic. As More described it, P & G discerned the trend to healthy foods before others and then looked around for a product that would match that trend. Canola oil is what they came up with. But since you cannot patent the desire to have a low-fat or a low-saturated fat diet, and you cannot patent the low saturated fat characteristics of canola, they are working on other things that you can patent, like high-oleic or low-linolenic fatty acid composition. The production of these specialty oils will be carried out by individual players contracting with each other. The background – the seed stocks – that interest P & G or McDonald's are those with low-saturated fats, and this is a generic, not a proprietary characteristic.

Access to information, and its free movement, are crucial issues for research, and both governmental and corporate attitudes have their effects. J.K. Daun, at the Canadian Grains Commission, commented that corporate sponsorship of research can lead to "much more interference, and a lot of information is simply not available."[18]

When the government cuts budgetary allocations to agricultural research in the public sector, it is, in fact, implementing a policy favouring private research with the consequent restrictions on the movement of information. Dwight More described the resulting dilemma facing the Council:

> If you support the theory that we need to have research information shared on a wide scale, and there are certainly benefits to doing that, then you also have to recognize that that will not provide an incentive for private organizations to invest in that research. So then you have to say that as a public we have to invest. But in the last ten years the decrease [in public investment in agricultural research] has been dramatic. So we came to a position that if, as a public, we are not willing to invest more in research, then we have to encourage private companies to invest in research in Canada if we want any research at all.[19]

The "public", of course, never came to this position. This is a position taken by the federal government for its own reasons and in response to specific pressures. There has never been public discussion and such matters are not the subject of Parliamentary debate. (We return to this point in Chapter 15.)

Funding for the Council's $2.2 million budget used to come 70% from the crushers and exporters through a $0.50 per tonne levy on raw seed exports and seed crushed domestically, but Canadian crushing officials complained that the Council is so broadly based that it is difficult for the crushers to get policies through the Council that work for them. In its 1992 budget, the exporters will continue to pay $0.50 per tonne while the crushers levy is reduced to $0.30 per tonne. Growers in Alberta and Saskatchewan are also funding the Council through a checkoff on their canola sales.

Of course, policy concessions favouring one sector of the industry goes directly against the original intent of the council and of its *modus operandi* since then. But it may reflect the changing nature of the Canadian crushing industry as well, with fewer, bigger players. The "Canadian" crushers said for several years that they wanted to set up their own organization, and the Prairie crushers did have their own association, Western Canadian Oil Crushers, headed by Bob Broeska.

> In the west there was quite a cooperative effort with the crushers and the public plant breeders – Ag Canada and the Universities. It was a sort of lock-step development, particularly with the Sask Pool industrial division. . . For the most part there is still quite a genuine cooperative effort on the crop through the Canola Council, though we are going over a rather rocky road right now because the crop is sold essentially to two buyers. The Japanese, who buy 55-60% of the crop, benefit both from their own protectionist trade policy and from Canada's export grain transportation subsidy. The other 40-45% is bought by Canadian crushers who have to purchase seed at the export price to Japan while selling and transporting products at North American commercial rates.[20]

Finally, in 1992, reflecting the changes in the structure of the crushing industry that left only two significant oilseed crushers both operating plants in the west and the east, the Canadian Oilseed Processors Association replaced the Canola Crushers of Western Canada, while retaining the same staff and office and their membership in the Canola Council. (The four members of the Association in 1992 are Archer Daniels Midland (ADM), CanAmera Foods, Canbra Foods Ltd. of Lethbridge, Alberta, and Northern Lite Canola Inc., Sexsmith, Alberta.)

It will be interesting to see how well the Canola Council brokers its members' interests in the future. With the industry now dominated by both foreign-owned transnational oilseed processors and foreign-owned transnational seed companies, with the trade in canola itself being on the open market where foreign transnationals also play a major role, the Canadian farmers growing canola may find themselves, along with Canadian public sector plant breeders and, indeed, the Canadian public, with a rather small voice.

Chapter 3

SCIENCE AS SPECULATION

There is no such thing as science. There are
only the activities of scientists.

Ruth Hubbard [21]

Brassica vegetables – the cole crops such as cabbage, cauliflower, broccoli and Brussels sprouts; condiment mustards *(B. juncea)*; root crops such as turnips, rutabagas and radishes; and oilseeds, as well as forage rapes and kales – are all close relatives.

Various members of the Brassica family are probably among the earliest domesticated food crops. There is evidence that some vegetable types were widely used in the neolithic age and ancient Indian Sanskrit writing of 2000-1500 B.C. mention these crops. Greek, Roman and Chinese writings of 500-200 B.C. also mention these crops and describe their medicinal properties. In the domestication of the Brassicas, roots, stems, leaves, terminal and auxiliary buds and seeds have all been utilized.[22] It is known that rapeseed has been grown in Europe since the 13th century, and quite possibly earlier, where it was used both in foods and as a cooking oil. The special industrial applications of rapeseed oil, such as in cosmetics, are widely recognized, and its uses are increasing as environmental concerns gain influence.

Rapeseed has been cultivated in China for nearly 2000 years and is the country's most important oilseed crop and fifth most important crop overall behind rice, wheat, maize and cotton. China is also the world's biggest producer of rapeseed. India is the second largest producer of rapeseed while Canada is the third, although the European countries considered as a whole would displace Canada for third place. Canada has been the leader in the development of "double-low" cultivars of rapeseed, though other areas of the world are now catching up.

The name canola is used to refer to the altered varieties of rape that meet the quality standards set for canola. (See box on page 27.) In Europe "rape" can refer to both the traditional rape and to the newer canola-quality rape. The new name began to be used in 1974 in connection with the introduction of the first "double-low" (low glucosinolate-low erucic acid) Canadian-bred variety of rape, Tower.

In 1986 the trademark "canola" was legally amended so that it could be applied only to varieties yielding rapeseed oil that contained less than 2% erucic acid and meal containing less that 30 micromoles per gram of glucosinolates.

The name "canola" was initially registered by the Western Canadian Oilseed Crushers Association for reference to oil, meal, protein extractions, seed and seed hulls from or of varieties with 5% or less erucic acid in the oil and three milligrams per gram or less of the normally measured glucosinolates in the meal. The canola trademark was transferred to the Canola Council in 1980... In 1986 the canola trademark was amended by the Trade Marks Branch of Consumer and Corporate Affairs to indicate that canola oil must contain less than 2% erucic acid and the solid component of the seed must contain less than 30 micromoles per gram of glucosinolates.

In response to a petition from Canada, the United States, in 1985, affirmed low erucic acid rapeseed oil (LEAR oil) as a food substance Generally Recognized As Safe (GRAS). The use of "canola" on food labels in the U.S. was cleared late in 1988.[23]

The trademark registration ensures that the term "canola" only appears on products which adhere to the canola definition. License agreements have been signed with 36 companies from Canada and abroad. The license agreement allows companies to use the word "canola", and the four petal flower symbol, on all canola products which meet the standards and specifications of the Canola Council of Canada.[24]

The more or less official history is that rapeseed was introduced into Canada when a farmer by the name of Fred Solvoniuk, who had immigrated from Poland in 1927, received an envelope of seed from a friend or relative back home and began to grow it on his farm in Shellbrook, Saskatchewan, in 1936. The descendants of these "Polish" seeds, (identified as being of the *Brassica campestris* species), later became low-erucic acid rapeseed.

Due to the absence of a market for the seed, little was grown in Canada prior to 1942 except in small research trials at experimental farms and research stations. Those trials did establish the fact that rapeseed could be grown in both Ontario and western Canada.

Prior to WW II, edible oil had been imported primarily from the Far East in the form of palm, coconut and cottonseed oil. The war disrupted that supply, while at the same time the rapid increase in the use of steam engines in naval and merchant ships created a demand for rapeseed oil. It had been found to be the best lubricant available for use in steam engines because it would cling to water and steam-washed metal surfaces.

Facing a loss of supply of imported rapeseed oil, T. M. Stevenson, Head of the Forage Crop Division of Canada Department of Agriculture, was asked by the Wartime Agricultural Supply Board to see if rapeseed could be grown in Canada. Stevenson assured them that it could and in the spring of 1942 he gathered up all the seed he could find and gave it to the Federal Experimental Farms and Research Stations. The harvest that fall was 52 bushels (1182 kg.) of *Brassica napus* seed. Since that was obviously not enough to permit a significant increase in planting, in 1943 Stevenson imported and distributed 18,640 kg. of *B.napus* from the U.S.

Farmers were guaranteed 6 cents/lb that year for the 2.2-million lbs. of rapeseed harvested. Production increased again in 1944 and 1945.

Early in 1942 the National Research Council had authorized J. A. Anderson to carry out a study of all possible sources of vegetable oil for Canada. Anderson focused on linseed and sunflower seed as potential sources of edible oils and on flax (linseed oil) as a source of inedible oil, but made no mention of rapeseed as a possibility.

Although Anderson simply did not consider rapeseed as a possible source of vegetable oil, another possible source was overlooked for reasons which illustrate the element of irrationality in the determination of the scientific research agenda. According to Baldur Stefansson, the Winnipeg scientist who developed the first double-low variety of rapeseed, Tower, another oil producing plant grows very well on the Prairies but is never mentioned (at least in polite company) as a possible source of oil. This is hemp, better known today as *cannabis*, the source of marijuana. Stefansson pointed out that hemp produces "a fine edible oil" and remembered

> talking with some of the immigrants who brought it with them and produced their own oil from it. We did not really do research on it because one of the best known plant breeders did do some work on poppies and the RCMP came and visited him. Hemp provides a good edible oil, and it grows so well here that government agencies are still trying to eliminate it from the old farmyards and the roadsides with herbicides. [25]

As Stefansson put it, "the research on hemp was eliminated before it got started, so we really don't know what its yield would be", even though it would certainly be possible to develop a hemp without the hallucinogenic alkaloids. The problem, as he saw it is that this would make "a perfect cover for growing the other kind for the trade."

Meanwhile, Fred Solvoniuk did his best to increase production of *B.campestris* by selling seed to his neighbours. The *B.napus* rapeseed took an early lead in production because it out-yielded the Polish culti-var, but the superior agronomic qualities of the Polish variety soon made it preferable. It was also discovered that while *B.napus* grew reasonably well in Manitoba, *B.campestris* by and large did considerably better in Saskatchewan. (*B.campestris* is shorter season and hence can be grown in more northerly areas than *B.napus*, which has a higher yield poten-tial.)

Saskatoon, Saskatchewan, was the centre of this research from the very beginning. As Burton Craig remembers it, H. R. Sallens did the first analytical work on rapeseed oil at the Oil Seeds Laboratory established in 1940 at the University of Saskatchewan in Saskatoon. In 1948 the NRC established the Prairie Regional Laboratory in Saskatoon (absorbing the older oilseeds lab) to look at crop diversification and to develop a re-search program to utilize agricultural surpluses and wastes. Sallens headed the oils and fats section and with Craig as one of his assistants, they focused on rapeseed, flax and sunflowers. Craig described the situa-tion then:

> Wheat had a history of recurring surpluses in Western Canada and thus was a major focus. Linseed oil was under pressure in the paint industry with competition from the synthetics coming from the petroleum industry in a new family of paints. Any pro-posed use of linseed as an industrial product faced competition from the petrochemicals derived from petroleum oils with a cost of $200 a barrel on Alberta crude. Consideration of the situation led to a decision to try for an edible vegetable oil which was needed both in Canada and as an export. If the crop could sub-stitute for wheat it would put another egg in the farmer's basket and could have a greater impact on the wheat surplus than trying to use wheat as a raw product for industrial processing, and rapeseed had been grown successfully by the farmers for several years.[26]

Seeing the potential of rapeseed oil, J. Gordon Ross built the first crushing plant on the Prairies, the Prairie Vegetable Oil plant at Moose Jaw, Saskatchewan, in 1945. The end of the war, however, brought an abrupt decline in the market for rapeseed oil, due to the availability of oil from other sources, the conversion to diesel engines for marine use, and the sheer decline in the number of ships. By 1950 barely 400 acres of rapeseed were harvested and the crop had all but disappeared, although Ross continued to keep the crop alive by contracting some production for crushing at his mill and the Dairy Pool in Saskatoon was operating a small margarine packaging plant. In 1952 Canada Packers was just starting to hydrogenate oils at its plant in St. Boniface (near Winnipeg).

Rapeseed, at this point in its history, was known to yield a high quality oil for specific industrial purposes and a meal which was useable only as a fertilizer. There was concern about the possible nutritional effects of rapeseed oil in the Canadian diet because it was already a high-fat diet compared to the grain-based diets of China and India, and it was known that when consumed in large quantities, rapeseed oil could be highly toxic.

In addition, the meal was not suitable for animal feed because the sulphur compounds (glucosinolates) it contained act as growth in-hibitors, although by the late 1950s the meal had been made acceptable (within specified and rather low limits) as a hog and poultry feed supplement by a processing technique worked out by C.G. Youngs of the National Research Council. He had found that by handling the meal in a certain way at the beginning of the oil extraction process (the seed is crushed before extraction), the glucosinolates could be kept intact and thus remain nutritionally innocuous in the meal.

It is ironic that farmers were learning how to grow rapeseed and discovering how well-suited it was to the Prairies and to their equipment used in the production of traditional grains just as the market for it was disappearing. In the early 1950s there seemed to be little prospect for rape being anything other than a high-quality weed, that is, a crop that could grow well but for which there did not seem to be any significant practical use, and which, being highly prolific and at home in the Prairie climate, could prove to be a real pest in more valuable crops such as wheat.

Fortunately, the plant breeders, despite the dim future for processing and marketing, never lost their professional momentum. William White, who had taken over the work on rape from Stevenson at the Dominion Forage Laboratory in Saskatoon, had already begun in 1944 the plant breeding that led to the registration of the first entirely Canadian rape variety, Golden, in 1954. As we have already seen, it was another 20 years before the first double low variety of rapeseed, Tower, was released. The Dominion Forage Lab was later incorporated into the Agriculture Canada Research Station on the campus of the University of Saskatchewan.

During this same period beginning in the late 1940s, North American agriculture was being introduced to industrial monoculture as a consequence of the immense amounts of public and private money being poured into the hybridization of corn and the breeding of varieties adapted to much wider growing conditions and responsive to increasing levels of synthetic fertilizer. Hybridization combined with the use of agro-toxins (herbicides and pesticides) and synthetic fertilizers, particularly nitrogen, embodied the spirit and process of modernization and industrialization, and modern corn production became a powerful symbol of the process and progress of "free enterprise."

While canola breeders today, at least in the private sector, seem to see in the development of hybrid corn the epitome of modern agriculture and seek to reproduce this model in canola (as we will see in Chapters 6 & 8), the plant breeders working in the public sector on open-pollinated rapeseed were flying in the face of this romance with corn. Stefansson, who was one of those, offered a simple explanation:

> Many people worked on corn and soybeans, and we have probably got them about as far as we are going to without a major breakthrough in genetics. Changing the adaptation of the plant is not easy. So we started with something that does grow in the area. We could grow wheat, barley, oats and flax, but we were importing all our edible oil, and I thought there must be an opportunity here. But the driving force was the need for an edible oil.[27]

The working environment at the time was described by Sallens, of the NRC in Saskatoon: "Without the co-operation of scientists in government laboratories, universities and industries, it would be impossible to carry a project of this diversity and magnitude through to successful completion. All workers contributed ideas, time and financial resources."[28]

Burton Craig remembers that this informal but highly functional research culture remained intact well into the 70s, when the benefits of this research became highly visible.

> But at the time we started it, there were no benefits. It was an impossible situation. There was no organization, just a group of people. I guess we were lucky with the people we had, and the fact that none of the universities, not even the Department of Agriculture itself, were involved in this business of having to submit programs and proposals and all this stuff. For the first years, there is just no way anybody would have bought the idea that the money invested in this thing was ever going to get a payoff.[29]

It was more than luck: everyone involved shared a common culture and concern. This point recurs again and again in conversations with the pioneers of canola: they were all white males of European/British descent; and, they virtually all grew up on Prairie farms during the depression and shared a profound and unique experience that their followers, born and raised elsewhere, whether in cities or eastern farming areas, could never know. They communicated easily and informally and shared a strong desire to find a crop that could provide at least a partial alternative to wheat as the mainstay of Prairie agriculture.

This common culture may have been the root of a complementary attribute: the willingness and ability to share information freely, whether it was information about success or failure in some experiment or information in the form of genetic information embedded in the seed itself. This was not, apparently, a matter of conscious ideology; it was just the way things were done.

This network of communication and information sharing included people working in Ottawa in the National Research Council, in Saskatoon in the NRC or in the university, and in industry, particularly in Canada Packers. These people came together in the National Research Council Associate Committee on Grain Research to form a policy board that played an important role in determining the direction the country's research efforts would take.

It was not difficult to get agreement on the importance of rapeseed research. At that time Agriculture Canada carried out more than half of the country's crop research, the NRC carried out their own research at about four labs, including the Prairie Research Lab in Saskatoon, and the Associate Committee of the NRC provided funding for much of the research carried out in the universities. This group of men represented, and to some extent constituted, the agricultural establishment of the day.

Keith Downey, a principal actor in the whole story, said that, "it helped that people in Ottawa came from a similar background and could understand us and our concerns and could make a judgement about whether these things were meaningful and important."[30]

An article published in 1975 drew the same conclusion:

Cooperation – this has been the most important aspect of the rapeseed story. Though emphasis has been placed on the teamwork among the scientists, it existed throughout the rapeseed industry as a whole: among farmers, oilseed processors, and businessmen of the food industry. The exchange of information in the arena of international agricultural science was also important. Without this cooperation, devoid as it was of formal structuring, rapeseed might have remained for Canadians what it was in the early stages of development – a laboratory curiosity. [31]

The structureless, apparently unorganized but cooperative work of publicly-employed researchers did confound some of those involved.

Craig recalls spending half a day in Ottawa with one of the NRC planers who was trying to understand what was happening with rapeseed: there was no organization and nothing in his plans for rapeseed research!

> I can remember the two of us walking out of the door at quarter to six or something, and he was shaking his head as he said, "I'll have to take your word for it that there was no one who master-minded this, but there are some other people who won't believe that this thing honestly was not planned."[32]

There is another aspect to these apparently close and easy relation-ships, however, highlighted by a contemporary report on the intimate relationship between the Department of National Defense, military con-tractors and lobbyists and retired military personnel. In the words of Paul Manson, retired general and now president of Paramax Systems Canada, Inc., the major Canadian contractor which received a $4.4-bil-lion order for new helicopters from the Canadian Government:

> These are people who know each other. They get along very well. They don't take advantage of it in an improper way – it's just that everyone knows each other very well, and they work together effectively for the good of the country.[33]

The public funds invested in rape/canola research, and the signifi-cance of the close relationships that existed between researchers and administrators, public and private, are insignificant in comparison to the billions of useless dollars spent on military hardware, yet there is a com-mon principle involved.

Neither in conversations nor in the available literature does the issue of the appropriateness of such elitist decision-making, or of accountabil-ity and responsibility, ever come up. It would appear that the whole process was – and still is – regarded as a technical matter to be decided by the individuals involved directly or by committees of experts in the field. There is no hint of farmers, except as some of them were repre-sented on the Canola Council, or people involved in other agricultural issues, such as soil conservation or long term sustainability, ever being consulted. Of course, farmers were much more numerous and consti-tuted a significantly higher percentage of the Canadian population at mid-century than they do now, and the culture of the country was itself much more cognizant of its rural and agricultural components, or simply more agrarian. So it was not entirely unreasonable for the researchers to assume that they were acting in the best interests of the farmers and the country.

This common culture is hard to imagine today when it has become so obvious that the corporate sector is transnational in character and regards agriculture as little more than a market for its "crop inputs" or a source for its commodity components. For its part, the federal government and its ministries, like Agriculture, function as little more than agents of transnational capital and propagators of free market ideology. One can hardly imagine the president of Hillsdown Holdings of Britain, which bought out Canada Packers in 1990, even knowing about what is happening in one of its regional divisions' research lab, much less permitting the kind of informal cooperation that Craig remembers with Canada Packers and its president, J.S. McLean.

J.S. McLean, Dr. Sallens, and J. Gordon Ross were known as the grandfathers of rapeseed. Hank Sallens used to visit Canada Packers quite often because CP was a Canadian company, and one time he was talking with McLean about what major problems Canada Packers had in terms of margarine, shortening, cooking oil, etc. McLean said one of the things they desperately need is a domestic oil because they had nothing they could use for margarine, all the oils were imported, and they had to pay whatever the import price was. One of the nicest things to have would be an edible oil in Canada that they could use both in manufacturing and for bartering.

So Sallens spent some time looking at oil crops. Soybeans could be grown to some extent in Ontario, sunflowers could be grown in the Red River Valley, but no self-respecting farmer out here was going to grow something where he had to cultivate between the rows, and sunflower was then grown as a row crop . . . the farmers just wouldn't grow them.

But rapeseed would grow. And if you looked at consumption worldwide, Japan, India and China were highly dependent on it. The Pakistanis liked it because it was hot like mustard oil. I had a post-doctoral fellow who was a Pakistani and he could not understand why we were trying to get rid of this stuff, ruining the oil! [It turns out that the "hot" in mustard comes from the glucosinolates that were being bred out of rape.]

Canadian companies were not interested, even though we were very short of edible oil during the war. Rapeseed was black, and who would want to eat it or use it if they knew it had been a lubricating oil? So in terms of developing the oil in Canada, it did not look as if it would go. And you couldn't feed the meal to livestock – they would go off their feed, off their milk production. So you couldn't use the oil or the meal. But Hank Sallens said, well, there is only one way to go, and that is up.

It started from there. The first trick was to get the farmer to grow a rapeseed that would all mature at the same time, with good, mature, well-formed seeds. This would help because as it was, some of it would freeze, some dry, and it would have the green colour in it which is what made the oil black. Bill White then picked it up and during the war years he developed the first rapeseed variety in Canada so that it did mature better, with a higher quality seed. But no one knew the history of the seed that we were growing here, so the chances were very good that we could improve it.

So I took a PhD at Minnesota and then came back here, and Sallens started me on this. The first problem was that we could not analyze the stuff. Well, I could analyze the oil, but it was two weeks work and took a pound of oil. So we did do some research using this slow analysis. . . This was 1950.[34]

Keith Downey, whose career has spanned the entire rapeseed-to-canola era, had a different start to his career.

I went to university and went into arts, but it only took me one year to realize that it really was agriculture that I wanted to do, and had seen being done. The other thing that turned me on to research was in my master's thesis where I was working on the problem of a line of dormant sweet clover seed that had a seed coat that seemed to be permeable to water. Water would break the seed coat. The problem was very strange: there were these spots on the seed coat. . . The question was, why did these things occur?

So I did a lot of seed sectioning and I had spent a lot of time looking in the microscope when suddenly it dawned on me that what was happening was that the seed coat was maturing and the embryo inside was continuing to grow. The embryo grew and crushed the seed coat and as a result there was an opening there for the water to get in. I had been working on this thing almost for two years before the light came on.

You don't come across that opportunity to explain a whole phenomenon very often and it's a very gratifying experience to have and to add to useful knowledge. . . It's a good life.

That was how I got into research, and the climate when I first came in was very positive. I came in on the forage crops side and there was a lot of interest in them and in developing superior varieties of alfalfa. But it was somewhat different than today because of the inefficiency with which we handled things in the plots. We probably had more hands, but we didn't have the technical assistance so the populations we could grow and evaluate were much smaller than today. We sowed the seed by hand or pushing a seeder and we didn't have the chemicals to control the weeds so we hand-weeded the plots. We used a motorized mower, but we still needed three people: one to cut, one to carry the cut materials to the scale and one to record the weights and take the moisture content. Today that is basically a one-man operation and you can seed far more plots than you can possibly harvest. You sow a whole plot as fast as you can run. It is very highly mechanized and very efficient.

When I came in the application of technical or mechanical devices for measurement were just getting nicely started: gas chromatography, multiple-row seeders – I worked on the designing of one, and I worked on one to weigh the forage on the machine and actually developed a couple of prototypes. So I guess I was one of the early innovators in trying to improve the efficiency of plot techniques, perhaps not as successfully as others, but I knew that was where we had to go if we were really going to make any mark.[35]

Downey's colleague Baldur Stefansson, though working at the University of Manitoba, has similar memories:

A substantial number of scientists shared the goal of developing alternatives to grain production, especially when the new products could meet domestic requirements. Increased edible oil production seemed to fit our country's needs particularly well.

At first the rapeseed breeding programs operated on a shoestring. Later, as an increasing number of individuals from research institutions and business understood the potential of increased edible oil production, they supported the development by performing much needed research and by making substantial resources available for rapeseed research and varietal development.[36]

Relations with the federal government were good, and Stefansson remembers that they had "some pretty good friends in Ottawa for quite a while, and they helped a great deal. . . There were a lot of people in Ottawa from this province [Saskatchewan], and this was more useful than most people realize."

This shared understanding of what should constitute the proper character and purpose of good crop science is very different from "the pressure for quick results", that characterizes the present situation, according to Stefansson, and "is very unfortunate for research." At the time the overall milieu was one of a self-selected group of government, industry and university men of highly similar background working together at a common task, largely unconcerned as to who got the credit, and, apparently, largely without institutional chauvinism. Their institutions were regarded as the tools or facilitators of the research, not its proprietors.

The fact that all the breeders worked in public institutions and that the results of their research were bound for the public domain meant that it really mattered little who happened to be responsible. Patent attorneys were not involved and Plant Breeders Rights were not even on the horizon. Personal ambition and competitiveness did not lead to legal ownership claims in those days, by either institutions or individuals. Burton Craig described how this affected his early work:

> Practically all the methods of analysis were developed at our place. I think that one of the secrets of the success of this thing was that we had the methods of analysis and were quite willing to work with other people. Practically all the research work that was done somewhere along the line went through us, so that if we were not directly in it, we were in it to help set the project up, and we knew everything that was going on, and it all fed into the NRC. We did Keith Downey's analysis for two or three years, and there is no way that could be done today, the auditor general would have a haemorrhage. A lot of people found the funding themselves for their particular area, and industry was very good in providing materials. . . There was no direction. The people who were interested got together and went ahead and did it.[37]

This attitude and style of work would more than likely be dismissed as utopian today, on the grounds that we cannot afford such vague, non-competitive and non-commercial attitudes. Today the emphasis is on short-term results, on commercial applicability if not outright private commercial purposes. R.K. Daun of the Canadian Grain Commission lab in Winnipeg, described the transformation:

> I did my PhD on Canola Utilization Assistance Program grants and the research was *to find something out about*, and I think today, if you went to a granting agency and said you wanted to "find something out about. . ." you wouldn't get the money. You have to have a solution to a problem. The change is that we are no longer finding out about, we are trying to solve a particular specific problem.[38]

Downey has said much the same thing:

> The one thing in the environment that has changed is that we don't have money to work with anymore. It used to be that we could say to the outside funders, give us enough to get the hands to run this stuff. We won't worry about supplies or travel, we have that in our basic budget, we just need hands. But then it

got to the point where we didn't have enough money in our budget to buy supplies, and keep the place operating, so we had to build that in. Now basically the outside money is running the whole show, and you have to stop and say to yourself, well how much outside money is really good, how much control do you have, are we doing technology or are we doing science. I feel today the proportion of science we are doing is getting smaller and smaller and we are just responding to technology requirements in the way we are approaching our work.[39]

To be sure, Downey, Craig, Stefansson and others were trying to solve a problem, but it was so broad that it was really a qualitatively different process than that of pursuing a commercial goal today. They wanted to find an alternative crop for the Prairies, so they started with a plant that actually grew well on the Prairies, as Stefansson said, and then they tried to find out what they could do with it in the hopes that it *might* become a commercially viable crop. Commercially viable in this case meant trying to find a way, whether through selection or discovery, to turn rapeseed into an edible oil and its meal into a useful animal and poultry feed.

Chapter 4

CREATING A PRODUCT

The first period of rapeseed development, from the mid-1940s through the 60s, might be labelled "playing with diversity." From seed to final product, farmers, breeders and processors were trying to find out what they could do with the unusually diverse genetic material that just one line of the Brassica family provided.

During World War II, rapeseed and linseed (flax seed) were available through a federal oil rationing program because they were domestically produced oilseeds. Canada Packers (CP), as a consequence, tried to process rapeseed for use as shortening, margarine being illegal until 1948. According to Bart Teasdale, who started work as a chemist with CP in 1944, CP found that there was a lot of chlorophyll in rapeseed oil, making it green and unappetizing, so as soon as the war was over it was dropped. At the end of the decade, the future looked dim for rapeseed – except that some farmers in the Prairies had learned how to grow it.

CP did not give up, however, and from 1951 to 1956 efforts to do something with rapeseed were largely focused on the processing side, in the hope of developing processing techniques or a technology that could transform it into an acceptable oil for margarine and salad oil. (See Chapter 10 on the continuing work of Leon Rubin in this area.)

According to Teasdale, CP's Winnipeg plant tried very hard to work with rapeseed oil and by 1958 they were making margarine that was 100% rapeseed oil. In Montreal they were making rapeseed salad oil for Kraft as well as 100% rapeseed oil shortening.

CP was also in the animal feed business, so they had an interest in the meal that oil refiners alone did not have. By the early 60s, according to Leon Rubin, who had joined CP as director of research in 1949, CP was using quite a lot of rapeseed.

> There was an element of self interest in our work on rapeseed, because if a crop were developed, then we were in a good position to utilize it, which is exactly what happened. What we did at Canada Packers was more in the nature of a service to the plant breeders in that it guided them, in both the chemical com-

position and processing characteristics, in producing new varieties.[40]

Then in 1956 the Canadian Food and Drug Directorate of the Department of National Health and Welfare ruled, largely on the strength of the work of K.K. Carroll of the University of Western Ontario, that rapeseed was not an acceptable edible oil and that its sale should be halted immediately. Carroll had been studying the anti-nutritional effects of erucic acid and rapeseed meal on rats. The plant breeders, at that time, were still preoccupied with the agronomic characteristics of rapeseed and with teaching farmers how to grow it, trying to increase yields in order to make it a worthwhile crop.

The judgement of Health & Welfare about the nutritional merits of rapeseed oil was, however, quickly reversed (pending further studies) in light of the very limited consumption of rapeseed oil at that time. The reversal of judgement was due, apparently, to the forceful intervention of J. Gordon Ross, among others, but the whole episode did serve to ignite the search by Baldur Stefansson in Winnipeg and Keith Downey and Burton Craig in Saskatoon for an acceptable low erucic acid rapeseed.

By this time the breeders had learned about the wide variation in characteristics of rapeseed, not only between seed from different locations, but among seed from a single source and even between seed of a single plant. Craig, having heard about the new gas-liquid chromatography method of chemical analysis, decided to try it and acquired the first gas-liquid chromatography for the National Research Council in 1957.

While Craig was busy adapting and developing this new analytical technology for use with rapeseed, Downey and his graduate student Brian Harvey discovered that erucic acid content in rapeseed was largely controlled by the seed's genotype, or the genetic constitution of the seed itself. They realized that if they could learn how to split a single seed, then theoretically they could analyze one half of it, saving the other half for propagation if the analysis was promising. This way they could obtain more seed with the identical characteristics of the seed they had analyzed. While learning how to do this they continued to collect seed from around the world.

In 1958 Craig's analytical technology and Downey's breeding and selection came together and the analysis of a single half-seed could be accomplished. Not long after that Baldur Stefansson in Manitoba was able to utilize similar technology. At that point the search for the needle in a haystack – the low-erucic acid characteristic – shifted gears. They all knew the needle was there, but they still had to find it.

In light of the current trend to claim discovery and ownership of everything possible (see Chapter 13), it is important to remember that the great diversity of the Brassicas, including the low-erucic acid characteristic, existed *a priori*, in nature, before discovery. Neither the diversity nor particular characteristics were created by either science or technology. The scientists invented nothing. They "simply" identified, isolated and subsequently reconstituted, the existing constituent components, or, more precisely, the existing genetic information.

When Stefansson isolated a seed from forage rape in 1960 with a erucic acid content of only 10% (it can go as high as 60% of the fatty acids present), it was only natural for him to send other seeds from the same plant to Downey to work on. That year Stefansson and Downey jointly published what they had discovered about rapeseed characteristics.

By 1964 Downey had succeeded in transferring this low erucic acid characteristic to the *B.napus* rape variety Oro through crossbreeding and contract production of the variety was begun in order to supply Canada Packers. CP, presaging developments decades later, obtained a patent on the production of salad oil from this LEAR (Low Erucic Acid Rape) seed. However, the year production was begun the Soviet Union dumped sunflower oil on the world market and this effectively pulled the plug on the project. (It took the nutritional scare about erucic acid in 1970 to rekindle interest in low erucic rapeseed.)

As we saw in the previous chapter, Canada Packers, Canada's largest food company, had been involved in the unfolding drama of canola from the very beginning. J.S. McLean wanted a domestic source of edible oil in order to free his company from dependence on imported crude oils. When CP opened its research lab in 1952, Bart Teasdale moved in as leader of the edible oils group. He continued to work there until his retirement in 1984. J.S. McLean died in 1954, but his son, W.F. McLean, carried on his father's dedication to research. According to Teasdale,

> They decided to have a project in the research centre to coordinate the work that was going on in their Winnipeg, Montreal, and eventually Toronto plants, and to exchange information through the research centre – that was myself. As we got more people together, we began to do more work ourselves to get rid of some of the problems they were coming up with. We dealt with the chlorophyll by using more bleaching clay which acted as an absorbent and took the colour out but added considerably to the cost. [The cold summer of 1992 produced a lot of green seed for processors to cope with in this way at considerable cost.]

> In the 50s the plant breeders had not really gotten all that far. They were dealing with the agronomic characteristics and the cultural practices of the farmers to increase yields to make it worthwhile for the farmers to grow it.

So the research was done in the processing plants to a great extent, until we got a pilot plant here in Toronto in the late 50s where we could work with a few hundred pounds at a time instead of 60,000 pounds.

Burton Craig was a great help to us with his analytical technology, and CP people trained in his lab. We worked very closely with them and whenever a problem came up we could talk with them. And with Jack Reynolds at Sask Wheat Pool, which was also very active.[41]

Teasdale shares the feeling of virtually all the other canola pioneers that it was a team project and that information of all sorts flowed freely between all the participants:

That was certainly my experience. We could call on them, and with Mr. McLean's approval we were able to pass our information on the work we were doing back the other way, too. I think this was unique, because we were in competition with some big operators - Unilever, etc. - and it was not normal. If you were trying to develop something new you tried very much to keep it to yourself, and while P & G in Canada were helpful, they were just not free, because of their control from Cincinnati, and it was the same with Unilever's control from Europe.

We were providing a service which wasn't available anywhere else. We had pilot plant equipment and research staff and could do the testing. I don't know where else it would have been done, and I guess I would have to say it would not have been done. Later on the POS (Protein-Oil-Starch) plant was put in place in Saskatoon, and it is possible that if Canada Packers had not been doing this, the POS plant might have come into being sooner.

I guess it was pretty much up to my own judgement what information to pass on, and by and large there was not too much restriction, really. The attitude of everyone was, "Let's get on with the job and get this crop in place." From our point of view, a local supply of oil, first of all for the west, would provide some economic advantage for our Winnipeg plant which would otherwise have had to bring oil in from Ontario, but even for our Montreal plant because it was cheaper to ship rapeseed from the Prairies than soybeans from Ontario due to rail subsidies. The alternative was cottonseed oil from the US, which was a long way away. It was also important to have another source of oil.

So the incentive was there, but the economic advantage was not a very big incentive because you never knew what problems you might have with rapeseed oil, it was not uniform and sometimes would be too green, or would not hydrogenate properly, or something, and that kept up right through the 70s. Specifications were pretty loose, but the absence of good analytical techniques meant you could not even set standards. Not until '78 could you set any sort of meaningful standards.

The financing of our research was quite informal, surprisingly so. The timing was such that we were just allowed to proceed as necessary. Toward the end of my time with CP – I left in '84 – the research there became much more structured and there were budgets for every project, every little project even. You had to stick to a budget. But during the 60s and 70s we really didn't have a budget. Even for the work that we did on Joyce Beare-Rogers's feeding studies, and other people's feeding studies, I never submitted a budget at all, even though it was very expensive. The individual plant managers were paying the bills because they were the profit centres and CP head office as such had no money. The money had to come in from the individual managers and they were willing at that time just to say, Yes, we want rapeseed, we want the improvements made, and if this is part of what you have to do, go ahead and do it.

Informality was a great part of our operation at that time too. But those were easier days.[42]

In talking with Teasdale, I got the same feeling that I have had with others who were involved in those free-wheeling days. They took that environment for granted, and when thinking about it now, they speak with some wonderment about their experience and considerable negativity about the current situation.

There is no question that the whole personality of the western researchers, their attitude, and the way they all got along with each other and tried to be helpful, was crucial. There were no negative voices there. And I suspect there were times when we did things that got them off on a wrong track, partly from our point of view and partly from what was fashionable nutritionally at the time. But they were always in good spirits and that was important. I was never part of that western culture, and they even used to make fun of that, from time to time.[43]

Teasdale also agreed with many other of the early canola people that canola would probably never have been created if the research attitudes and funding in the early days had been what they are now.

Canola as such would never have developed as a Canadian oil, but you can't say what might have occurred in other countries, like Sweden, with whom we worked very closely. They might have developed a very similar crop. We got processing help from Sweden, from the independent people, that is, non-Unilever. That kind of cooperation would probably not take place now.

I think the situation at Canada Packers started to change when Dr. Rubin retired as research director in 1979 and a new one was put in his place. What his mandate actually was, and whether it was the board of directors or whether it was his own initiative, we gradually began to get into more rigid budgeting.

The restriction in the flow of information began to come into place about the same time. Up until 1982 I was still giving papers, and giving quite specific information about what we were doing, and the results of our analytical work were published. We had been pretty open on trade secrets, on formulation etc. We saw our advantage in being there and doing it first, in collaboration with the men out west. That was what lay behind our commitment to research from the beginning: being there first, and hopefully having some advantages in product quality and cost.

Now, if you have to go through patent lawyers and whatever, that's a pretty tricky business, and you cannot publish anything or discuss anything, and you have to keep it all very tight in the notebooks until six years later when you get a patent, and the coverage is as broad as you can get and the information you give out is as narrow as you can get away with.

If you can get a very broad patent, even though it is eventually thrown out, who is going to challenge it? It would have to be overthrown by the courts, and then you've got a multimillion dollar expenditure. It's unfortunate, I guess.

When Hillsdown came in, the research went and the lab was closed. The records are all gone. Of course we had kept lab books and research reports were written, some even monthly, and I guess those were simply all thrown away. Whoever wanted anything took it - universities got some equipment and books, and Mr. McLean took what he wanted, but Hillsdown didn't want anything. So all those records of the work that we did is just gone. It is strange when you think about it.[44]

Leon Rubin, who was director of research for CP in 1949 and director of their research centre from the time it opened in 1952 until he retired in 1979, described the collapse of CP's research in much stronger terms. According to Rubin, when W.F. McLean retired the company started going downhill: "It just seemed to be lacking direction, and eventually they had to do something, but the way Hillsdown did it was cruel, unconscionable. They closed down the lab in six months, scattered the staff and destroyed the library. It was an act of vandalism."[45]

The role of Canada Packers in shaping the development of canola can be known at the level I have described, but what its more subtle influence might have been on the decisions made by the researchers remains unknown. If it had been the Shur-Gain Feeds division of Canada Packers assisting the breeders, the outcome might have been different. As it turned out, Canada Packers was a great help in developing the oil, but not the meal. That still had to be cleaned up so that it could be used as an animal feed, and it was due to work being done at the Prairie Regional Lab in Saskatoon that equipment was developed to test for glucosinolates, which had been identified as the problem in the meal.

When the technology became available to Downey in 1967, he began to test every seed he had. Once he and his colleagues had identified the low- glucosinolate characteristic in a *B.napus* forage variety from Poland, they had to introduce this trait into a variety that was both agronomically satisfactory and had a low erucic acid profile. They also needed to transfer this characteristic to the *B.campestris* varieties that occupied the other half of Canada's rapeseed acreage. They decided to do this by inducing *B.napus* and *B.campestris* to interbreed, thus transferring the low glucosinolate characteristic of the *B.napus* variety to the low-erucic acid, agronomically desirable, *B.campestris* rapeseed.

Because of the breeding program followed to develop these varieties, the low-glucosinolate characteristic for both *B.napus* and *B.campestris* came from the same source, with the consequence that "all low-glucosinolate rapeseed grown in the world – and today that means almost all rapeseed – can be traced back to the single batch of Bronowski *B.napus* seed," a variety developed in Poland before WW II.[46]

By 1973 the breeders were able to supply seed with no more than 5% erucic acid in the oil, and in 1974 the first double-low canola- quality *B.napus* rapeseed was given the name Tower and released by Baldur Stefansson at the University of Manitoba.

While all this searching and researching was taking place, nutritionists were still wondering about the effect of rapeseed oil on human health. The problem, as mentioned earlier, was not that the oil by itself was so bad, but, as Joyce Beare-Rogers (with training in science, food chemistry, nutrition and biochemistry) put it, it was a matter of quantity. Up to this time it had been used only as a cooking oil in very low fat diets. Now retired, Beare-Rogers talked with me about her experience:

> We do not know how the high erucics would have been dealt
> with in high concentrations because Canadians were already de-
> veloping a low erucic acid rapeseed when we became con-

cerned. The country had a policy of becoming self- sufficient in fats and oils, and all that was available domestically was high erucic acid rapeseed oil and herring oil.

Herring oil contains an isomer of erucic acid, cetoleic acid, and when herring oil is partially hydrogenated, you can get a great assortment of C-22 acids with one double bond, which are isomers of erucic. You get the same thing when you hydrogenate rapeseed.

What was being proposed for Canada was an increase in the intake, higher than humans had ever consumed before, of a vegetable oil that was high in erucic in a country where, at that time, herring was the principle marine oil. So the question was, does this have any implications for man? We did not have any answers for that.[47]

Unilever in The Netherlands was working on this problem, and their test results showed that rapeseed oil could cause "fatty hearts" in ducks.

Health & Welfare decided that they should do some work on their own, on rats. They came up with similar results, so they tried it on several other species of animals as well and the results were consistent: rapeseed oil resulted in fatty hearts in young animals. (This had been Carroll's conclusion in 1956.) As Beare-Rogers put it, "If there was an alternative, why subject man to something about nine kinds of animals responded to unfavourably?" She continued with a not-uncommon story providing an insight into the social construction of science and technology, which is discussed further in Chapter 14:

There was an international meeting at Ste-Adele, Quebec, in 1970, and I was asked to organize a nutrition session for that meeting. I did, and prepared a paper on our work, and panic struck when the rumour circulated that rapeseed oil caused heart attacks. After the meeting there were so many phone calls that I did my work in Montreal for a few weeks just to get out of the lab.

I wanted the information from Unilever to come out first, so we pried the data out of Unilever by telling them we had similar results, but that they should get credit for it because they had it first. So they published, and I sent my paper to the *Canadian Journal of Physiology and Pharmacology*, which was supposed to be the organ of the Nutritionists' Society of Canada, and I heard nothing. I wrote the editor, and got a letter back saying it had been through peer review and there was no problem scientifically, but it was against the policy of the journal to accept anything of this nature. It was very strange, actually. But that editor who wrote me was very much involved in agriculture.

My boss felt that if I was doing decent research I ought to be able to get it published. The reviews came back to me and there was nothing that discredited the paper scientifically, so I sent it, with the reviews, to the *Canadian Institute of Food Technology Journal*, and they accepted it as a reviewed paper and published it (Vol.4, No.2). As far as I know that is the only science "citation classic" that journal has ever published. That was in 1971.[48]

In light of what was happening in all the animal studies, in 1970 H&W decided that a high erucic acid diet "should not be inflicted on humans", as Beare-Rogers put it, and suggested that low-erucic acid rapeseed be phased in as quickly as possible. By 1974 the changeover to low-erucic acid rapeseed was 95% complete, and by 1984 the conversion to the double-low varieties was virtually complete, though the breeders pressed on to reduce the erucic acid and glucosinolate levels even further. The progress made in that work made it possible for the Canola Council, in 1992, to agree to further restricting the definition of canola (thereby further decreasing its genetic diversity). Effective in 1997 the erucic acid level of canola must be less than 1% of the oil content and the allowable glucosinolate level will be lowered to 18 u-moles per gram.

Beare-Rogers, however, questions the logic of this drive. Just because 2% erucic acid is good does not mean that 1% is better and 0% is best. Nothing is quite that simple.

It doesn't make a lot of sense to me to see big programs to lower the saturates still further when we are not even sure it is a good thing. Erucic acid is under 1% now, I don't think it matters two hoots to lower it further. People eat mustard and horseradish to add zip to things. It's all marketing. Nutritionally it doesn't make any sense.[49]

Perhaps it was no accident that in 1978 the a.d.m. of Health and Welfare said that there should be no more work done on rapeseed oil, according to Beare-Rogers. If the rest of the game was to be a matter of marketing, then nutritional issues could be left to the corporate nutritionists. If diversity in the seed is something to be overcome, then diversity in the finished product is also something to be overcome, and how better to achieve this than with a zero rating for what had once been labelled as problematic.

Up through the 70s public sector research had been focused on open-pollinated varieties of canola, which made sense since public sector breeding was not organized or financed to provide a return to the government. It was organized to serve the interests of the Canadian people by serving the interests of Canadian farmers. This being the case, it was only logical for the public sector researchers to focus on the agronomic characteristics of the seed and on commercial production of the crop. The establishment of six or seven regional canola production demonstration sites was an expression of this orientation.

This does not mean, however, that the plant breeders were immune to the lure of hybridization or to the assumptions of chemical agriculture. Canola production has been limited because of the problems of weed control and disease. Being a broadleaved plant, it is susceptible to most of the herbicides used in wheat production. Given the cultural orientation of dealing with weeds by treating them as enemies to be eliminated, canola researchers chose the now-conventional path of trying to produce herbicide tolerant canola. Alternatives would be to seek the collaboration of other disciplines or even farmers themselves to find ways to overcome the weed problem through cultural practices and farming systems that placed less reliance on agro-toxins.

As early as 1979 work was started at Guelph and Saskatoon to develop a triazine-tolerant canola, for two reasons. First, so canola could be grown on land previously used for corn, where the use of triazine herbicides is routine; and second, so that triazine could be used on canola to deal with wild mustard. Seed was on the market in 1984 and by 1986 half the Ontario crop, or 40,000 acres, was in triazine-resistant OAC Triton or OAC Tribute, although Prairie farmers were little tempted to try much of it.

Progress in this project was illusory, however, for it was found that in commercial production, yields of these triazine-tolerant canolas were 30% lower than regular varieties grown under completely weed-free conditions and 12% below canola grown in commercial production. This did not stop Dale Adolph, of the Canola Council, from stating that "triazine-tolerant canola is a success from the standpoint of excellent weed control."[50] Another problem with using triazine is the toxic residues left in the field that limit what can be grown in the following years. With a crop like canola that requires a minimum four-year rotation, such residues can be extremely detrimental to good crop rotations. In addition, the crushers complained that they were paying for oil they could not get out of the seed, since its oil content was 40% rather than 42%; the oil they did get was higher in free-fatty acids and, therefore, less stable.

In sum, it appears that going the chemical route was not a glowing success, at least in that round. One must wonder at the total cost of that research and the consequent development work, and what could have been achieved by applying the same level of resources to learning how to grow canola well with a weed population. A 12-30% drop in yield and an inferior oil quality is a high trade-off for being made herbicide resistant. Allowing for either significant weed populations or different cultural practices and no herbicide usage might produce the same net results at a lower cost. The problem with such an approach, as Wallace Beversdorf of the University of Guelph and others have pointed out, is that wild mustard is a major weed in some canola-growing areas, and it has an erucic acid content of 20-40%. As well as reducing yield of the desired crop, this can cost the producer in terms of dockage (price reduction) for more than 5% wild mustard in the crop. In other words, there are trade-offs whichever way one goes – but that is the point to remember.

Chapter 5

RESHAPING RESEARCH:
THE POWER OF MONEY

The corporate sector isn't willing to do a lot of
the research that is necessary for Canadian producers. They just aren't. There isn't the money
in it for them. It was not the corporate sector
that developed canola.   *Wallace Pigden*

The intellectual curiosity bit doesn't count for
much in the private sector.   *Peter McVetty*

Through the 70s and 80s the research environment underwent substantial, if slow, change. What the men working in the 50s and 60s took for
granted would appear as utopia by the late 80s.

> When I think back on it, it's quite amazing, the cooperation we
> had, and the way everybody worked together, even within
> Canada Packers itself. . . For people nowadays it is an unbeliev-
> able story. Now everything has to be so structured.[51]

Wallace Pigden was an animal nutritionist with Agriculture Canada in
Ottawa for many years, and then an administrator after he earned his PhD
at the University of Saskatchewan. Around 1968 he was asked to serve
on the committee responsible for research planning and evaluation and
then on the committee overseeing the Rapeseed Utilization Assistance
Program of the federal Department of Industry Trade and Commerce. He
had an insider's view of the changing scene in research from the 1950s
up to the present, and remembers that when the Research Branch was
expanding in the early 50s,

> there were all kinds of opportunities to build research programs.
> If a chap came in and said he had a bachelors degree and was
> anxious to get further training, the department would probably
> send him off with half-pay to university to get a masters and even
> a doctorate. A lot of veterans got an education that way, but in
> 1955 they started to cut back gently on research, although the

Research Branch as an organization had a lot of resources and a lot of freedom.

From 1965 on there was some restriction of funding and in the 70s we were cut back by the amount of inflation every year. Since the Conservative government came in in 1984 there has been a drastic decrease in opportunities to do agricultural research in government, along with a tremendous drop in morale and a tremendous loss in interest and capability in doing research. A lot of the research stations are being starved of funds and personnel. Corporations will only work on the projects that they consider will make them money, not whether it is good for Canada or for the producers. That's just the fact of life in a free market society.[52]

Canada Packers seems to have been the exception to the rule, at least until the 80's, although, as already indicated, they had their own reasons for cooperating in the development of canola. In the long run, they obviously regarded it as good business.

Pigden's sense of what he was doing as a scientist working in the public sector stands in sharp contrast to what the situation seems to be in the 1990s:

I was proud of what I was doing. I felt I was doing something valuable even if I wasn't paid as well as I would be paid in industry. I could have moved into lots of better paid jobs. But when you are doing something you really enjoy . . . well, I was a combat soldier before that, and I felt that working for the Canadian government was a prestige job. And I was very proud of the fact that I had gotten myself trained as a scientist and that I was also trained under the veterans' program and was prepared to work for the government. There was good morale, lots of encouragement, good resources to do a job and do it right. Now I walk down among the scientists and the older ones are just looking at the calendar wondering when they can get out without a big penalty so that they can get away from this atmosphere – this terribly negative atmosphere. And the younger ones do not feel that they are protected, in terms of pension. . . I never had to worry about my job. At the time I left we were just getting into this, and I thought that maybe it was time for me to leave. . . From then on it has just been downhill, in terms of morale.[53]

Baldur Stefansson shared Pigden's enjoyment of his work. He told me of the satisfaction he got from going out to see farmers at a time when prices were depressed and finding that the farmers who were growing canola seed were making a few bucks, as he put it, out of seed propagation:

> I enjoyed that more than anything else. When farmers got their foundation seed from me, they could make some money – maybe $3000 per acre – out of maybe 20 acres of seed. That was a godsend at the time, and it helped a few farmers pay off their debts. There was a real contribution there to the economy of the country.[54]

But like almost everyone who worked on the development of canola, whether for the private or public sector, Stefansson expressed his doubts that canola would exist at all if the research climate were then what it has become today,

> because the austerity is getting too severe. A lot of people want short term research and they want lots of results, but that is not the way it works, they are not going to get them. You have to slog away at a problem for a long time and maybe you will solve it and maybe you will not.

Because he continues to work as a consultant, Stefansson is aware of the restriction in the sharing of information that has taken place over the years. Now,

> the flow of information is basically dictated by corporate strategies which must restrict it in order to make a buck, or at least they think so. . . For example, I was visiting Proctor & Gamble, and when I finished my presentation I was escorted out of the conference. . . It stands to reason, if you are going to make a buck out of your research, you have to keep it secret.[55]

Funding cutbacks, dropping morale, increasing secrecy; Peter McVetty, who followed Stefansson at the University of Manitoba, described the current situation as one in which, "We try to get money to do the things we want to do, but we only get to do those things we can get money for."

McVetty and his department are still, as he puts it, working on the research agenda set by Stefansson, whose focus was always on quality improvement. That is not necessarily what corporations want to fund, and the net has to be cast wider and wider. In 1990 McVetty could still say that they had not done any work for interests outside Canada, but he felt that they were getting closer to having to do so with every passing day.

McVetty raised the interesting issue of conflict of interest that could, and does, arise with funding from outside Canada: "Who would benefit, for example, if P & G asked us for a cultivar which they could grow in the U.S.A. and completely undermine production here?"

We are public servants here – one tends to forget it – and we interact directly with the Canadian canola industry. We go out and talk to farmers when they call and say they have a problem. We are more or less here for the good of the Canadian canola industry, and this is perhaps a rather major difference in the way we view our role. The private canola breeders in Canada are breeding for the world and they do not care where they sell it, but we take the view that we are publicly funded to serve the Canadian industry. It's an old-fashioned idea at this time, but we're hanging on to it.[56]

McVetty has emerged as one of the strongest voices for public sector research. In addressing the Annual Meeting of the Canola Council in 1992, he pointed out that there has been a steady reduction in funds available and that, "as competition among canola breeding programs increases, the market share available for each cultivar decreases." McVetty's major concern is that "the opportunities for high risk, innovative research are declining. This could lead to the loss of opportunity for the type of discoveries which led to the development of canola."

Two years earlier McVetty could see the handwriting on the wall and told me that he felt that public sector breeding would be reduced gradually in Canada in the 1990s and eliminated sometime early in the next century, to be taken over in its entirety by the private sector.

In talking about the difference in emphasis between his public breeding program and privately funded research, McVetty described the three routes being tried in the quest for hybrid canola varieties:

The hybrid heterosis is there, but the second step is a useable, practical and competitive seed production system, and we still don't have that, and in my opinion it's going to be a number of years before we do. Pollination control is the major problem. Canola is a perfect-flowered plant, with both female and male parts in every flower of every plant. In order to produce hybrids, you have got to control pollen production in your female line. One of the ways to do this is the cytoplasmic male sterility (CMS) system, which just eliminates pollen production. The other, more devious approach is the self-incompatibility (SI) system where there are still anthers there and pollen, but the pollen is genetically unable to fertilize the ovules on that plant. The third way is to use a chemical gameticide which kills the pollen on the female side [the pollen-killer gene approach].[57]

Because of problems with all three paths, McVetty has concentrated on long-term varietal improvement of open-pollinated varieties rather than the development of new varieties. His approach is crucial to the distinction, in practice, between public and private breeding programs: Rather than spending millions in pursuit of hybridization, McVetty feels that

> we need to look at alternative ways of maximizing the increase of yield on canolas without relying entirely on hybrids, looking at all possible methods to increase yield from inbred lines, population reconstruction, as they call it. . . My job does not depend on releasing one, two or three commercial hybrids every year.[58]

The "disposal" of unwanted genetic material is another potential area of difference between public and private breeding which McVetty pointed out, and it merges with the issue of secrecy. Because the major plant breeding enterprises are really breeding for the world rather than for a particular location, they create a wide spectrum of material. In his case, McVetty might keep the early maturing material that works really well in Manitoba and send the late-maturing seed to someone else for evaluation. Rather than throw away the breeding material that cannot be used in Manitoba, why not let someone else try it out?

The movement of seed, however, is the movement of information, and information of any and every sort is increasingly regarded as commercial property. As the envelope of genetic information, the movement of the seed takes on increasing significance even for the public sector. As McVetty put it,

> We are all public servants of sorts, while at the same time we run a program in competition with other public sector programs, and since the total amount of research dollars is steadily shrinking, we all wish to get as many of those for our own program as possible and let the other programs do without. To maintain the competitive position of this program tends to necessitate keeping ideas at home, keeping material at home, capitalizing on the natural advantages of that which you already have. For example, we could divide all our early and late low linolenic material into three piles and send a pile to each of the other two public stations, which would provide a good public service, but who knows who would get the funding to carry on that work in a year or two?
>
> Of course this can have a negative effect on our research in terms of inhibiting the flow of information because one of the ways you make rapid progress is by getting together with other knowledgeable people in your field and brainstorming and that happens less and less with each passing year.
>
> Funding by industry also brings with it restriction on flow of information, but we have to distinguish between product devel-

opment and genetic advance with specific objectives in mind. For example, I can tell you that we are running a high-palmitic acid breeding program, but I won't tell you what level we are at or what our objective is because that would provide information which could be used against us by other organizations. We can give you general information, but if you want specifics, sorry, that is proprietary, and if you want the material, no.

I think I have experienced all possible scenarios here in terms of release of information in only six years in the canola area. I've done some collaborative work with private industry without any funding on the understanding that the information generated would be co-authored and published and then gotten down to the final publication being put together when my private industry collaborator said, "Well, we don't think we can let this be published after all because it tells our competition something about our material we don't want them to know." It's very frustrating. On the other hand, I've had some excellent experience with private companies that have funded research and then said, "Publish everything you want, let it go, we are interested in the overall good of the industry."[59]

Canola research at the University of Manitoba is not confined just to plant breeding and quality. Sue Arntfield is a nutritionist in Food Science working on the utilization of canola oil. She, too, has experienced the limitations of privately funded research, being told by others in the field: Look, if you are going to get funding from this source you need to concentrate on these variations; you should work with a crop that has a high economic profile; this is the type of thing that will get funded by NSERC (The Natural Sciences and Engineering Research Council). Speaking from experience, Arntfield described the necessity of choosing which way one wants to work:

If you want to go the industrial route, then you have got to look at very specific applications that will be acceptable to Weston [or any corporation], and you have to be careful because you can get tied up in terms of publication which means that you can't get grants from other places if you don't get a publication out of your work.[60]

So Arntfield is working on basic molecular interactions "because NSERC will support looking at basic properties, not applications or applied situations." In other words, public funding will go to work that will provide the basis for commercial application, but the goodies of research that will produce a commercial return will be reserved for the private sector. Coupled with a continuing reduction in public funding, this means that public sector research is bound to become a handmaiden of private industry, and to be funded only as long as private industry can capture private benefit.

As funding becomes more product-oriented (teleological) and subject to corporate direction, so do the genes. We will see in Chapter 8 what has happened to canola breeding at the hands of the private sector in the last decade, but the direction was well articulated by Mark Forhan, a canola breeder working for ICI Seeds Canada, at the 1992 annual meeting of the Canola Council:

> Canada had only a public breeding effort until the early 1980s when a rapid shift toward private involvement occurred. . . The first private variety in Canada was licensed in 1985 and the first private breeding company was established at about the same time. Since then the number of Canadian private seed companies involved in canola has grown to ten.[61]

One might be inclined to take satisfaction in this presentation of the progress achieved in the increase in "choice" marked by now having ten private companies involved in canola breeding in Canada. But this is hardly significant diversity when their research is focused primarily on hybrids and based on years of public-sector research, and the adjective "Canadian" hardly describes reality when the companies are foreign transnationals merely working in Canada to build on what was done in the public sector. Forhan lists, among others, Agrigenetics (USA), Hoechst (Germany), ICI Seeds (UK), King Agro (France), Monsanto (USA), Palladin Hybrids (USA), Plant Genetic Systems (Belgium), Pioneer Hi-Bred (USA), Svalov (Sweden) and Calgene (USA).

At the same time, the deliberate throttling of public sector canola research could hardly produce anything other than what Forhan describes:

> The private industry effort into canola research currently totals 83 research scientists with a conservatively estimated total research expenditure of $17 million Canadian. This is above the public sector investment and is a very conservative estimate. [A current estimate is that the split in funding of canola research is 40% public, 60% private.] . . . In 1992 there will be an estimated 26 licensed varieties of canola on the market, 15 of which are private varieties.[62]

Getting 26 varieties, or even 15, onto the market is not cheap. Proliferation and competition are expensive, and maybe the result is less real choice than there might be with fewer varieties with really different characteristics. When the industry is conceived of as 17 competitors, with every one of them hoping to recoup their investments from seed sales, there will be few winners, and someone has to cover the losses: "too many players, too many varieties", is the way McVetty summarized the situation today.

Other breeders, however, would take issue with McVetty, pointing out that of the 26 varieties, some are on their way out, others are on their way in, and some are there simply because some farmers want them (or like their name?). They say, quite rightly, that no one variety can or should do for every situation, every ecology, and that western Canada is a huge area, with different soils, different moisture levels, different weather, day lengths, and so on. On the other hand, the diversity that is offered very often has more to do with marketing proprietary seed than with providing locally-derived genetics and genuine diversity.

Forhan's recommendations for the canola industry are self-serving and, unfortunately, little different than those of every other corporate voice:

> Private industry has proven itself to be a positive influence in the canola seed industry. However, I think that Canada's best bet is to build on the synergies between the public institutions with their well established research excellence, and the private sector with its proven ability to deliver product to market.[63]

Such a statement does not prove the point: getting inferior varieties to market is no big achievement, and for 20 years before the private breeders appeared on the scene, the public sector seemed to be doing a good job of getting tested varieties out to Canadian farmers. The argument will be made that the biggest "improvements" have been the work of the private sector, but the problem is that there is no adequate reference point; what constitutes an improvement depends on one's values and perspective.

So the lines are drawn. The private breeders argue their notion of "choice" and the public breeders argue quality. Both support cooperation, but that means different things to different people. The private sector claims that they can do a better job of getting varieties to market while admitting that they want the public sector to do the basic genetic work that the corporations can't see making money on. The public sector breeders point out that without being able to commercialize the varieties they develop, they will soon have no money for research. The corporations argue that if the public breeders would treat their materials as private property and charge royalties on protected varieties and materials, they could carry on their work with their royalties. One plant breeder went so far as to suggest that if Keith Downey, with close to 100% of the western Canadian canola market with his Westar and Tobin varieties, had been collecting royalties, he wouldn't have any problem funding his research. "He could have put money in the bank and paid all of his summer students and research assistants."[64]

With this scenario, there would be no funding for work at the University of Manitoba, or Guelph, or much of anywhere except Saskatoon. Despite its amazing short-sightedness, the corporate sector continues to increase its power over canola, leaving the university researchers, as McVetty puts it, "selling chunks of our program to private industry, with exclusive first option rights to varieties that we produce. "

> As a consequence, we are less open than we perhaps used to be, with less publication of some of the research. But what is being commercialized is, to some extent, variety development and the varieties that come from it. The breeding programs still provide training ground for grad students and spin-off projects, but we are not as free- speaking because there are all sorts of organizations competing directly with us – public and private. Everybody pretty well keeps to themselves. There is no point in letting too many good ideas slip out.

> There was a point in time, I guess, where a public institution like the university was an idea generator. . . but we don't do so much of that now. You can't have it both ways.[65]

Chapter 6

REPROGRAMMING THE SEED

> Every fact has its *factor*, its maker. It exists as
> an autonomous unit only within the world in
> which its makers perceive a need for that partic-
> ular "fact" because they want to build theories
> and actions on it or with it. But in the larger
> context these facts may be artifacts, and the the-
> ories and actions built upon them may disfigure
> or even destroy important aspects of nature.
>
> *Ruth Hubbard* [66]

The fact that seed selection has been carried out by farmers for as long
as they have been growing crops does not mean that what corporate
science is doing today is just more, faster. The criteria of selection, its
narrowness, and the speed of the process are distinguishing marks of
modern plant breeding, and the technology of plant science is determined, like the science, by a cultural context. The analytical technologies
that were essential to the transformation of rapeseed were appropriate
to the task as defined, but like the approach to seed characteristics, the
technology as it was developed was a reflection of the reductionist culture out of which it came.

Seed can and has been selected for widely differing traits beyond the
obvious ones of food value and local viability. For example: tolerance of
extremes of moisture or drought; ability to be cooked quickly to conserve
fuel wood; long stem or straw in order to provide material for thatching
or weaving; or, ability to take advantage of symbiosis or allelopathy when
grown together with another crop. None of such characteristics fit the
typical reductionist criteria of yield per hectare or uniformity of height
for mechanical harvesting. Yet each one is valid and should properly be
described as scientific in the cultural context that values these traits.

Criteria such as these are not, however, generally recognized by a
culture that has a narrow reductionist definition of science. In spite of
the fact that the research agenda of science and technology must reflect

the values and culture of the scientists and their sponsors, what is selected as the subject of research, who selects it and who funds it, are seldom recognized as political decisions made within an identifiable context. In Canada, at least, those who have made the decisions in any particular field of scientific or technological research have represented a highly homogeneous elite. There has been virtually no public policy debate or discussion of alternatives to the views of this minority. (We will return to this in Chapter 15.)

This is clear enough when we recall the process by which the agenda for the original rapeseed research was established. As we have seen, the group which set the agenda, which became the agenda of the seed itself in due course, was composed primarily of a small number of men of European origin who all shared a common history and culture. Within the Canada of that time they were fairly representative of a significant portion of the white male population. Within any larger framework, they represented a very narrow cultural tradition, whether considered by race, class, gender, geography or schooling.

This high degree of cultural homogeneity was, according to the records, not tempered in any way by what might be referred to as a larger democratic process. Neither Parliament nor any parliamentary committee had any role in the decision to carry out research on rapeseed, nor, apparently, did any farmers. This is not to say that the decision was wrong or contrary to what might have been decided if some larger democratic process had been operative. But when we come to look at the research agenda today and how it is determined and by whom, to say nothing of who pays for it, we might well wish that long ago there had been instituted some means of ensuring public debate on the subject.

This issue becomes all the more important when the dimension of biotechnology and genetic engineering is added. Biotechnology magnifies the speed and power of scientific research, along with its potential negative consequences.

The first years of rapeseed research were characterized largely by the application of then-current science to the question of what could be done with rapeseed, from its cultivation through to its use as an edible oil and useful animal feed. The initial research agenda is best described as one of discovery. Over the years, however, and particularly since the mid-80s, the agenda has increasingly taken on the character not of science, but of technology applied to the political and economic goals of identifiable commercial interests.

The selection of herbicide resistance as a subject of research, for example, has many implications, and cannot be described as a choice made on the basis of science, yet substantial amounts of both private and public money are being spent on the science of developing resistance (tolerance) to certain herbicides in a number of crops, including canola. Stefansson reported in 1983 that a triazine-resistant form of *B.campestris* had been found in corn fields in Ontario and Quebec and that triazine-resistant cultivars of rapeseed were being developed using backcross methods. While at the time yields of these crosses were quite low, Stefansson recognized "that a high level of weed control can be achieved using triazine herbicides on a triazine-resistant form of rapeseed."[67] In commenting on the consequences of such breeding, and of the work to develop hybrids, Stefansson highlighted the difficulties of producing hybrid varieties of canola quality without significant decreases in yield and, more significantly, "a temporary decrease in genetic diversity."[68]

The attitude of modern reductionist science is that such negative consequences for yield, genetic diversity, and possibly other characteristics can and will be overcome through further research. The assumption is that adequate solutions can be found if only enough money is invested in the research and development. In other words, the basic assumptions of the "science" being pursued are not questioned, regardless of the consequences. But just in case the science is questioned, there is a back-up strategy that suggests that if there are negative consequences, they can be overcome through a public relations campaign and other non-scientific measures to convince farmers and others that there are no alternatives and that the consequences, though problematic, are the price of "progress."

The reductionist selection of certain characteristics for targeted change, such as selection for the absence of erucic acid or resistance to triazine, can often lead to a very narrow evaluation of the results. When triazine-resistant canola, for example, was developed, "no nutritional studies on the meal residues or the oil were conducted prior to its commercial release."[69] In other words, a single characteristic was targeted and only that single characteristic evaluated. Apparently no recognition was given to the potential effects of symbiosis or of the possible changes to the nutritive value or safety of either the oil or the meal.

In 1990, the Agriculture Canada Research Station in Saskatoon and the Scott Experimental Farm reported on five canola projects and one sunola project. The canola trials focused on: screening for varieties resistant to a new race of white rust; a study of the glucosinolate preferences of flea beetles in the search for varietal resistance to the flea beetle; research on the feasibility of a European parasite for biological control of bertha army worm (a canola predator); rapid and inexpensive identification of canola quality by means of a new technique and technology; and the breeding of two new Argentine *(B.napus)* varieties, one for Blackleg resistance and the other a triazine-resistant variety.

These last two trials are interesting because they both focus on introducing resistances into canola, one to a major disease, the other to a very popular herbicide. Blackleg is a major disease problem, usually dealt with by maintaining a minimum four-year rotation (canola every fourth year). Up to now, breeding Blackleg resistance into canola has resulted in low yield and quality, while inbred triazine resistance in canola is accompanied by reduced yield and high susceptibility to Blackleg. In other words, the reductionist approach to solving one problem at a time seems to produce negative unanticipated side effects, resulting in little or no net gain.

The sixth trial was with sunola, which is the name given to an extremely early-maturing, miniature sunflower developed at the Saskatoon Research Station which "appears to offer several advantages over canola in many areas. . . Unlike most, if not all, sunflower cultivars available in North America, sunola will be open-pollinated, not hybrid. This will keep seed prices low and make higher seeding rates practical."[70] Being deep-rooted, sunflowers are more drought tolerant than canola and they are also more heat tolerant. Downey commented that the major problem was birds, but added that the answer to that is simply to plant enough for both the birds and the farmer!

What is most notable about all this research, particularly in sunola, is its public character, that is, its probable unattractiveness to private interests due to the lack of significant capturable return. (Only the new Blackleg-resistant AC Excel *(B. napus)* variety which is supposed to be superior to the reference variety (Westar) in oil content, yield and Blackleg resistance, might be considered an exception.) Typical of the tradition of public sector research, the focus is on open-pollinated rather than hybrid varieties, and on agronomic advantages, so that if there is a return on the research investment, it will be widely dispersed among growers rather than concentrated among seed or chemical interests.

This kind of research is in rather striking contrast to the research carried out by ICI Seeds, King Agro, or Allelix Crop Technologies/Pioneer Hi-Bred, all private corporate breeders of canola. (Pioneer now describes itself as a "genetic crop supply company."[71]) In the U.S., Calgene, of Davis, California, offers an example of yet another approach. (These companies and their strategies are discussed in Chapters 8 and 9.)

The problem of maintaining genetic diversity while trying to find and utilize very specific traits is an unending challenge, and the results are not always the most desirable, which suggests that the search for specific characteristics may itself be at the root of the problem. As Manitoba plant breeder Peter McVetty describes it,

There is a fair amount of genetic variability because there are 15-17 different breeding organizations, world-wide, putting materials into the western Canadian co-op trials, and most of the off-shore programs are private companies with their own in-house germplasm that I think is probably fairly distinct genetically. In Canada, however, our canolas are discouragingly Westar-based.

In *napus*, many are working on a Westar base for both inbreds and hybrids. I know that the SI system that King Agro is working with, which they bought from Guelph, and that Allelix is working with, works well with Westar but not all that well with anything else and Westar is susceptible to Blackleg.[72]

It would seem logical that if Blackleg is the major disease of canola, breeders would, if at all possible, stay away from a variety that was susceptible. Since the hybrids currently on the market or under test all share Westar's susceptibility to Blackleg, it is a reasonable guess that they are, as McVetty suggests, derived from Westar. McVetty's own *B.napus* low linolenic fatty acid program is an exception, he says, having no Westar in it. The *campestris* varieties are also limited, no matter where the genetic material comes from, says McVetty, because it has to be related to the variety Tobin to get the White Rust resistance that is a mandatory requirement. As a result, "you end up with default happenings: you work with what works."[73]

Private sector research is likely to take the path followed by Monsanto for development of a Westar canola resistant to its broad-spectrum broadleaf herbicide Round-Up (glyphosate). It announced in 1992 that such a canola variety could save canola growers as much as $100 million by reducing their average expense of $20 per acre on weed control to $11 per acre, even allowing for an extra $3 for additional seed costs. (Spending on herbicides for canola in 1989 was at the rate of $87 million per year!)

In addition to the $3 million it says it has already spent, Monsanto promised to spend $11 million more for field trials and testing of the glyphosate-resistant canola variety in the next five years. (Monsanto's Round-Up-resistant strain was entered in the co-op trials in 1992 along with Hoechst's Ignite (glufosinate ammonium) resistant strain of canola.)

Monsanto's strategy to reprogram canola so that its herbicide will be widely used is to make the glyphosate-resistant gene, and the technology for transferring it, readily available to both public and private plant breeders. Monsanto prefers to make its money by selling herbicides rather than by making and selling seeds, which it will happily leave to others if they will incorporate its technology and its demands, which are applicable to both hybrid and open-pollinated varieties of canola.

Harvey Glick, research and development director for Monsanto Canada's agriculture group, described for me Monsanto's approach as of mid-1992:

> We have been working specifically to *improve* canola for about five years. The first *improvement* that we would like to bring to canola is a trait that allows it to be sprayed with Round-Up herbicide. Right now it will kill all the weeds [particularly wild mustard] in canola but it will also kill the canola. [my emphasis]

> This research is driven by farmer response, as most of our research is. Farmers have not been happy with the level of crop protection chemicals available for canola. They have been limited to one (Treflan) that has about 80% of the brand share right now, and farmers have said that, a) they would like to have more options; and, b) they don't think that what they have right now is giving them the maximum return on their acre. We hope to bring this to market in about 3-4 years. We know it is controversial, but what is really driving it from the industry's perspective is that it is going to take costs out of production. That is why, unlike so many other new increases in technology, it has such a tremendous pull-through from the producer segment. It is going to lower costs, improve yields, increase the flexibility they have in managing their canola.

> We are not doing our own breeding, but we are saying to the breeders, we can give you an improvement [coming out of Monsanto's lab in St. Louis] that will provide a benefit to the grower. You develop the best lines of canola and we will give you this gene. Here is another benefit that you can add in.

> We hope to work with all of the breeders so all varieties of canola will all have the ability to withstand Round-Up and it will not be an issue in purchasing. The reason canola got picked is because its system lends itself very nicely to this kind of work and because farmers would see this as a very clear benefit and would like to have it.

> We have several genes that work in different ways, from bacterial and plant sources, and we are still evaluating which one works the best. In some plants one gene system works better than it does in another plant. The concept is not new. What has changed is our ability to be more concise and efficient.

Since he had used the words "give" and "offering,, I asked Glick if Monsanto was going to "give" this technology away? "

We are still discussing this with the seed companies. We are asking them, If you sell two varieties – Westar and improved Westar – and the farmer can save himself $5-15 per acre in weed control with the improved Westar, should some of that be recaptured by the improvement we have put into the seed, and how should we share that? We are still a few years away so we are still trying to fine tune a lot of those details.

And then there is hybrids, because of course if you have hybrids you have a greater possibility of capturing the value you have put into the seed. With o.p's, where a farmer can use the same seed year after year, you have to be careful because if you try to capture too much value he will say, I think you have enough value and I am going to use my own seed.[74]

Monsanto has also come up with another way to sell its famous herbicide, and that is as a pre-harvest desiccant. This is expected to be a solution to the problem of green seed in canola. Glick explained that the use of Round Up as a desiccant will hasten physiological maturity, and while seeds that are mature will not be affected, "we're going to help the seeds that are not quite there yet so they mature in the time between spraying and harvesting."

There is a pronounced tendency among those actively involved in scientific research to describe the use of such chemicals as a "technology", and claim, as one breeder did, that "technology isn't good or bad, it's how you apply it that's good or bad", Such an attitude ignores the structural issues and the alternatives. What else might Monsanto's $11 million have been applied to that would not increase dependence on its agro-toxins, such as research into how to handle weeds through better cultural practices and more diversified agriculture? (We return to this issue in Chapter 12 on Product and Process.)

It has not been difficult for companies like Monsanto to secure the cooperation of the universities, not only because their commercial contracts are attractive, but because their personnel obviously share the same culture, having been trained in the same institutions and sharing, by and large, the same gender and race.

The Ontario Agricultural College at the University of Guelph is one of the institutions that has allied itself, ideologically and practically, with the private sector and the interests of corporations like Monsanto. This has been consistently reflected in its research agenda both in animal and plant science. For example, the Department of Crop Science has been engaged in basic herbicide resistance research for some time. They developed the first triazine resistant canola and are currently working to replace both that and the current herbicide of choice, trifluralin, with a canola resistant to "a more environmentally friendly herbicide", as department head Beversdorf puts it.

> Most of the canola crop now gets treated with a herbicide family called trifluralin (Treflan) which on the Prairies has to be incorporated in the top three inches by fine working in the fall. Many of us would like to do away with that family of herbicides and that practice of leaving the soil exposed to erosion, so most of the canola research is looking for resistance to broad spectrum post emerge herbicides, like Monsanto's Round Up or Hoechst's Ignite.[75]

Another illustration of the reprogramming of the seed is found in the work being done to further alter its oil composition, and this is being done in a variety of ways by a variety of players.

The amount of linolenic acid in canola and soybean oils is unique among common vegetable oils. It causes susceptibility to oxidative flavour and odour changes that are troublesome in storage and when the oil is used for frying. The most promising approach to this problem appears to lie in the reduction of linolenic acid by genetic modification of the seed. Low linolenic acid canola oil has been shown to be much more stable in storage.

Stellar, developed at the Univ. of Manitoba and registered in 1987, is the world's first low linolenic canola variety, with linolenic acid levels in the order of 3%, or about one-third that of the usual canola crop. It is being used as source material for the development of improved low linolenic varieties of canola. McVetty says he hopes that their new low linolenic variety, Apollo, will lead the way to the same kind of total conversion of canola to low linolenic character as happened with low erucic acid rapeseed, but this depends on achieving superior agronomic characteristics as well.

This type of research utilizes *B.napus* strains that have high levels of palmitic acid as well, while also selecting for the yellow seed coat colour trait that has yielded higher oil and protein content with reduced percentage of fibre in both *B.napus* and *B.campestris*.

Although researchers may claim that all this work is concerned with increasing genetic diversity and strengthening the genetic base of canola, the commercial goals really have to do with producing designer oils via "identity preserved" canola varieties, herbicide tolerant varieties that will encourage the use of specific herbicides rather than more complex farming systems, and canola varieties more responsive to capital intensive farming practices rather than more extensive diversified systems (including the choice of hybrids over open-pollinated varieties). While the corporate breeders extol the virtues of the choice of canola varieties now available to farmers, they do not dwell long on the subject of the very narrow cultural and commercial framework that has produced these choices.

Having a lot to choose from does not necessarily work to the benefit of the farmer. I was recently told by a Cargill salesman, who was haranguing me about how "the market should decide", that there are 250 varieties of hybrid corn on the market. He admitted that there was no way a farmer could make an informed choice! How is the farmer even to know which of the 26 varieties of canola on the market in 1992 (15 private varieties and 11 public) is best for the particular location and conditions of his or her farm? Competition between seed companies to get a return on their investment is fierce and one can be sure that each will put their own variety in the best possible light and downplay any shortcomings.

The issue of choice should not be passed over too quickly, because there is little similarity between genuine genetic diversity and varietal differentiation for purposes of marketing. It may be in vogue to proclaim "freedom of choice" for the farmer as much as for anyone else in a neo-liberal society, but, as McVetty puts it,

> All this choice, choice, choice. . . all the farmer really needs is a list of good varieties. And they need seed readily available at a local dealer. They don't need a list of 75 look-alike Chevys coming off the production line one after the other. Boring. "I like Vanguard, that's a nice name, maybe I'll grow that this year." That's kind of insane. What you need is good varieties that promise reasonably good agronomic performance for the growers and carry with them minimal production risk or minimal risk for anyone through the system. They have some oil, they have some protein, they'll mature before they're frosted and they have enough disease resistance that you succeed. You don't need to get all fancy about this.[76]

The Seeds Act, which governs the inspection, quality and sale of seeds in Canada, has been in place since 1923. The objective of the law was to ensure that varieties licensed for sale in Canada met certain agronomic standards. Every new seed variety had to be entered in trials and prove its superiority to the varieties already on the market in order to gain registration for sale. The Cargill salesman referred to above described all this as backward and socialist, pointing out that there is no such system in the U.S., where any seed can be put on the market by anyone.

The Canadian licensing system has, however, assured farmers of a minimum level of agronomic performance and set standards of quality and uniformity so that the buyers of the crops being produced would have some idea of what they were getting. One might describe this as the institutionalization of the principle of equity: customers at every level, big or small, have some assurance as to what they are buying.

This approach is in obvious conflict with the neo-liberal ideology of competition and de-regulation, and consequently has been under pressure from private breeders, transnational seed corporations and Conservative politicians in the government and their bureaucratic shadows. In mid-1990 the Conservative Government pushed though Plant Breeders' Rights legislation and then watered down the provisions of the Seeds Act so that new varieties could be registered for sale if they were simply *as good as* the mean of a number of checks for existing varieties. Again to quote McVetty, "The declining degree of meaningful information will make the decisions on what to seed in the spring more difficult than ever."[77]

To ensure the success of its de-regulation, the federal government has steadily cut back on funding for the co-operative registration trials that have provided the objective data for comparative seed evaluation. The consequences are obvious when coupled with the increasing number of privately-generated varieties being pushed onto the market. It will become simply impossible for the test stations to carry out their mandate and farmers will become increasingly dependent on the information supplied by the seed salespeople themselves or on their neighbours who may or may not have had good luck.

The social principle of equity, so easily lost sight of in the ideological culture of competitiveness, has been embedded in every aspect of Prairie agriculture, from seed variety testing and registration to the Canadian Wheat Board and the rail transportation system. The current attack on this principle is based on the assertion that it denies diversity and choice. It is true, to some extent, that the CWB system favours uniformity and specialization and works against diversity. The Canadian system has been built on the practice of rigid grading, and pricing according to grade, thus ensuring every farmer of the same price for grain of like quality. Uniform quality in large volume is also key to efficient large-scale grain handling and to inter-governmental trading. To the private traders who want to gain control of grain marketing in Canada, all this is, of course, a disadvantage. Using a rhetoric of diversity and choice, they claim they want to be able to supply niche and specialty markets with a wide variety and quality of grains and specialty oilseeds but are blocked from providing that "service" to farmers by the system now in place.

The question of diversity is not simply one of supplying the consumer with thousands of variations on six basic staple foods, nor, on the other hand, of ensuring that the food system is not under monopoly control. The development of canola provides a good illustration of the practical problems of maintaining diversity in the face of conventional reductionist science, as described by Beversdorf:

> Canola is a classic example where market demands – for low erucic acid and glucosinolate levels – tightened up the specifications, which initially meant that most germplasm available in the world could not be used. So then it is a slow process of reintroducing genetic diversity while maintaining the desired characteristics. This took a good ten years for spring canola and 20 years for winter canola. [78]

While recognizing the limited genetic diversity of canola, because the sources of the double-low characteristics are the same early *napus* and *campestris* varieties that the breeders started with 30 years ago, Beversdorf insists that there is more diversity today than there was in the late 1960s and early 70s. This is because there has been a gradual re-assimilation of the double-low germplasm into new varieties with different genetic backgrounds and with a fair bit of diversity in other traits, such as disease resistance, early maturity and yield. Numerous varieties have been registered in the past few years, he says, from a diverse array of Australian, European and Scandinavian genetic backgrounds, as well as traditional Canadian germplasm.

A parallel process has gone on in the winter canolas grown in Europe where a single variety, Jet Neuf, occupied about 80% of the Western European acreage at one point. According to Beversdorf, "There was about an 18 year period in Europe for single-zero and double-zero winter rapeseed that had very limited germplasm."

Since disease and insect organisms evolve and adapt to the host they feed upon, growing one individual genotype for a long period of time gives the disease or the insect a good opportunity to adapt itself. While disease can be controlled by increasing genetic diversity and by breaking its life-cycle through crop rotation, the susceptibility of virtually all canola varieties to Blackleg and white mold *(Sclerotinia)*, as I have already pointed out, limit the growing of canola in the same field to once every four or five years.

The disaster that can befall a crop with limited genetic diversity that is grown continuously over a long period of time was illustrated by the very severe increase in disease problems that resulted when a single cultivar of *B.napus* (Westar), constituting nearly 80% of that variety grown in Canada, was grown continuously for about eight years. Even though it may have been the best variety available, the consequence was that white mold and Blackleg became epidemic on the Prairies, and remain epidemic in some areas, severely limiting canola production.

Dwight More, of the Canola Council, described how the combination of Canada's registration system and the significant achievement of the publicly developed variety Westar contributed to this situation:

> Our registration system said, if a new variety cannot at least equal Westar in each category and be better at least in some of them, then it won't get registered. As a result, hardly any varieties got registered for a period of about five years. The varieties from Sweden that tried to come in hit a barrier because they were longer in maturity, etc. So over its lifetime Westar was probably grown on 20 million acres, and that set up a situation where its weakness, Blackleg susceptibility, came through.

> We kind of did the same thing with Tobin, a *campestris* variety. It was so superior to everything else that from 1985 to 1990 it was grown on the rest of the acres, Westar and Tobin together making up a total of 95% of the acres. The 1991 crop is the first time those two varieties were not dominant. Now we have changed the system and I don't think we will ever see that situation again. And we have private companies along with AgCanada.[79]

One might, on these grounds, be tempted to take sides with the Cargill salesman, except that, as usual, there were alternatives to creating this situation. Westar gained its place of dominance on the grounds of yield (itself a consequence of a number of factors). If yield had not been seen as such a singular requirement, more attention might have been paid to disease susceptibility. In addition, if scepticism were a more prominent characteristic of reductionist science, such crop uniformity, however heterogeneous a single variety might be, would never have been permitted simply on the grounds of the potential vulnerability of such a uniform crop. Uniformity has become, however, a fundamental and essential attribute of industrial agriculture.

Increasing genetic diversity in a crop that is built quite literally on the genetic composition of one seed is a long and difficult process, particularly when the product has to meet the rigid specifications that are laid down for canola quality, to say nothing of what must happen when product characteristics are even more rigidly defined by end-users.

The apparent increase in canola diversity that has taken place in the past decade must be evaluated in light of the privatization of the seed industry that has accompanied it. The kind of diversity that appeals to Proctor & Gamble or McDonald's does not necessarily introduce any significant genetic diversity into the crop. If McDonald's or Proctor & Gamble specifies certain characteristics for canola oil, and is willing to pay for it, the process of suddenly narrowing the genetic base in search of specific characteristics and then having to broaden it again repeats itself. This type of cycle can occur with any monoculture crop, that is, any crop where uniformity is an overarching requirement.

The same thing happens when you find a new type of disease, as Beversdorf pointed out to me:

> Wheat went through epidemics every 10-20 years in the first years of this century, and every time there was an epidemic there was a scramble for a new gene for disease resistance. And every time a new gene was introduced the germplasm became very focused on the source of that gene for disease resistance. Then there would be a gradual broadening over the next few years and when the next epidemic hit we would be back to another single source of resistance. Eventually the science got sophisticated enough, I think, that we were able to predict the next epidemic quite accurately and usually have the resistant varieties in place before the epidemic arrived. Even so we will go thorough cycles of narrowing and broadening, but hopefully without severe epidemics.[80]

What is happening at the same time, however, is that the disease continually develops its own modes of survival by developing mutations to handle every new resistance gene introduced into the plant. It becomes an endless game of tag as long as the underlying uniformity of the crop is the dominant characteristic.

As I pointed out earlier, traditional plant breeding has been a matter of the selection of obvious characteristics, such as time to maturity, disease resistance, drought tolerance, etc. As the Western science of plant breeding has developed, and analytical technology with it, the selection process has become increasingly refined and deliberate. Yet it remains a process of selection out of what nature chooses to provide, and the step beyond selection, deliberate crossing, still depends on what is there to start with and what nature permits or encourages.

With the advent of biotechnology in the 1980s, it has become possible to both select and move genes with a speed and deliberateness that is quite unprecedented and non-natural. The process has moved from selection and crossing to direct intervention to determine the character of the progeny. The development of canola is a good illustration. From simple selection of seeds and the reproduction of those with desirable characteristics, rapeseed research moved into a period of more specific selection and breeding, and now it is a matter of actually *introducing* desired characteristics through genetic engineering, as indicated in the 1990 annual report of Pioneer Hi-Bred International: "The Company's application of biotechnology is focused on planned plant transformation as opposed to an experimental approach where the objective is to achieve a major breakthrough largely by chance."

The intentional movement of genes, not only within a species, but also between species, and the creation of transgenic plants as a result, is not simply a matter of evolutionary continuity. It is different from Beversdorf's description of the genetic flow (information exchange) that has always occurred:

> Genetic material seems to flow, if not from population to population at one time, it certainly flows across evolutionary timeframes, so you probably share more genes than you realize with bacteria, right down to basic sequences. There is a flow between species, and there is probably a flow between related populations, naturally, though at a low level, and there are probably a remarkable number of genes in rapeseed that are the same as your genes.[81]

One has to wonder what happens when this very slow evolutionary process is short circuited, and something is put into a system to which it has had no chance to adapt.

The deliberate and accelerated movement of genetic material is, at this point, from the natural ecosystem into the agro-ecosystem (from wild to agricultural) as far as we know. Beversdorf says that he does not think the reverse can be done deliberately by plant breeders, but it can and does happen naturally.

> When there is a selective advantage in the weed population for an agronomic gene (such as being resistant to some particular disease or insect) and there is a natural system for crossing, even at a low frequency, I am sure that eventually there will be movement. There is some flow of specific genes from agricultural to wild populations. Herbicide resistance is a classic: if you put a resistance gene into a specific crop from some alien source, there could certainly be a backflow into weedy species that grow around it. I don't think there is a risk to the agricultural ecosystem in introducing selective herbicide tolerance into crop varieties, but there might be a risk in introducing pathogens in order to select plants that are carrying resistance.[82]

Just as the plant gets reduced to its seed, the seed gets reduced to a set of genes, and the genes get reduced to a genetic code. But this reductionist process, even if we might eventually be able to identify all the bits and pieces, tells us little about the functioning of the whole and its relationship to its environment. There really is little reason, other than self-justification, for claiming that the genetic manipulation carried out by Monsanto or Allelix researchers is just what nature does, only more directed. What we know about canola may be a whole lot less than what we don't know about rapeseed. The problem lies not so much with ill will as with the arrogance of our science.

Chapter 7

SQUEEZING OUT THE OIL:
THE PROCESSORS

On the processor side of the story the restructuring of the seed was in many ways being replicated.

Oilseed crushing refers to the process of extracting oil from oilseeds, the Canadian ones being flax seed (linseed oil), sunflowers, soybeans and rapeseed/canola. Corn oil is also a vegetable oil, but corn is not treated as an oilseed because its oil comes only from the germ or embryo of the corn seed. The other 80% of the seed is processed into starch, corn syrup, HFCS (high fructose corn syrup), and other products.

Elsewhere in the world industrial and edible oils are produced from cottonseed (cottonseed oil), oil palms (palm oil/palm kernel oil), peanuts (peanut oil) and others. Depending on the character and use of the oil, it may require refining after extraction. Each oil has its own characteristics and applications.

The oilseed crushing industry in Canada has been divided historically into a western, or Prairie, sector and an eastern, or Ontario, sector. The distinction between the two regions is due both to large differences in growing conditions and to the role of transportation policies and subsidies. In the East (Ontario), oilseed crushing (primarily soybeans) has been for the nearby domestic market for both oils and meal and has been protected by tariffs on imported oil. Since markets were close to the crush plants, transportation costs have not been a significant issue. In the West, however, the crushing and refining industry was built to meet the limited needs of the local market as well as the distant eastern domestic market and beyond. In the 1970s and early 80s the export market was expanding at the rate of 8-10% per year, but since the mid-80s exports of canola oil to the U.S. have increased significantly.

The western Canadian crushing industry has long been burdened with high fixed costs relative to the local market demand since it was assumed from the beginning the oil would be exported. Dependence on distant markets, combined with rail subsidies on whole (raw) seeds and high transportation costs has added to its instability.

In 1991, 8 million acres of canola were grown in Canada, producing 4.3 million tonnes of seed, of which Japan imported 1.84 million tonnes, or about 95% of its domestic requirements, with the remainder processed in Canada.

To understand the Canadian oilseed processing industry, then, one has to understand how the operating context of this industry is determined by the Japanese buyers of Canadian canola seed.

Japan has been importing rapeseed, and subsequently canola, from Canada since the 1960s. During the 60s and early 70s, Japan controlled rapeseed imports by means of an import quota system initially in order to protect its domestic growers, and then to protect both growers and small inland crushers. This was part of Japan's traditional protection of its domestic food supply.

In 1964 Burton Craig made his first trip to Japan as a member of a trade delegation sponsored by the federal Ministry of Industry Trade and Commerce and the Rapeseed Association to promote the utilization of Canadian rapeseed. Craig remembers that,

> The Japanese told us that rapeseed was not competitive with other [domestic] crops, and they could therefore import it without a problem. The meal was used as fertilizer. Rapeseed was the only oil allowed to be used to light the lamps in the Imperial Palace. Japan deliberately phased out the crop, even though it meant the destruction of a widely dispersed cottage industry. The old stone mills in the villages were supplied by farmers who grew the rape in their small fields and brought the seeds to the mill in sacks. The government's choice was to establish a few big mills on the coast and import the seed.[83]

When domestic production of rapeseed began to decline due to the withdrawal of price supports, the government continued to protect the small inland crushers by allocating to them a percentage of the increasing amount of seed being imported by the few large crushers, situated on the coast, which were allowed to continue to expand their capacities. Gradually the small inland crushers sold their quota to the large coastal crushers – a pattern of consolidation that is very familiar to every aspect of agriculture where the farm product requires processing, dairy being the prime example.

Different tellers tell different stories, or at least different versions of the same story. According to Downey, after the Second World War when young Japanese left the farms for the cities, there was not enough farm labour to transplant the rapeseed after the rice crop and rapeseed production almost disappeared. The government tried to maintain local production, but when this failed, they continued to support the small local crushers by giving them import quotas. However, according to Downey, one man organized these small inland crushers and began to sell their import quotas to the big crushers on the coast for very high prices. By the late 60s, the big crushers had succeeded in breaking the hold of the inland crushers.

By the late 70s the import quotas had been replaced with a flat rate import tariff on oil only. The import restrictions that had been initially put in place to protect domestic growers and then small crushers had been captured by the very large crushers. The beneficiaries of the protective tariff on imported oil are now the crushers who depend entirely on imported seed. Accompanying these changes in Japan was Japanese encouragement of the western Canadian canola growers and the Canola Council.

As Bob Broeska describes it, two processing industries, both based on western Canadian seed, had been structured simultaneously: one in Japan and one in western Canada. The Japanese processors had the handicap of a distant seed source but the advantages of the Canadian rail subsidy and a protected domestic market, while the Canadian processing plants had the benefit of a local seed source and the handicap of no control over domestic seed price and no corresponding transportation subsidy for their products.

Japan's high import tariff on canola oil, but not on canola seed for domestic crushing, amounts to effective exclusion of foreign competition in the Japanese edible oil market. The structure of the industry makes it possible for the crushers to pass the cost of the tariff on to the Japanese consumer, thus allowing the Japanese crushers to outbid the Canadian crushers for seed. Broeska explained that,

> by the late 70s the oilseed crushing industry was dominated by the giant mills and Japan was importing large amounts of soybean and rapeseed from Canada, the U.S. or Brazil. In the late 70s Japan abandoned import quotas on edible oils because they no longer had a domestic rapeseed industry to protect. They shifted to a flat-rate fixed tariff of 17,000 yen/tonne on crude canola and soybean oil, and 22,500 yen on refined oil. But then the value of the yen skyrocketed in 1979-80 so that flat rate also went up from 11.5% to as high as 36%, a rising barrier behind which the crushers could buy their raw seed at a higher price to sell the oil on a protected market.[84]

The Japanese oilseeds industry is neatly summarized in the primary trade journal of the global oilseeds industry:

In the last 20 years the edible oil and fats industry has changed from a large number of small companies each serving a specific region to bigger companies servicing a large area, some on a national scale. Thus the number of processors has fallen from 800 to 125, with only 10 having a daily production exceeding 1000 tonnes and the top seven accounting for 99% of the market.

Market leaders in the edible oil for domestic use sector are Nisshin Oil Mills with 39%, Ajinomoto 25%, Hohen Oil 14%, Showa Sangyo 10%, Rinor Oil Mills 5%, Yoshihara Oil Mills 4%, Nikka Oil and Fats 2%; all others the remaining 1%. In addition to this consolidation, major processors now have fully integrated production, from extraction via processing to finished products.[85]

The agenda for canola seed in western Canada, then, is shaped by five companies in Japan. In fact, says Broeska, the Japanese have controlled the market for western Canadian canola since 1967: "Yukio Sakaguchi was there with James McAnsh and Mac Runciman from the start, and even now the Canola Council meets twice a year with the Japanese, once in Japan and once in Canada."

The western Canadian crushers naively participated in the Council believing they were equal partners, only to discover that their "finely crafted trade policies, as a result of joint industry-Government strategy", had given the Japanese a distinct advantage. This has left the Canadian crushers in a position where there is nothing for them to discuss with the Canola Council or the Government except trade and transportation policy "distortions" while the Japanese focus on seed quality and crop development. It is hard to carry on a conversation about industry policy when the speakers are talking about different subjects. Speaking on behalf of the crushers, Broeska describes how they felt about all this:

Canadian crushers felt duped: they had participated in the Council with the Government in order to develop a Canadian crop and they had made investments in Canada only to have a distorted set of trade and transport rules dictate negative economics.

The sell-out of the entire Canadian crushing industry to stronger interests in the late 80s and early 90s is a direct result of this situation. New owners in 1992 will reiterate all the same trade and transport problems of the earlier era that require Government action if the industry is to be viable.[86]

The Canadian canola industry has developed within this context. On the one hand canola was to be the Cinderella Crop for Prairie agriculture, but on the other its welfare was to a great extent determined by outside forces that bought nearly half the Canadian production for direct export as raw seed every year, leaving the Canadian processing industry to settle for access to only half of the Canadian crop. The industry has not been static, however, and over the years it has undergone an almost continuous process of restructuring that in many ways parallels the restructuring of the seed itself. The apparent condition of equilibrium reached in 1992 may be short-lived.

The Processors

[Note: Information in this section is detailed because there is no other account to which researchers can be referred. The general reader is invited to observe the trends and major players and not worry about the details if you do not share my fascination with how the corporate sector organizes and reorganizes itself and others.]

The first crushing plant in the west was the Co-op Vegetable Oils plant at Altoona, Man., which was conceived in 1939 when it was discovered that sunflowers could grow well in Manitoba, and built in 1943. It continues to operate, crushing and refining both sunflowers and canola.

J. Gordon Ross started a plant in Moose Jaw, Saskatchewan, about 1946-7 but he dismantled it in the 1950s and literally integrated it into the Saskatchewan Wheat Pool plant in Saskatoon, where they crushed both flax and rapeseed. It later became a solvent-extraction plant.

E.P.Taylor built the first sizeable oilseed crushing plant in Ontario on the Toronto waterfront in 1946, naming the company Victory Mills Ltd. in honour of the Canadian military effort in World War II. Taylor had made a fortune in food, ammunition and other enterprises and saw new opportunities in oilseeds. Originally his plant crushed soybeans imported from the U.S. to make pig feed but the Western Grain Transportation Act of 1941 established low, fixed rates for shipping whole grains out of the Prairies, making the utilization of western grains and oilseeds in feed manufacturing financially attractive. (There was also a preferential tariff on exports of feed to Britain.)

In 1940 Australian businessman Sir Walter Carpenter saw an article written by Stan Boulter, who was then working for Canada Packers in Edmonton. The two got together and began processing copra (coconut oil) in Vancouver in 1941. The war soon cut off the supply and there was nothing for the plant, R. W. Carpenter Canada Ltd., to process. According to a story in *The Hamilton Spectator* in the late 70s, Mrs. Phyllis Turner, (mother of the Liberal politician John Turner), was then head of the Wartime Prices and Trade Board oils and fats section, and she promised to supply the company with oilseeds if they would move the company to Ontario or Quebec – thus illustrating that business decisions are not always based on the kind of rationality claimed by the economists. So it was that in 1942 Carpenter and Boulter moved their plant to Hamilton and began processing a variety of oilseeds: flaxseed, sunflowers, rapeseed and soybeans. They apparently even tried producing fish oil.

While he was in the process of setting up the Hamilton plant, Boulter was asked by E. P. Taylor to set up the Victory soybean plant in Toronto with the promise that he would get a cut of the action. When that did not happen, Boulter went back to Hamilton in 1946 as managing director of the Carpenter plant which was renamed Canadian Vegetable Oils Ltd. In 1950 Boulter bought out the company and renamed it Canadian Vegetable Oil Processing Ltd. (CVOP).

C.M. McLean of Canada Packers was one of Boulter's backers in Hamilton, and eventually Canada Packers bought the CVOP plant (c.1967). In 1983 the canola processing plant, which had been built quite literally in and around the soybean plant, started processing western canola seed. At that time there was no canola grown in Ontario, though since then Ontario production has peaked at 100,000 tonnes.

Canada Packers ran the Hamilton plant until selling it in 1989 to Central Soya. The plant currently runs two separate lines, one for canola with 600 tonnes per day capacity, and one for soybeans with 1200 tonnes per day capacity. The plant runs continuously except for a two-week maintenance shut down every summer. It employs about 120 people, although it takes only seven people to actually operate the processing operations at any one time. The rest are maintenance, supervisory, clerical, and so forth.

The Toronto plant (which came to be called Victory Soya Mills) was sold in 1954 to Proctor & Gamble which later sold it to the Shamrock Group, a Walt Disney investment group, which in turn sold it to Central Soya in 1986. In March, 1991, Central Soya, which is owned by Ferruzzi of Italy, shut down the Toronto plant, which was capable of crushing 1200 tonnes per day of soybeans only. The reasons for closing the Toronto plant were its location on the changing Toronto waterfront, an hour further for truckers hauling beans from SW Ontario, and its higher operating costs, since its overhead was spread over 1200 tonnes while the Hamilton plant can spread its overhead over 1800 tonnes per day, according to Ted Hamill of Central Soya in Hamilton.

This has left only two operating oilseed crushing plants in Ontario: the Windsor plant belonging to Archer Daniels Midland (ADM) of the U.S.A. which, like Central Soya, processes both canola and soybeans, and the Hamilton plant belonging to Central Soya. Hamill described this plant to me:

> We run the Ontario harvest from mid-July through early September and then run the western harvest on through the year. There is on-farm storage, and substantial storage at the Lakehead. It goes by rail to the Lakehead then by laker [lake freighter] to here. We have had two ships tied up here for the winter, and we unload them as we require the seed for processing. We need 600 tonnes per day, and a small laker carries 11,000 tonnes, enough for 20 days, and the large ones, self-unloaders, carry 25,000 tonnes, about 40 days supply for us.

> We purchase crops on our own, but when it comes to purchasing other things, like our solvent, hexane, we do it as Central Soya, with seven plants. They negotiate the contract, and then we draw on it.

> We have stayed close to Canada Packers, and they are more up to date in research and facilities than someone like Proctor & Gamble, so in terms of knowing what the industry wants, we get more out of Canada Packers and the people on both sides know each other. Even though they sold us, they remain our major customer.

> We have made a commitment to stay in the market. ADM will step right out of the market, whether over bad quality or whatever. They have always been a lot more secretive, so in terms of research, they have let us carry the ball, knowing that what we want is what they will want.

> I think we will be here quite a long time. Central Soya wouldn't want to allow ADM to have Ontario. If we were to walk out of Ontario in terms of crushing soybeans, ADM would just sit there and pick them off as they went south and make money hand over fist. It's like two gas stations on opposite corners in a gas war, and they get down to five cents a litre and neither is making money, but no one's going to blink.[87]

The 1200 tonne/day capacity Windsor soybean processing plant (actually capable of processing up to 2000 tonnes per day) was built in 1976 by Maple Leaf Monarch, a partnership of Maple Leaf Mills and Monarch Foods (Lever Bros./Unilever). The mill was forecast, at the time, to cost $21 million, "partially financed with $9 million in Federal funds, in part repayable depending upon the profitability of the project."[88]

The mill was planned to operate in tandem with a deep-water grain terminal on the Detroit River which was nominally built by United Cooperatives of Ontario (UCO) at the same time. Grain unloaded at the terminal can be moved by conveyor into the adjoining mill, and there was a long-term agreement between Maple Leaf Monarch and UCO for oilseed handling. When ADM bought the mill from Maple Leaf Monarch in 1985, UCO continued to operate the terminal, but in 1987 ADM leased the terminal from UCO and then bought it outright in 1991. ADM acquired both facilities in Windsor for something like 20% of their actual value, by all reports.

Extraction of the oil from the canola seed is only the first step. It still has to be refined, and this is a separate process. The initial extraction process produces a crude oil cleaned up so that it can be stored for weeks, but the refining process removes the gums so that the oil has a shelf-life of months or years. (The gum residue from soybeans is used to produce lecithin.)

Canada Packers was for many years the major Canadian refiner, with six or seven plants around the country. With the recent takeover of oilseed processing by ADM and Central Soya, the processing and refining plants have been brought under common ownership.

This is illustrated in the person of David Sommerville, now president of CanAmera Foods Ltd. Sommerville says he has worked for 35 years in virtually the same location, although for four different companies. He started with Swift Canadian in 1958 at its edible oil refinery adjacent to the Toronto stockyards where the major meat packers were also once located. When the refinery was purchased by Gainers they kept Sommerville on and then, in 1983, when Canada Packers bought the plant they too kept him on, making him manager of the refinery. In 1992 Canada Packers, having been taken over by Hillsdown Holdings and renamed Maple Leaf Foods, sold its entire edible oils division to CanAmera Foods, a partnership between Central Soya and CSP Foods (see below). Sommerville's new employer made him president.

Western Processors

The story of western Canadian oilseed processing is not a happy one, except perhaps for the contractors who built the various mills scattered around the three Prairie provinces. Political opportunism – a new crushing plant is certainly good for the votes if not for the voters – coupled with the notions of "value-added" and diversification and greased with visions of grandeur generated by the promoters of Canada's Cinderella crop, led simply to the construction of more crushing capacity than crop. The continual drain on the public purse finally, in 1991, resulted in the takeover of the industry by foreign transnationals.

Sexsmith, Alberta:

The oilseed crushing plant in Sexsmith, Alberta, was proposed in 1973 as a farmers co-operative, Northern Alberta Rapeseed Processors Ltd. It had already cost $14 million by the time it opened in 1977. The plant went into receivership in 1985, taking with it $34 million in farmers' investments and provincial loans. In 1987 the government bought the plant from the receivers for $8.6 million and turned it over to Alberta Terminals Ltd. The Agricultural Development Corp. purchased $14.6 million in preferred shares and the provincial cabinet issued a $20 million loan guarantee. The government also agreed to spend another $6.9 million to cover past losses and make plant improvements. The acknowledged total of spending and write-offs by the provincial government was $49.5 million, but with the preferred shares and the loan guarantee added in, the public investment came to a total of $84.1 million by the end of 1991. As if that was not enough, in March, 1992, the Alberta Government put in another $7 million to keep the plant – now Northern Lite Canola Inc. – going until a buyer could be found.

One possible buyer for the Sexsmith plant is ADM, rumoured not to want it as a functional mill but rather to get rid of it by taking it apart and selling it to Russia, where ADM has positioned itself to become a major presence in a restructured agriculture.

Cargill Ltd:

One company noticeably absent from the oilseed crushing business in Canada is Cargill, but it is not because they weren't paying attention. In 1972 Cargill wanted to be in the originating business, according to Cargill v.p. Dick Dawson, and rapeseed was the only grain not under control of the Canadian Wheat Board, so it made its first investment in western Canada by building a rapeseed collection terminal at North Battleford, Saskatchewan. Cargill intended to build a crushing mill as well on the 40 acre site, but they never got around to it since the terminal was sufficient to give them fair access to the rapeseed trade. The location was chosen because it was equidistant, for rail purposes, between the West Coast and Thunder Bay, the two export positions on water, so that the shipping costs to an export terminal would be the same either way.

The terminal was a success, according to Dawson, and two years later, when Cargill had a spare $20 million as a result of selling grain to the Russians during what is referred to in the trade as The Great Grain Robbery of 1971-73, they bought National Grain, giving Cargill a major presence in the Canadian west. The Great Grain Robbery refers to the prolonged episode during which the Soviet Union bought up nearly all the grain available around the world. They did this through a series of deals with private traders that caught national governments off guard and drove up grain prices very substantially as grain stocks were pulled down to nothing. [For the complete story of Cargill in Canada, see my book *Trading Up*, NC Press, 1990.]

In the early 80s Cargill bought land at Melfort, Saskatchewan, to build a crushing mill. Word has it that Cargill did not build the mill because when the Saskatchewan Wheat Pool got wind of their plans, they, together with Manitoba Pool Elevators, quickly built a mill at Harrowby, Manitoba, with help from the Federal Government courtesy of then Agriculture Minister Eugene Whelan. (Whelan also assisted construction of the Windsor mill.) When Whelan refused to help Cargill, Cargill scrapped their plans, figuring they would be the victims of unfair competition if their plant was not subsidized in the same way their competitors were. Today Dawson says Whelan saved them $25 million since they are much better off without a crushing mill given the vast overcapacity as a result of government subsidies.

United Oilseed Products Ltd. (UOPL)/ADM:

UOPL was incorporated in 1973 and the crushing plant at Lloydminster, Alberta, began operations two years later. The company was 50% owned by United Grain Growers (UGG), 35% by Mitsubishi Corp. and 15% by Nisshin Oil Mills Ltd.

In late 1990 the mill was closed. Six months later the plant, which was capable of processing 250,000 tonnes of canola (10% of the Canadian crop) into 100,000 tonnes of oil each year, was sold to ADM Agri-Industries Ltd, the Canadian subsidiary of ADM. ADM also bought Soo Line Mills Ltd., Winnipeg's only remaining flour miller, and McCarthy Milling of Mississauga, Ontario, from Weston Foods, Ltd. at about the same time.

In 1990, just before its expansion into western Canadian oilseed crushing, ADM had shut down its Velva, North Dakota crushing plant. In its 1989 annual report, ADM had described the "newly acquired" Velva plant as its "first canola processing venture in the U.S."

CSP Foods/Central Soya/CanAmera:

In mid-1991, CSP Foods formed a joint venture with Central Soya of the U.S. CSP Foods is itself a joint venture of Manitoba Pool Elevators and the Saskatchewan Wheat Pool and operates crushing and refining facilities at Altona, Manitoba and Nipawin, Saskatchewan, as well as a crushing plant at Horrowby, Manitoba, and a refining plant at Dundas, Ontario.

The new company, named CanAmera Foods Ltd., then bought out the edible oils division of Maple Leaf Foods Inc. (formerly Canada Packers, which had been bought by Hillsdown Holdings of Britain), consisting of a crushing plant in Fort Saskatchewan, Alberta, refining plants in Montreal, Toronto and Wainwright, Alberta, a seed-gathering plant in Humboldt, Sask., and 50% ownership in Prairie Margarine Inc. of Edmonton, of which CSP owned the other 50%. The price was reported to be about $105 million in cash. Maple Leaf Foods reported that its edible oils division had annual sales of about $250 million.

The net result is that CanAmera Foods owns five oilseed processing plants and five vegetable oil refineries with a combined processing capacity of 1.6 million tonnes of oilseed annually. The company employs about 800 people and should have gross sales of $700 million and about 50% of the Canadian crushing capacity, leaving ADM with about 35%.

While it may be big by Canadian standards, CanAmera will have only about 3% of the North American edible oils market compared to 33% for ADM, 20% for Cargill and 12% for Bunge. For comparison, Ferruzzi (which owns Central Soya), Cargill and ADM together process in Europe about 7 million tonnes of rapeseed/canola, 4 million tonnes of sunflower seed, and 1.5 million tonnes of soybeans per year.[89]

CanAmera is a 50-50 partnership, run by a board with 3 directors from CSP and 3 from Central Soya. CSP is stronger in the west and Central Soya in the east. CanAmera's creation is a recognition of the fact that there will be a full North American market in 1995 when tariffs on soybean oil come off. Tariffs on canola oil have already been removed.

According to Sommerville,

ADM's style and strategy in the U.S. is what we can expect to see here, and have seen in Windsor: high throughput, totally integrated, a narrow approach to a few products, like canola and soybean only, and they're a production driven, low cost producer with high market shares. They are pretty predictable in what they want to do and how they want to do it. You have to admire that, without necessarily agreeing with it. In some cases, its almost like a predatory approach to business, but that is typically the way they have entered a region. They attack it, and try to drive the fringe players out. With Central and ADM, it's the difference between being number one and number four. Central is being narrower in market focus, more regional, more specialized, value-added. Cargill is like ADM.

I don't particularly want to slug it out with the ADMs and the Cargills, I just don't think we want to get into the kinds of things these guys get into in the States, like 3000 tonnes a day crushing plants – it's hard to compete with that. So we like to position ourselves in specialty oils.

We are not far enough along to see what role we should play, except in processing these special seeds. Being a small player in the North American market, it makes sense for us to seek niche markets, and we want to support research where we can in the development of specialty oils, and we have done that with HEAR oil. There are different patterns that could evolve, but we have only been in business eight weeks.[90]

Just to indicate how intertwined the whole business is, Canada Packers had previously purchased the Alberta Food Products Plant in Fort Saskatchewan, Alberta, from a partnership of Alberta Pool and C.ITOH. C.ITOH is a major purchaser of canola, buying about 13% of the raw canola seed exported to Japan annually. In crop year 1990-91 a total of 1.88 million tonnes of canola seed were exported. C.ITOH has a close relationship with Fuji Vegetable Oil.

There are about 35 crushing companies in Japan. They crush 3.8 million tonnes of imported soybeans and 1.8 million tonnes of imported canola seed per year. The rationale for importing whole soybeans and canola seed rather than oil and meal is that the freight for importing whole soybeans is $25 per tonnes compared to $43 per tonnes if crude soybean oil and meal are imported. Canola oil for edible use surpassed soybean oil in Japan in 1989. Currently about two-thirds of the meal is used in animal feeds while one-third is used as fertilizer for citrus and fruit trees.[91]

As usual, there is more to the story. Japan has requirements for oil and high protein meal. They can come from canola and soybean in varying percentages since soybeans produce about 80% meal and 20% oil when crushed while canola yields about 60% meal and 40% oil. Since imported oil of any sort is virtually excluded from the Japanese market by the tariff, the crushers can import whole soybeans and canola in the amounts required to balance the requirements of the market. Because they are integrated, the crushers are able to also control the prices of oil products in the retail market as well as the prices for canola meal for feed and fertilizer.

The recent shifts in the ownership of Canadian processing facilities has blurred the line between crushers, refiners and traders. ADM and Central Soya are both major traders as well as crushers and refiners, in

Canada, in the U.S. and globally. At the same time the Japanese buyers are either themselves crushers in Japan or so closely related to crushers that it is difficult to separate the categories. As described above, C.ITOH has a relationship with Fuji, while Mitsui, another Japanese buyer of canola, exporting about half a million tonnes of Canadian canola annually, is also related to a Japanese processor. Mitsubishi Canada is another canola exporter (with ties to Lakeside Packers in Brooks, Alberta) and a sister company to Nisshin Oil Mills, and both of these companies used to own a share of UOPL in Alberta, as noted above.

Relationships between players in the industry can be just as important as the capabilities and strategies of the individual companies, and just as the processing plants have been subject to an almost continuous restructuring, so have the relationships between them and with the trade. For example, UGG had a working relationship with Mitsui for about 20 years, but in 1989 UGG broke that off in order to form a joint venture, Canagrain, with Continental Grain of the U.S.

According to UGG c.e.o. Brian Hayward, there are two ways of selling canola: one is FOB Vancouver, which is the way UGG was selling to Mitsui, which means that UGG bought the canola from the farmers, assembled it in Vancouver, sold it to Mitsui and put it on a boat, and Mitsui took it from there on. The alternative is to buy the grain, ship it to Japan, and sell it directly there.

> When you sell grain FOB you have less control over the movement of that grain from the farm right on. When you sell it delivered in the importing market, you have a lot more control over your own destiny. We did it both ways. As a result, we have gained a lot more understanding about how the international marketplace works.[92]

The $1 million per year cost of maintaining a sales office in Japan was one of the reasons UGG decided to change its strategy and form the marketing alliance with Continental. Now, as Hayward put it, "we are using Continental's people to do our bidding over there. We do the Prairie end and they do the offshore."

Mitsui now works closely with Pioneer Grain; the Pools and XCAN Grain work with Mitsubishi, which has its own affiliated crushers; and UGG works as Canagrain with Marubeni as their major customer and Mitsui as their minor customer, according to Hayward. UGG is not obliged to deal with Continental, but there is a definite benefit in working together. Both UGG and Continental retain the right to deal elsewhere.

> The fact that there are these large entities around in the marketplace does not mean that they have such leverage and clout. . . There may be fewer firms around, and they may be bigger, but as long as you have four or five choices, that's all that it takes.[93]

The standard measurement of corporate concentration is four firms controlling 50% of the market. Hayward's evaluation of the situation would seem to be a bit ingenuous. Given the general pattern of developments in the trade, it seems more likely that UGG had little choice but to form a substantial relationship with a much larger company if it was going to continue to be a player at all.

Dwight More, from his sensitive position as president of the Canola Council, saw the association of UGG and Continental, "as much stimulated by Continental's decline as it was by UGG's need. It came down to Continental saying, there is this part of the business we just cannot stay in, and UGG said the same thing in another area, so it ended up a natural fit."[94]

Bob Broeska, one of the franker commentators on the canola industry, suggests that the constant refitting of the industry in recent years is at least in part due to the irrationality of the way canola processing developed:

> Putting plants in the middle of Western Canada a thousand miles from a port, never mind how many thousands of miles from a marketplace, might have had good logic at the time the crop was being developed because you had this dialogue and cooperation going on between plant breeders and growers and crush plants, but once you were into the real economics of edible oil and protein meal, that's all dictated by the nature of market demand and transportation costs. If freight rates are equitable, it is more economic to process seed in the region in which it is grown and ship the oil and meal separately to distant markets than to ship the whole seed. Look anywhere in the world: crushers are not located at the source of the seed supply, but either at a port, an export position with access to cheap transportation, or at the marketplace – unless there have been non-market factors at work, such as the disparate freight rates in western Canada.[95]

Broeska, who previously headed the Canola Crushers of Western Canada, became head of the Canadian Oilseed Processors Association when it took the place of the Canola Crushers in mid-1992. While the new association represents four companies, CanAmera, ADM, Canbra Foods (see below) and Northern Lite, Broeska is candid in remarking that "working for two U.S. firms is a whole different ballgame."

Looking ahead, Broeska sees a more radical restructuring of the industry taking place:

> North-South movement will make ADM and Central Soya's move make much more sense. This will depend on the payment of the Crow. [The Crow refers to the historic agreement, first made in

1941, between the government of Canada and the railroads that established a statutory rate for hauling grain to a deep water port. In recent years the federal government has been trying to weasel out of the agreement in order to improve the profits of the railroads, so that as of 1992 the railroads receive a compensatory lump-sum payment.] Right now it all goes to the Japanese, in effect, [because the subsidy is paid on whole grains and oilseeds moving to an export position] and works against the western Canadian oilseed crushing industry. This would explain UGG's break with Mitsui, too, so that if UGG can sell itself in Japan, then it too can get the benefit of the Crow payment.[96]

Canbra Foods

There is one other piece of the western oilseed crushing story that remains to be accounted for, and that is Peter Pocklington's Canbra Foods. Pocklington is best known for his extreme individualistic right- wing attitudes and his willingness to go to any length to break a union or keep a union out of his businesses. (The story of Gainers Meat Packers in Edmonton in the 1980s is a tale of robbery of the public purse combined with a vicious anti-union campaign by Pocklington, but that is a story for another book.) By 1990 Pocklington's business empire was reduced to little more than Canbra Foods Ltd. of Lethbridge, Alberta, which has produced canola oil since the 1960s. Pocklington purchased Canbra in 1987. The original purpose of the plant was to process safflower, then sunflower, and finally canola. It is not in a growing area for any of the three, so it now operates three collection points in Saskatchewan and Alberta.

In September, 1989, Canbra announced that it would build a $15 million edible oil refinery in Butte, Montana, U.S.A. At the same time, Canbra president Bob Burpee announced the start on the second phase of a $29 million expansion to its Lethbridge crushing plant to double its crushing capacity to 1200 tonnes per day and its refining capacity to 250 tonnes of canola oil per day. The Butte refinery was to be built in a former Safeway warehouse made available to Canbra by the Butte city council. The refinery was also to receive loan guarantees from the Montana government as well as an interest rate "break". The proposed 400 tonne a day Butte refinery was to be supplied by seed grown by Montana Agricultural Producers Inc. and crushed in Lethbridge before being shipped to Butte for refining.[97]

Two years later the Butte facility was engaged in packaging only as a Canbra subsidiary under the name Heartlight Corp. of America, Inc. Montana farmers grew 16,000 acres of canola under contract to Canbra in 1989 through Montana Agricultural Producers, and 26,000 in 1991. Canbra has no plans to build crushing or refining facilities in Montana until it has access to about 500,000 acres of canola in the U.S.

Recalling the comments of Joyce Beare-Rogers about the marketing strategies of the manufacturers of canola oil products, it is interesting to note what happened to Canbra after it launched Heartlight brand salad oil in the U.S. in early 1989. The name on the label was accompanied with a big red heart and Canbra spent $2.5 million in 1989 and again in 1990 promoting the product. Early in 1991 the Food and Drug Administration (FDA) decided to clamp down on the growing number of health claims being made in food promotion and ordered Canbra to remove the heart and change the name. Canbra complied by changing the name to Canola Harvest.

Not only is the Canadian crushing industry now dominated by foreign transnationals, even some of the best people are being bought out to work in the U.S. and elsewhere. The U.S. chemical giant DuPont, for example, is building a specialty oilseed processing plant in Idaho Falls, Idaho, and according to Broeska, they have offered employment to every single good person that has been let go by the industry in Canada.

DuPont

Intermountain Canola, a joint venture between DuPont and DNA Plant Technology Corp.(DNAP), was formed in 1991 after six years of collaborative research between DuPont and DNAP. Their objective is to put a "superior quality" canola oil on the market in 1991, according to their c.e.o. What they have developed is a new variety that produces an oil with enhanced heat stability that can be used in processed foods.

The company estimates the market potential for such an oil is 10 billion pounds per year.[98]

The close relationships that exist in agribusiness are illustrated by DuPont in other ways. It might seem at first strange for DuPont to be investing in an edible oil, but then one notices that DuPont is the manufacturer of an herbicide designed for use on canola. Muster is "the first to control wild mustard and stinkweed in all canola varieties" according to a company press release.

With the major players in the Canadian Oilseed Processors Association being two very large foreign transnationals, the people and organizations responsible for representing the canola industry in Canada face an increasingly tough task. (As we will see in subsequent chapters, the seed breeders and seed trade are also dominated by foreign transnationals.)

In referring to the crushers, Dwight More described the reality as he saw it late in 1991 as a choice between having none or having two. Given his job, it is hard to know what else he could say.

In the face of going from nine [crushers] to zero, I would take two over zero any day. The bottom line is that the producer and the consumer are demanding a corporate system that takes less profit and provides more service. Under that scenario, the corporations involved have no choice to become more efficient and there is no room for them all to make a profit, so some get squeezed out or go into joint ventures or amalgamation.[99]

Dwight More deserves credit for creative interpretation, but it is not obvious to me that the "corporate system" is taking less profit while providing more service. Nor can I see ADM or Central Soya working with the plant breeders in the public sector the way Canada Packers once did.

Then there is certainly a question about what "the consumer" is demanding – but this has never really been a part of the equation.

Chapter 8

BREEDERS AND ENGINEERS:
THE SEED TRADE

> Nobody knows really why canola is so
> amenable to genetic manipulation – so geneti-
> cally plastic – you can reproduce the plant from
> anything.   *Ian Grant*

If open-pollinated, "public" seed was characteristic of the first 30 years of canola development, the last five have seen seed research and development increasingly taken over by hybridization and patenting while control has been gained by transnational capital as expressed through a limited number of very sophisticated corporations.

UGG, ICI Seeds and King Agro, which we examine in this chapter, appear to be pursuing similar corporate strategies. In the next chapter we continue with the most significant private Canadian canola breeding organization, Allelix Crop Technologies, now a subsidiary of Pioneer Hi-Bred International of the U.S. Because it is pursuing a similar corporate strategy, in that chapter I also include Calgene, of California, the dominant U.S. canola breeding organization.

Mapping out current canola research and the activities of seed breeders and their corporate sponsors is a challenging exercise. While some of those involved claim that genetic diversity is being conscientiously increased by the breeders, the corporate structures behind these efforts are not as diverse as they may appear.

Apparent corporate diversity, whether in size, strategy, culture or attitude, should not cause us to forget that these corporations share a singular goal: profit and the accumulation of capital. It is this common goal that enables them to work together in the Canadian Seed Trade Association. A brief look at the CSTA and the ideological leadership exercised by its executive vice-president, William Leask, provides a useful introduction to the strategies of specific corporations.

The CSTA has about 150 members, identified as the companies with international seed sales and research and development programs. The Association is funded by members on the basis of a percentage of sales, with one member one vote, regardless of size; but naturally it is the bigger ones that have the resources to devote to organizational activities and the personnel to serve on committees and attend meetings.

This phenomenon, while true of many other organizations, must not be overlooked in trying to evaluate any organization and the differences between those it officially represents and those who actually form policy.

William Leask, executive vice president of the Canadian Seed Trade Association (CSTA), has had a distinct influence on the way people in the seeds industry conceive of what they are doing. He has come up with a three-wave theory that fits right in with business theory. The first wave is sort of pre-history, when seeds were just plain common seeds, traded among farmers, and, as Leask put it, "the business that developed around them simply focused on farmers and their needs, seed was sold as common seed, and the criteria were visible, such as cleanliness and uniformity."[100]

What is missing in this description are the characteristics of the seed that would either have been known within the community within which the seed was traded, or would have been known by the producer of the seed and conveyed verbally to the recipient or purchaser of the seed. This information would have had to do with agronomic characteristics invisible in the seed itself, but nevertheless embedded in it, and the utility characteristics of the seed, whether it was used for food or fibre or both, likewise invisible to the naked eye. The value of the seed would depend in great part on the availability and reliability of the invisible genetic information embedded in the seed and on the cultural information about its production and use embedded in the culture familiar with the seed. (We come back to this subject in Chapter 11.)

This first wave, in Leask's typology, started giving way to the second wave in the 30s and 40s as plant breeders developed specific, proprietary, varieties, whether open-pollinated or hybrid, that are sold by name. Common seed traded among farmers was pushed out by proprietary seed developed and sold by companies to farmers. Corn is the primary example of this, where virtually all corn is now traded by a variety name, and this is the dominant mode of the seed business today.

Now Leask applies the term "third wave" to what the industry refers to as "identity preserved" commodities, "where the processor is the final arbiter." "Many of our vegetables and fruits are already in this category, sold by variety or brand name to the consumer", says Leask. In this third wave, the seed remains, functionally, the property of its creator, and is loaned out for production, under contract, to farmers.

In the case of canola, all three waves are found. There is still some trading of commodity seed, particularly in Alberta, there are a lot of proprietary varieties, and now specialty seeds are beginning to be grown under contract.

Leask is obviously much enamoured of the marketing possibilities and their rewards for those who want to enter his third wave, though others might remain sceptical of the ultimate benefit to either farmer or consumer.

> The premise of the whole identity-preserved thing is that the ultimate product can command enough of a premium, ultimately from the consumer, to adequately reward all the participants in this process.[101]

> Plant breeders would receive more corporate sponsorship for their research, the seed trade would have a new line of products, farmers would receive premium prices for their crops, and food processors could offer exciting new products.[102]

There is an interesting aspect to this "identity-preserved" product that neither Leask nor anyone else has mentioned. If such a product has to command a premium price all along the line, then it will have to be an "exciting new" product for the top 20% of the market that can afford it.

As Joyce Beare-Rogers has commented, this is all marketing, and probably has very little to do with health and nutrition.

Thirty years ago the only research on rapeseed conversion anywhere in the world was being done at the Agriculture Canada Research lab in Saskatoon and at the University of Manitoba in Winnipeg, with funding for this work coming from the provincial governments and the federal government through the National Research Council.

Between 1981 and 1991 the public sector research base began to expand, with 190 projects funded by the Canola Utilization Assistance Program of the Canola Council, carried out at the Universities of Guelph, Manitoba, Saskatchewan, Alberta and British Columbia and at the Saskatchewan Research Council, the POS (Protein, Oils, Starch) plant in Saskatoon, and Ag Canada stations in Ottawa and Saskatoon.

While these are all public institutions, and none of the research reports or summaries make any mention of private sector (corporate) partners or sponsors, the appearance is deceiving. In a 1991 report, the Canola Council mentions only that "other breeding programs exist, particularly in the private sector, but the Canola Varietal Development Program and the Canola Council assist to establish and co-ordinate breeding priorities for the entire industry."[103]

Corporate research may take place both in a corporation's own facilities or, under contract, in university facilities. King Agro (Senofi), for example, has a very attractive two-year old research facility in Listowell, Ontario, that includes laboratory, greenhouse and farmland, where they do most of their work now, though they have, in the past, contracted with the University of Guelph. Similarly Allelix Crop Technology (Pioneer Hi-Bred) has had very elaborate lab facilities in Mississauga as well as a research farm in Georgetown, Ontario, while also contracting research to universities. PGS (Plant Gentic Systems) of Belgium has contracted research at the University of Guelph with Wally Beversdorf to develop canolas with herbicide and antibiotic tolerance, but in mid-1992 set up its own research facility in Saskatoon.

(The antibiotic tolerance work has to do with using kanamycin resistant genes *(kan)* coupled with herbicide-resistance genes as markers to identify plants that have accepted and express the herbicide resistance characteristics. If the trial plants survive treatment with the antibiotic, they have incorporated the herbicide resistance as well.)

Cargill has contracted with the Agriculture Canada Research Station in Saskatoon for research in combining in one canola plant both triazine herbicide tolerance and cytoplasmic male sterility.

The "9th Project Report, Research on Canola Seed Oil and Meal – Canola Council of Canada 1991" presents 618 pages of research project descriptions and data without any mention of who has paid for any of it, how it will be used, or who has "rights" to the information produced, including that of genes and processes.

Instead, we are presented with a vast collection of fragmented "information" as if these fragments are self-validating and in no need of explanation as to their genesis, context or purpose. It amounts to a denial of the teleology of current science in the corporate interest. A conclusion drawn from one experiment, "No chemical method gave complete agreement with the sensory results", either signifies a failure in method or in the formulation of the experiment. Or it may reflect a natural disposition of life to increasing complexity rather than to reductionist simplification.

The Canola Council does not conduct any of its own research but rather allocates funding, primarily from the federal government, to existing research groups. The Canola Research Priorities Committee of the Council has emphasized the importance of increasing the oil and protein content of the seed, increasing seed yield, and working on oil quality.

The development of larger, yellow-seeded canola is on-going. Seeds from such varieties are lower in hull, higher in oil and protein and produce a meal higher in protein and energy and lower in fibre. . . Hybrid development is ever increasing *with the belief* that canola hybrids will significantly out-yield pureline varieties.[104][emphasis added]

The statement above is an interesting, if unintentional, acknowledgement that hybridization as the way to achieve increased yields is more a matter of faith than science. What is equally interesting is that the substantial amount of research devoted to creating herbicide tolerance is not mentioned as a priority, yet a report on work done by Agriculture Canada at the Ottawa research centre would suggest this is a major activity. The report also gives an indication of who will benefit from the research:

> Major progress has been made in the isolation of *B.napus* genes for AHAS (Aminahydroxyacid Synthase) which is the target site for sulfonylurea (DuPont, Ciba-Geigy) and imadazolinone (Cyanamid) herbicides. One of four *B.napus* AHAS genes has now been fully sequenced. The other genes should be fully characterized within the next year. These isolated genes will be modified to induce resistance and subsequently transferred into *B.napus* with the aim of engineering high levels of resistance to specific herbicides.[105]

In 1992, corporate expenditure for canola research, according to Mark Forhan of ICI Seeds, should total at least $17 million[106] which he suggests is above the public sector investment in canola research. By comparison, the Canola Council disbursed a total of $1,112,000 in 1991: $814,359 for research directly and another $305,000 to researchers under the Canola Utilization Assistance Program.

The number of researchers in each sector – 93 in the corporate sector and only 28 government and university scientists – reflects this same ratio. (Obviously the above is not a complete accounting of research funds, but it is a good indicator.)

United Grain Growers

The changing mix of players and purposes in canola research and seed production is well illustrated by the associations that United Grain Growers (UGG) has been involved in. UGG is a conservative, free-market farmers' cooperative, odd as that may sound. It has consistently lobbied for destruction of the Wheat Board and sought its fortune, if not that of its members, in alliances with transnational corporations, as we saw in the previous chapter.

In mid-1992 UGG announced that it intended to make a public share offering on the Toronto Stock Exchange, and its president admitted that this would end its status as a co-operative, though he claimed that new by-laws would require that 12 out of 15 board members be farmers. Of course, this would not prevent the by-laws from being changed again, and a company like Cargill might see this as a golden opportunity to increase its control. The announced change stirred a great deal of discussion, but it is doubtful that the farmer-members of the co-operative who object to the proposal will prevail in the final decision.

UGG's 1991 Annual Report mentions "business relationships with various plant breeding organizations" including AgriPro Biosciences (wheat, sunflowers), Allelix Crop Technologies (pure line and hybrid canolas) and Weibulls (canola, feed barley and oats).

UGG has had a joint venture with Allelix since about 1985 to develop hybrid canola varieties for western Canada. In spite of the "fits and starts at the beginning of such a venture" and the lack of agreement on which path to hybrid canola is better, according to UGG president Brian Hayward, "the venture is moving along. We do not want to be in the science game and they don't know the dynamics of the market, so Allelix does the science and we do the marketing."[107] Sales of "Proven" brand canola seed, produced by Allelix/Pioneer and sold by UGG, amounted to $7 million in 1992.

> Our goal in life is to be sure that that voice out there is heard, and heard back in the [Allelix] labs in Mississauga. Our marketing approach, as a company, is to say, What do you want, Mr. Farmer? I believe the competitive dynamic exists.[108]

Since Allelix has another venture with the Swedish seed company Weibulls, UGG is also able to market Weibulls' canola varieties for Allelix while Allelix gets the genetic material it wants. Weibulls has a lot of material, according to Hayward, but no idea of what will work in western Canada, so they send it to Allelix for evaluation and then UGG works with certified seed growers to reproduce the desirable seed which UGG then markets through its grain and farm supply system. In 1991 UGG & Allelix had their first hybrid canola on test hoping for registration in one or two years.

ICI Seeds

It is very easy to get lost, or at least confused, by the kaleidoscope of corporate names and alliances. For example, depending on when you look, you will find references to Conti Seeds, Garst Seeds, Super Crost and ICI Seeds. They are now all one and the same.

ContiSeed Division of Continental Grain Co. of the U.S. entered the canola scene in 1989 with announcement of the first hybrid canola for the Canadian Prairies. Hyola 40 was developed after nine years of research, according to the company, as a spring hybrid with resistance to Blackleg and high yield potential. About 3000 acres were to be grown in 1989, but the hybrid was not without its drawbacks. While costing (at $3.25 a pound) five times as much as other canola varieties, Hyola 40 had lower protein and oil content than Westar, the reference variety, and yields only 14% or so higher. While 14% might seem like a lot, the industry figures that hybrids should yield 40% more than open-pollinated varieties to justify their use and cost and has priced hybrids accordingly.

The problem, as all the breeders have admitted, is that the theoretical gain of 40% has yet to be achieved. It seems to be particularly difficult to get lab and small plot yields to translate into actual field results.

Behind the facade of Hyola 401, which was registered for sale in 1991 and replaced Hyola 40, the corporate scene was changing, much the way it did for David Sommerville (president of CanAmera Foods) in the edible oil refining business.

ICI entered the international seeds business in 1983, bringing together Garst Seed Company of the U.S.A., (founded in 1930 to produce and sell hybrid corn), Société Européene de Semences sa (SES) of Belgium, Pacific Seeds in South America and ICI Seeds U.K. to form ICI Seeds. Through SES, (which it bought from Ferruzzi of Italy), ICI is involved in Europe with sugar beet and corn breeding and through ICI Seeds U.K. and Unisigma in cereals.

In 1989 ICI Seeds, a unit of ICI Americas, Inc., which is in turn a wholly owned subsidiary of Imperial Chemical Industries PLC, (ICI) of London, purchased the Conti Seed Division of Continental Grain Co. of New York, including their Canadian operations.

Late in 1990 Garst/ICI purchased BP's U.S. subsidiary Edward J. Funk and Sons with its "Super Crost" lines of hybrid corn, creating one of the largest research, production and distribution networks in the U.S. seed industry, with more than 7000 sales agents and dealers and an annual research and development budget of $20 million. The companies' combined product lines include corn, soybean, sorghum, alfalfa, sunflower and canola seed varieties.[110] ICI's purchase of Funk and Sons moved it into second place behind Pioneer Hi-Bred in the U.S. corn seed market. [111]

Just to confuse the picture, "Funk's G" brand belongs to CIBA-GEIGY Seed Division and is distributed in Canada by ICI's Agromart Group.

Today, ICI Seeds is the 3rd largest seed corn company in North America and the 5th largest seed company in the world. Our goal is to become the leading seed company.

1985: Garst Seed Co. ends 50-year history of producing/marketing Pioneer Brand products.

1985: ICI acquires Garst Seed Co.

1986: British Petroleum acquires Edward J. Funk & Sons

1989: Garst Seed Co. acquires Conti-Seeds

1990: Garst Seed Co. acquires Edward J. Funk & Sons

1991: Garst Seed Co. changes name to ICI Seeds[109]

[Along the way four other U.S. seed companies were acquired and folded into what has become ICI Seeds.]

Like other companies of its size, ICI has sought ways to rationalize its diverse interests. In August, 1992, ICI announced that it would split its own embryo, forming two companies out of the one: ICI to hold the company's industrial chemical business, and ICI Bio made up primarily of its drugs, agrochemicals, fertilizer and seeds businesses. This latter grouping has been responsible for about 31% of ICI sales, but has accounted for 70% of both profits and research expenditures.

ICI is quick to proffer its promotional material, which is attractively and tastefully designed to convey its corporate business philosophy to the public. Its materials use lots of colour and expensive white space to present the image of a conservative, environmentally and socially conscious corporate friend. ICI Agrochemicals is one of the top three [agrochemical] companies in the world and ICI Seeds has grown, through investment and acquisition, to become one of the top five seeds companies in the world. The following quotations from their promotional materials give the flavour and convey the culture of their message:

The growing need for food in most parts of the world can only be satisfied with the help of advanced technologies, including new agricultural products. . . In order to maintain the current standard of living for an ever increasing world population, they will be required to produce more food on smaller amounts of land. . .

A unique vision is needed to see the fullness that lies waiting within this tiny kernel [of corn]. Yet, an astounding vision is required to manipulate the seed's genetic potential, unravelling and rebuilding its genetic codes to unlock bountiful yields. . .

Here in Canada, producers need new ways to compete interna-
tionally. New land, new machines, new chemicals were the engines of past growth. These options are not compatible with the
1990s. . . Plant breeding and biotechnology are the key to continued improvements in agricultural productivity. Plant bio-sci-
ence will produce higher yielding crops, better adapted to specific climatic conditions and resistant to diseases and pests.
Plant bioscience will make for better farming, a healthier environment and improved quality of life. . . The future of agriculture
is seed. The future of seed is hybrids. . .

Canola is a Canadian plant breeding success story. Thanks to the
dedication of leading breeders, this crop has undergone a Cinderella transformation, from an ugly sister industrial oil crop to
one of the premier food products in the world. . . Hybrids have
tremendous yield potential. . . [Uniformity is] another characteristic that separates hybrids from traditional varieties. . . Hyola
hybrids, with their narrow genetic make-up, produce a very even
crop. . .

If harvested seed from a hybrid crop is planted, the resulting
crop will have uneven maturity, poor disease resistance, poor
lodging resistance and low yield. Therefore growers must purchase new seed every year. . . Hyola seed costs more than traditional varieties. But Hyola isn't an expense, it's an investment.

ICI Seeds is not a minor player. They have a full-time staff of 15
people working on canola in western Canada, which constitutes 95 per-
cent of their work in Canada. They also have some joint ventures in
research, according to manager David Hansen.

Hansen's description of the problems encountered when trying to
get Prairie farmers to grow hybrid canola is interesting:

In the last two years we have spent the majority of our time trying
to educate the canola farmers about hybrids because the farmers
in the canola growing regions haven't got a clue what hybrids
are, simply because the crops that they grow – barley, wheat,
oats, flax and rape – are not hybrid crops.

We are working predominantly on hybrids to be able to exploit
the benefits that will bring, with different breeding tools available to us through the ICI Seeds research groups. Here in Winnipeg we are focused on spring *napus* hybrids for western
Canada and the North American market.[112]

One of the questions raised about large conglomerates like ICI that
have interests in both seeds and chemicals is whether the seeds are not

being deliberately engineered to require, or perform optimally, with the companies chemicals. Hansen reacted quickly to this question:

> Just because we are a seed company associated with a chemical company does not mean that we are in collusion to create seeds dependent on ICI chemicals. Each division within the ICI network has to survive on its own merits. The chemical business will develop their programs and their strategies based on the needs of their marketplace. There isn't the amount of collaboration that people would assume there is between the agro-chemical division and the seed division any more than there would be with the films division or the pharmaceuticals.
>
> The prime example of this is seed treatment. ICI Chipman has a fungicide called Premier, very similar to a product produced by Gustafson called Vitavax. [Gustafson is a business unit of Uniroyal Chemical Ltd.] We went through a long period of testing and evaluating those products to find out which was going to be best for our particular needs. It wasn't an automatic decision that we were going to use an ICI product. We are trying to do what's best for our program and what's best for the customer at the other end. You have to have a product that is saleable, and the last thing we want to be seen as is that there is a hidden agenda standing between us and the farmer.

But it really isn't quite that simple. One of the more fascinating aspects of the seeds business, as of agri-business in general, are the constantly shifting strategic alliances formed between TNCs, including ICI. For example, ICI and Plant Genetic Systems (PGS) of Belgium are cooperating on a breeding program to develop a transgenic canola with disease resistance and modified protein quality and in mid-1992 PGS set up shop in Saskatoon to work on its patented hybridization technology. (One of Monsanto's approaches to these linkages was described in Chapter 5 and 6, and more discussion of the linkages between seed and chemical development and their corporate sponsors will be found in the next chapter.)

Since ICI has focused its efforts on the development of hybrid canolas, and has already put two on the market, it is only reasonable to ask if this is the only route to take. Hansen gave a candid response to the question of whether or not the same results could be achieved in open-pollinated varieties:

> I'm not a plant breeder, but I'll give you the scenario that is repeated for me, and you can take it for what it is worth. It is the belief of canola breeders in general that open-pollinated varieties have a ceiling of opportunity or of exploitation of yields and various other characteristics. They know genetically that there is

a plateau which they will eventually reach, and there is a feeling in the industry that we are likely nearing that edge. Hybridization allows us to extend that curve and provide results that are an improvement over where that plateau is going with the open-pollinated types. The other key to that is the incorporation of biotechnology as a breeding tool locked in with the hybridization process.

We have seen ceilings in other crops, such as open-pollinated corn, which in the 1930s and 40s was reaching a plateau of 30-40 bu/ac. Hybridization techniques have increased the ultimate performance of corn to the 200-plus bu/ac. level, not on average, but as possibility. It is the belief of breeders that canola hybrids will bring a similar increased potential.

When asked again if the same results could not be achieved with open-pollinated varieties under similar development and management, Hansen responded: "We really don't know the answers to that question. Like I said, I'm not a breeder, and I cannot argue that point, and even the breeders disagree."

The growing concern about the ecological and structural consequences of industrial agriculture is causing a reevaluation of these supposed "ceilings" in crop potential. In some cases, as in the traditional waru waru agriculture of the Peruvian Andes, scientists have discovered that when they reconstruct traditional agricultural forms and practices, the resulting crops are superior to the High Response Varieties of the Green Revolution grown under "modern" industrial conditions with maximum inputs.

There are problems with hybrids that faith alone will not overcome. In 1991 Blackleg was a severe problem, and the two hybrids on the market, one from ICI and one from King Agro, were affected. The former is listed as "susceptible" while the latter is "highly susceptible" to Blackleg. Westar, the industry standard for *B.napus*, is also highly susceptible, and it is probable that the hybrids have inherited their susceptibility from common parent stock. Hansen may, as he says, wish to see hybrids succeed and be distressed at a bad reputation for them as a result of a competitor's problems (HC 120 is more susceptible than Hyola 401), but that is not going to alter the fact that so far, for all the efforts put into them, hybrids have fallen far short of the claims made for them.

Nevertheless, Hansen feels that the publicly produced varieties are falling behind the privately created hybrids, and that this shows up in the co-op trials. But then this raises the question of whether this isn't inevitable given the deliberate policy of the federal government to starve public research and force it into the hands of the private sector?

I don't think we should be taken to task for this, and I don't want to sound defensive, but is it wrong for us, as a private breeding company, to benefit from that? We didn't come into this business with the assumption that the public breeding programs were going to come under more and more pressure. We had nothing to do with that.

Perhaps Garst did not have anything to do with federal policy, perhaps they really were just going about their business, but that does not mean other companies, like Cargill, were not lobbying, in effect, on their behalf. Hansen did not want to comment on Cargill's possible lobbying activity, but did feel that ICI's approach was different and more dependent on their relationship with farmers.

Hansen, like others working for transnational corporations, does find advantages in their global linkages that are not as readily available to public sector breeders:

The beauty of being involved with an international business is that we're able to access technology from somewhere else. It's a two-way street: other places in the world are accessing technology that we have developed here, and our farmers benefit because we're able to access technology from somewhere else. So we don't get caught up in country to country politics as competitors in that regard. We look at ourselves as a business trying to do what is best for each of our individual operating units.

ICI's global activities are not merely a matter of philosophy. To facilitate their corporate activities and the work of their researchers in biotechnology around the world, ICI has invested heavily in communications technology and is developing the hard- and software to allow data from the one million trial plots which ICI Seeds plants every year worldwide to be collected, summarized and made available on a database.[113]

While there may be technology transfers of this sort, an ambiguity remains. The corporation may prefer secrecy, but as the research director of one large company said, he is continually amazed at the conversations that go on between breeders right under his nose, as it were, on official delegations. Hansen pointed out that,

There is still an exchange of germplasm between the private and the public groups and there are relationships that have developed over the years, not necessarily between company and public breeders, but person to person, and there is an exchange of resources, not just of seed but also of knowledge. There is a lot of interaction between the private and the public, and they should not be separated as on different sides of the fence, though there does come a time when you have to protect your investment and your future. Absolutely.

But that is not necessarily bad. There have been no international connections for exchange of germplasm in the past, but now we are working with a bigger group of people with a wider resource base. Canada has been very up front in the past, and continues to be, as an educator to a lot of the more underprivileged countries of the world, but ultimately we've been shooting ourselves in the foot in some instances where we have provided the technology and the information. India, for example, has changed from being an importer of oilseeds from Canada to being more self-reliant, and a lot of that technology comes from right here in Canada. (See Chapter 10 on the activities of IDRC in India and China.)

Of course this is not necessarily bad for Garst/ICI, for they owe no particular allegiance to Canada, and ICI could just as well set up a canola breeding program in India to help India become self sufficient as they could anywhere else. ICI, after all, is interested in selling their hybrid seed, anywhere and everywhere. Their return is not in breeding programs, but in seed sales. So, as Hansen put it, "We are able to be flexible and take advantage of different shifts in business in any corner of the world."

King Agro

While Garst was busy developing hybrids in Manitoba, King Agro was working on the same project in Ontario. Apparently at least one of the companies was good at keeping trade secrets, because in late 1990 Kees Kennema, King Agro's director of marketing at the time, was still under the impression that King Agro had followed a completely different route than most other companies by going into the hydribization of canola.

King Agro entered the Ontario canola market in 1982 with a winter near-canola quality *campestris* rapeseed. Recognizing how small the Ontario market for canola really was, King Agro then started concentrating on spring *napus* varieties for western Canada. Their work on canola hybridization began in 1985 when they financed a graduate student at the University of Guelph who was working under David Hume transferring SI genes from *campestris* to *napus* varieties. Once the genes were transferred, King Agro took the germplasm for plant production. At that point, according to Zenon Lisieczko, who has been in charge of King Agro's canola breeding since 1985, they did not know how to put things together, "and that is where I came in, to put it together and make it work."[114] By 1992 King Agro's contracts with Guelph were ending and all work was being done in their own facilities.

The two commonly known ways of hybridization, as we have seen, are the cytoplasmic male sterility (CMS) system and the self-incompatibility (SI) system. Self-incompatibility occurs naturally in nature, making the flower refuse its own pollen so it has to accept foreign pollen. (See Chapter 11.) This system has been used in vegetables for many years, and all the Brassica vegetable hybrids are based on SI. The trick, said Kennema, is that you have to find the genes, which are available in nature, and transfer them into the plants.

U.S. Patent #5,043,282 was granted Aug. 27, 1991, to Kingroup, Inc. (King Agro) for its SI hybridizing system, with patents pending in Canada, Asia, etc. Lisieczko is justifiably proud of this patent – justifiably, that is, if you believe in the privatization of information. (We will return to this issue in Chapter 13.)

Lisieczko explained to me that, "SI is not really a biotechnology, it is a system invented by nature. We just learned how to utilize it. What we patented is basically a method of hybrid production." But if it occurs in nature, I wondered, how can it be patented? Lisieczko explained that even though what they patented was found in nature, it was found only in other species. It was the *application* of this natural "technology" to canola for which the patent was granted:

> SI occurs in nature in different species. Through traditional breeding we transfer the gene responsible for this trait from *B. campestris* to *B. napus*, which belong to the same Brassica family. As a result, we can make *B. napus* self-infertile, self-incompatible, and because of that, and knowing how to maintain them and reproduce the seed, we can produce hybrids. The SI gene prevents the flower from pollinating itself through the mechanism of refusing to accept its own pollen, though it will accept pollen from other plants. It's a system invented by nature as a way of survival by preventing inbreeding.

Lisieczko agreed that it would be possible for other companies to develop different SI systems, but said they believed that, "we have done this patent in such a way that it covers the system we have chosen as the most economical way of creating hybrids. If someone else wants to use this system, they will have to get a license from us."

This led me to ask what kind of reward he personally got out of this, and his response reminded me of what both Downey and Stefansson had said about the satisfaction they got from their work:

> Nothing – but satisfaction. It is nice after hard work to find something works. And it is recognizing our efforts, that we did something. But it is much more complex. You cannot say, I did it, because that would be wrong. It is not me personally. We had

a group of people and everyone was involved, I was one of them and the one who was in charge of the group, but everyone has a little piece.

While the goal of King Agro is hybridization, to go in this direction they need in-bred development. This requires self-compatible lines, and these can be used as normal open-pollinated crops. So while they are aiming at hybridization, along the way they are getting open-pollinated varieties.

Theoretically a 40% increase in yields can be achieved with hybrids (heterosis), but practically a 10-20% increase is what may actually be achieved because yield in the field is dependent on weather, soil, precise locations, i.e., less controlled conditions. King Agro was marketing two spring *napus* hybrids in Canada (HC 110, HC 120, both registered in Canada in April 1991) and about four in other countries, but, as Lisieczko said, "these are not the best hybrids, they are hybrids to start with. It took 40 years to get hybrid corn where it is today. "

> In a very short time with hybrids our company has come further than anyone else, but we still have many weaknesses, many things to fix. We have learned a lot, but we have to learn by our own mistakes, while others can follow us and learn from our mistakes. I think that in many companies people have not judged properly the efforts needed to move from production of very small amounts of seed to very large amounts of seed. We know what it takes. But at the same time we have made mistakes in some processes that we have to clean up. One of our hybrids is very susceptible to Blackleg. In a normal situation it yields very well, but when the disease hits, it just fails. We knew this might be the case, but because of our lack of knowledge about the genetic differences, we had to choose certain genotypes, even though we knew they were susceptible, because we needed other characteristics.

> This does narrow the genetic base, but then we spin off, and in that spin off there is enough variability already to easily get 20% heterosis.

By mid-1992 King Agro had decided to take HC 120 off the market. Its Blackleg susceptibility had caught up with it. (Remember that in Chapter Six we pointed to the Blackleg-susceptible Westar base of virtually all hybrids.) King Agro's director of Research, Frank Scott Pearse, was candid in describing what happened:

> We made an error. We are a small company, and did not have the opportunity to do everything at once. For the past seven years we worked on the SI system, not on the hybrids. We feel

that we now have a system that works, and now we have to put the best hybrids together. HC 120 was the first hybrid we brought out in western Canada. The biggest problem we had was Blackleg, and last year they had the biggest Blackleg problem ever, and the hybrids we had out were not as good as our open-pollinated variety, Cyclone. It all goes back to the fact that we were working really with only one female, and it had anything but good tolerance.[115]

Nature, it seems, has her own way of doing things, and as has been often mentioned, what can be made to happen in the lab or even in the test plot may not translate into a full-blown field trial or commercial production. When this happens, the scientists try to understand what went wrong, or at least to offer some rationalization. When the oilseed processors in Ontario complained that they were getting a lot of free-fatty acids in the 1991 canola crop, Scott-Pearse reflected his obvious respect for the ways of nature in trying to understand what had happened rather than saying it was a freak occurrence or that it was simply a matter of engineering. He pointed out that in 1991 the crop was under stress at harvest time and then offered his understanding of what might have been happening:

> Plants which have the higher potential tend to be the ones with the higher free fatty acids. Free fatty acids are primarily in seed that is immature, and if you are trying to mature 3000 seeds per plant under stress conditions, you are going to have a higher percentage of seeds that never mature properly.
>
> I don't have all the data I need to prove my point entirely, but if you look at seed size, you can start seeing the difference. If you know what seed size is under normal conditions, and you start seeing seed half that size, you know you have immature seed, or seed that did not mature properly. This was turning up in about everything, as a function of increased yield.
>
> If you take the seed from the top of the plant, or the tip of the branches, you get smaller seeds. If the plant is tending to be more vigorous, setting more flowers, then you are likely to have a problem.[116]

Chemistry all too easily lends itself to, or produces, a reductionist mentality. Biology, on the other hand, seems to nurture more holistic inclinations. Or one might suggest that chemistry seems to be little more than technology or engineering, while biology, at whatever level, seems to encourage more organic approaches, at least in thinking, if not in organization, even at the corporate level. King Agro's Lisieczko, for example, described how,

Each company now is strongly on their own and we are each doing our own homework. It would be easier if companies shared information, and sometimes cheaper, but there are different methods and different ideas, and by doing the work independently we are creating variability.

I find it hard to understand why variability could not also be the consequence of deliberate public policy that encouraged sharing and cooperation among researchers working on different theories and lines of research. The kind of growing individualism described by Kees Kennema, two years earlier, must carry with it a high price tag, in terms of duplicated research and capital investment, costs of espionage and communications, and total expenditure:

Ten years ago it was much freer, researchers talked to each other without restraint. Five years ago it started to change, and people do not talk to each other between companies. They see each other, but the conversation stops at a certain point. Now they communicate freely, but within the corporation, as within Senofi.[117]

In that same conversation I asked Kennema the question about whether the hybrid route is inherently more fruitful, in terms of the seed and its productivity, than working with open-pollinated varieties:

I think you can reach the same yield level with an open- pollinated crop as you can with a hybrid, but I think it takes longer. But there is another reason that hybrids have been developed and that is that hybrids provide insurance for a seed company's revenue.

Lisieczko described how the price of hybrid seed depends on marketing strategies: "We try to relate it to the farmers return on investment. We were looking at five times the return: if the farmer invests an extra $5 in seed per acre, he should get $25 back. But in Canada seed is very inexpensive to begin with, so it may be very different. But this should change in Canada. Our winter varieties are for Europe. If something fits here, that is fine."

Because winter varieties, where they will grow, are nearly twice as productive as spring varieties, it is much more worthwhile for a breeder to produce winter varieties for which much more can be charged. Then the problem lies in adapting varieties to geographies where they will grow. Thus King Agro is interested in producing winter varieties for either the southeast of the U.S. or for Europe.

Kees Kennema described the way a small seed company such as King Agro works:

As seed people our place is on the land, close to the farmer. We are not publishing papers, we are not in the news. Our policy is good seed, good farmers. Fancy stuff is possible to do, but it costs a lot of money, and we do not believe, in this state of economy, that farmers can bear this. This is our King Agro philosophy, not Senofi policy. I am always against heavy investment. You can do it, if you can see the return, but I know that in our company we are almost getting back what we have invested. Other companies, even if they controlled the whole of Canada, would never get their investment back. Eventually they are spending taxpayers money to enjoy themselves in so-called science. I think this is not proper.

Senofi may be a large, global seed company, and its parent may be a vastly larger energy company, but as a small piece of this whole, King Agro seems to be pretty much on its own. Unlike Allelix/Pioneer Hi-Bred or Calgene, King Agro's seed development has to be paid for out of its sales on a reasonably short-term basis. Scott-Pearse pointed out that what he has spent over the years is less than what Allelix spends in one year, and he wonders how Allelix could ever recoup what they have put into canola research and development – or Calgene and DuPont either, for that matter. He is inclined to suggest that the reasons they have spent so much money is that they did not know what they were getting into – or what they were doing when they did get into it.

Chapter 9

APPLIED SCIENCE AND TECHNOLOGY

> What kinds of product do you want and what
> kind of plant do you want it in? Canola, soy-
> beans, sunflowers? *Wm. Leask*

Canola is both biologically pliable and agronomically adaptable. The
same canola grown as a spring crop in the cool crop area of western
Canada (an arc north and east of the Palliser triangle) can be grown as a
winter crop in the southeastern U.S., planted in November and harvested
the following May. If the plant will do virtually anything it's told (except,
maybe, hybridize successfully!), then the issue of who gives the order,
and how, is indeed important.

The commercialization of research has become a major preoccupation of public authorities, including university administrators, who feel a
need to justify to the corporate sector the investment of public funds in
scientific research. At the same time, private interests are eager to seize
the benefits of public investment in spite of their ideology of private enterprise. This is one aspect of the rape of canola, though it is in no way
confined to canola.

In Canada, at least, there is a long tradition, nowhere better illustrated than in seed breeding in general and canola in particular, of public
funds and institutions being used not only in the research and development of new seeds, but in their commercialization as well. Public sector
research produced Marquis wheat and Westar canola, both standards of
their commercial species in Canada. SeCan Association "works closely
with all publicly funded Canadian breeding programs" to ensure "that
newly licensed varieties are increased as rapidly as possible and offered
to farmers along with the information required to make them aware of the
advantages." Most of the varieties developed in the public sector are
released through SeCan. The Association itself is a non-profit corporation funded entirely by its members through an annual membership fee
and a small levy on all Certified seed that they use. Membership is open
to any individual or firm who has access to facilities for multiplication,
processing, storing and merchandising of seed.[118]

It is this public sector commercialization through a non-profit organization that private or corporate breeders are apt to regard as unfair competition. Of course, it all depends on your perspective and whether you see providing good seeds to the farmer as an essential social responsibility or whether it is simply another corporate profit-centre.

Another aspect of the presence of this non-profit sector in the seed business is its effect on the prices that can be charged to the farmers.

The net returns to the farmer for using proprietary seed have to be significant if the seed suppliers are to make what they regard as a decent profit. Or the proprietary varieties have to offer a perceived advantage not otherwise available.

Allelix Crop Technologies subsidiary of Pioneer Hi-Bred and Calgene are the two most aggressive and innovative companies in the seed business, but neither started out in seeds, which distinguishes them from the companies we discussed in the previous chapter. Both have chosen canola as profit vehicles because they see particular opportunities in patenting, hybridization, and contract production of specialty oil-producing canola, or some combination of the three. In contrast to King Agro or ICI Seeds, these two companies have built their corporate strategies from the end-product back, rather than from the seed forward.

Calgene, Inc.

"There were no plant molecular biologists because nobody ever had engineered a plant."[119]

". . . altering of the plant's genome to achieve such benefits as better pest resistance, reduced spoilage, improved flavour, or even production of new classes of value-added products."[120]

Calgene, Inc., of Davis California, is a brilliant example of the new wave of biotech companies utilizing teleologically oriented, privatized science and technology to redefine the agenda of the seed. For this reason it is worth a close look.

Calgene is a publicly owned biotechnology corporation founded in 1980 in Davis, California, by Norman Goldfarb, who recruited the best biochemists and molecular biologists he could find to develop biotechnology for agriculture, "the world's biggest business." During the 80s Calgene's work was exploratory and broad in scope, utilizing the research and the discoveries of the public sector – such as that of the University of California at Davis, with whom they were collaborating on research in rapeseed/canola by 1985. "The idea was to do the science and get the products developed and registered and market them. . . We started out developing basic science, not even exploiting it", explained Calgene's c.e.o. Roger Salquist.[121]

Calgene has experimented almost as much with corporate associations and business strategies as with plants, and at the end of 1991 Calgene described itself publicly this way:

Calgene is a biotechnology company that is developing a portfolio of genetically engineered plants and plant products for the seed, food and oleochemical industries. Calgene's research and business activities are focused on three core crops – tomato, cotton and rapeseed (canola) – where Calgene believes the products resulting from its research and development will provide a substantial business advantage in both agricultural input (seed) markets and output (such as food and oleochemical) markets.[122]

Calgene, unlike many other biotech companies, is both publicly owned and very public about what it is doing by way of annual reports, stock prospectuses, and frequent press releases. Calgene is precise about its corporate objectives and provides some clear insights into how biotechnology can be – and is being – applied in the food system.

Calgene's corporate and scientific strategies, and what they have already achieved, also indicate the extent to which the privatization of information and control can be carried by means of biotechnology and intellectual property rights.

In a 1989 prospectus, Calgene stated that its "business strategy is to build operating companies focused on its core crops in order to facilitate the market introduction of genetically engineered products and to maximize the long-term financial return from its proprietary products."[123] At that time, its core crops were rapeseed/canola, cotton, alfalfa, tomato and potato. Proctor & Gamble Company became Calgene's single largest shareholder in 1988 when it invested $5 million to support Calgene's canola research in return for 7% of its common stock.

In its 1989 annual report, Calgene chairman and c.e.o. Salquist (who has been with Calgene since 1983) stated: "Our number one goal is to successfully commercialize the genetically engineered products now in field trials, beginning with superior processing and fresh market tomatoes and herbicide tolerant [Bromoxynil] cotton. Secondly, we must genetically engineer rapeseed to demonstrate our ability to modify the oil composition of the plant." Calgene's work with cotton has produced a proprietary *BromoTol* gene "which encodes an enzyme that detoxifies the herbicide within the engineered plant." Calgene received a patent for this gene, which was developed in partnership with Rhône-Poulenc of France, in 1988.

Calgene subsequently granted Rhone-Poulenc Agrochimie the exclusive, worldwide license to the use of its *Glyphotol* glyphosate-resistance gene in most major field crops including soybeans, cereals, sugarbeets and sunflower, while retaining exclusive rights to glyphosate tolerance in its core crops of cotton, rapeseed, alfalfa, tomato and potato.[124]

Calgene acquired its Davis, Cal. next-door neighbour, Plant Genetics, in 1989 and with it its *GelCoat* technology for encapsulating seeds in general and somatic embryos (which are referred to as synthetic seed) in particular. That same year Calgene and Gustafson, Inc., announced their collaboration

> to use Calgene's patented *GelCoat* technology to encapsulate novel strains of *Bacillus subtillis* and *Trichoderma* as a means of enhancing their biological activity. The initial project will be aimed at potentially enhancing the efficacy of a proprietary strain of *Bacillus subtillis* that was discovered by Morinaga and Co. Ltd. and licensed by Gustafson. The strain has shown promise for controlling aflatoxin. Gustafson, a subsidiary of Uniroyal Chemical Co., Inc., is the world's largest seed treatment company.[125]

Business strategy

In a 1992 prospectus for a new stock offering, Calgene used words almost identical to those of its 1989 prospectus referred to above to describe its strategy:

> Calgene's business strategy is to build operating businesses in its core crop areas to facilitate the market introduction of genetically engineered products and to maximize the long- term financial return from such proprietary products. Implementation of this strategy can provide the Company with direct access to both agricultural market inputs, where it intends to sell seed that has been engineered with value-added agronomic traits, and to agribusiness output markets, where it intends to sell fresh and processed plant products having value-added quality traits, cost of production advantages or both.

The prospectus goes on to describe the reasons for Calgene's choice of cotton, tomato and rapeseed/canola as its core crops, including "market characteristics such as fragmentation or the absence of a dominant competitor." To achieve its chosen goals, Calgene has engaged "primary corporate partners:" Campbell Soup Co. in tomatoes; Rhône-Poulenc in herbicide resistant cotton; Proctor & Gamble in edible oils and detergents; and Nippon Steel Co. in metal-working lubricants. (The starting point for canola in Canada, you will remember, was the use of rapeseed oil as a marine steam engine lubricant.) These associations have meant an investment in Calgene research and licensing fees of some $37 million as of Feb. 1992.

As for its research, Calgene is again explicit:

Calgene's research strategy has been to establish itself as a recognized world leader in the application of recombinant DNA technology to plants concentrating its research efforts and resources on developing broad-based expertise in modification of the plant oils biosythesis pathway and in fruit and vegetable postharvest physiology, building a portfolio of potentially useful agronomic genes from both internal discovery and external licensing and developing the most efficient and effective plant transformation and regeneration systems and gene expression systems applicable to targeted core crops.[126]

Tomatoes

To the public observer, it appears that King Agro has been very quiet about its SI patent, referred to in the previous chapter. Calgene's behaviour is much more extrovert, whether as a function of its leadership or of its public persona, utilizing press releases to mark every development it regards as significant. Calgene's tomato activities are detailed here because they illustrate clearly how Calgene's strategy is to be implemented, not just in tomatoes, but very likely in canola, particularly in relation to intellectual property and corporate partnerships.

In February, 1989, Calgene received the first U.S. patent to be issued covering the use of antisense technology in genetically engineered plants. The patent specifically protects the use of the tomato polygalacturonase gene sequence, including the antisense orientation of the gene and tomato cells expressing such sequence.[127]

Calgene's antisense tomatoes have been engineered with a gene that significantly reduces the expression of the naturally occurring enzyme polygalacturonase (PG). The activity of PG causes the breakdown of pectin, a major component of fruit cell walls. The process involves isolating the naturally occurring PG gene in tomatoes and reinserting it into selected commercial varieties in the reverse, or antisense orientation.

In mid-1989, Calgene and Campbell Soup Company reported that results from the first field trials conducted with antisense tomatoes had validated greenhouse results, demonstrating reduced fruit rotting and increased total solid content, viscosity and consistency. The advantage of reduced fruit rotting in producing a higher yield percentage is obvious. Consistency and viscosity "improvements" would appeal to the processor who would like tomatoes with less water that has to be removed in processing and greater uniformity for the production of tomato paste or whatever. These "improvements" would allow for greater distancing in the tomato system, i.e., easier mechanized handling, more travel time, greater shelf-life and more centralized (under Calgene) control.

The field trials were conducted, out of reach of citizens concerned about environmental release of genetically altered plants and organisms, at Campbell's research facility in Sinaloa, Mexico. What they found was that the 92% reduction in PG activity did not affect normal fruit ripening, initial fruit softening, fruit colour, pH or acidity. Calgene and Campbell have since then conducted field trials with antisense tomatoes in many growing areas in the U.S.

Calgene's strategy of forming strategic corporate alliances is well exemplified in its arrangements with Campbell since 1985. Campbell has co-funded the tomato program, owns worldwide tomato plant quality rights, and is Calgene's commercialization partner for biotechnology-developed tomato products.[128]

In addition to obtaining the U.S. patent which protects the tomato PG DNA sequence, including the antisense orientation of the gene and tomato plants engineered with such sequences, Calgene filed patent applications in the U.S. and elsewhere directed at protecting broad rights to the use of antisense technology in plants generally.

In 1990 Calgene received a U.S. patent covering the genetic regulatory sequences, or "promoter", of a naturally occurring tomato gene, designated the 2A11 gene. At the same time, Calgene announced that it had selected "Flavr Savr" as the commercial trademark for its antisense polygalacturonase (A-PG) gene.[129]

Calgene then requested that the U.S. FDA issue an Advisory Opinion regarding the use of a selectable marker gene, *kan* (discussed already in Chapter 8), in the production of genetically engineered plants. This gene is inserted at the time of the "antisense" manipulation to make host cells resistant to the antibiotic kanamycin. Subsequently the genetically engineered plants can be treated with the antibiotic and those that succumb are identified as the ones in which the engineering did not "take". Further breeding will utilize only those plants "marked" by their antibiotic tolerance (resistance). This was the first submission to the FDA requesting an evaluation of a component of genetically engineered plants to be consumed as whole food. Calgene also announced its intention to file future FDA petitions for specific genetically engineered food products and that, in recognition of the high level of public interest in the federal approval process for genetically engineered food plants, it would make its complete *kan* data submission package directly available to all interested parties.[130]

In mid-1991, Calgene requested the U.S. FDA to issue another Advisory Opinion, this time confirming the status of its genetically engineered Flavr Savr tomato as food. At the same time, Calgene also announced that it had purchased from Campbell Soup Company, for $2 million, an exclusive license for the use of the "Flavr Savr" antisense PG gene for fresh market tomatoes in North America. Campbell retained the exclusive rights to use the gene in processing tomatoes. [131]

170,000 acres of fresh market tomatoes are grown annually, primarily in California, Florida and Mexico, to supply a $5 billion annual U.S. retail market, according to Calgene's 1992 prospectus. As Calgene sees it, the majority of the consumers of those tomatoes will be dissatisfied with the taste of their purchase. Calgene intends to cash in on that dissatisfaction with its Flavr Savr tomatoes.

To take maximum advantage of this market, Calgene formed Calgene Fresh, "to develop, produce, market and distribute genetically engineered, branded, premium-priced, high quality fresh tomatoes." Calgene claims that these vine ripe tomatoes will deliver "superior taste and shelf life to consumers."

Calgene's applications for proprietary rights to bio-technologies, however, has gone far beyond tomatoes. In January, 1992, Calgene received a Notice of Allowance from the U.S. Patent Office regarding its patent application entitled "Anti-Sense Regulation of Gene Expression in Plant Cells."

With unusual speed, the U.S. Patent Office followed up with Patent #5,107,065 on April 22, 1992. This patent grants Calgene exclusive rights for "the use of antisense technology to regulate genes in plants, and is not restricted by any limitation as to the type or species of plant cell." Calgene has said that it plans to license this technology to other companies developing plant products that are not directly competitive with its own.

In commenting on the success of their patent application, Calgene pointed out that the patent covers application of this genetic technology to produce products as diverse as naturally decaffeinated coffee, carcinogen- and nicotine-free tobacco and higher quality fresh fruits, vegetables and cut flowers. [132] In other words, unless challenged legally, this patent will allow Calgene to control and benefit by the application of this technology in any and every plant cell application. This is what is referred to a broad patent – in this case, very broad indeed.

If this patent stands, it will also further entrench the principle that life forms and their expression (process and product) can be patented, at least in the U.S. (We will return to this issue in Chapter 13.)

Armed with such a patent, Calgene is in a position to forge alliances with companies many times its size for the production of specific products, such as it has done with Campbell Soup.

The world of patenting, however, is not as certain as its proponents might like to believe. ICI Seeds, which we discussed in the previous chapter, has also been working on anti-sense genetic engineering and in mid-1992 decided to contest one of Calgene's anti-sense tomato patents. Calgene c.e.o. Salquist is reported to have commented, "I didn't spend $95 million in research in order to give it away to some bozos from Great Britain."[133]

The Flavr Savr tomato is due on the market in 1993. To get it there, Calgene has signed up one packer in California and two in Florida to supply Calgene Fresh "with tomatoes grown to the company's specifications for its proprietary Flavr Savr[tm] tomato product line."[134]

As part of its Plant Genetics inheritance, Calgene already markets five hybrid processing tomato varieties developed through conventional breeding and grown under contract by companies in Taiwan, India and China.[135]

Canola

"Calgene's longer-term strategy is to utilize the canola plant as a factory for producing novel oils to its specifications."[136]

Calgene established its U.S. canola breeding program in Davis, California, in 1885 but has since shifted all of its rapeseed/canola research to Tennessee. It has breeding nurseries and variety trials in 23 states and is the largest producer of canola seed in the U.S. In 1987 Calgene established the Ameri-Can Seed Company as its canola seed marketing subsidiary. Ameri-Can claims to supply 40% of the winter canola seed market in the U.S. (compared to Cargill's 35%) and to have the only U.S.-based winter canola breeding program. It plans to introduce commercial hybrid varieties in 1993 and claims these will offer up to a 20% yield advantage over existing open-pollinated varieties.[137]

The global network of, and tight control over, the seeds business is reflected in Calgene's arrangements with other seed companies. In 1987 Calgene entered into an agreement with L. Daehnfeldt A.S., a leading Danish seed company to develop and commercialize its canola varieties in the U.S. In 1989, Calgene and Ameri-Can became the exclusive producer and marketer of canola varieties (except in the Pacific Northwest) developed by Hans-Georg Lembke, Hohenlieth, Germany. Lembke was the first company in the world to actively breed rapeseed, and it introduced the first winter canola variety, Ledos, in Europe in 1978.

In 1988 Ameri-Can obtained rights to Cascade winter canola which was developed in Idaho by the Idaho Research Foundation (University of Idaho) for U.S. production. Agronomic research programs for canola have also been established with Calgene funding at major universities in Tennessee, Arkansas, Missouri and Mississippi.

On the downstream (output) side, Calgene formed a 50-50% joint venture with Central Soya to crush, refine and market canola in 1988. Operations of the new company, U.S. Canola Processors (USCP), did not begin until mid-1989 (in a modified soybean crushing facility in Chattanooga, Tennessee that had belonged to Central Soya) and were terminated in 1991 when Central Soya "decided to close the processing facility used by USCP."[138] The future of USCP remains undecided, particularly since it is strongly influenced by the actions of Central Soya's competitor, ADM.

Calgene's focus on canola is not simply whimsy. As it points out in its 1992 prospectus, total U.S. consumption of edible oils is approximately 13.5 billion pounds (6.14 b.kg) per year, with canola oil supplying only 725 million pounds of the total. It is estimated that in 1991 only 90,000 acres of winter canola was planted, while it would take 975,000 acres to meet domestic demand. In other words, Calgene sees a bright future for canola simply on the basis of current demand, which is one of the reasons it pushed for the inclusion of canola as an eligible crop in the 1990 U.S. Farm Bill.

In its 1989 prospectus, Calgene reported that Ameri-Can was instrumental in the formation of the U.S. Canola Association. "The organization, whose primary objective is to facilitate domestic growth in the cultivation of canola, successfully solicited sponsorship of federal legislation enacted in August that will allow winter wheat growers to plant up to 20% of their acreage in oilseed crops and still qualify for wheat subsidy payments on their actual wheat production."

This activity was explained a little more fully in Calgene's 1992 prospectus:

> Seed sales are affected by changes in U.S. government agricultural policy, which generally imposes limitations on planting acreage as a criterion for farmers' eligibility to receive government subsidy payments and other benefits. . . Prior to 1990, farmers received no subsidies for the planting of canola. The 1990 Farm Bill contained provisions entitling farmers to 92% of their wheat subsidy if they planted canola.

Neither Calgene nor anyone else can force farmers to grow canola, nor are they in a position to determine all the factors influencing a farmer's decision. But it certainly is a big help if government policy can be shaped by the efforts of an industry association.

As the company has developed and its focus has sharpened, Calgene has wasted little time in reshaping its corporate vehicles. Thus in 1989 Calgene changed the name of its subsidiary Agro Industries to Calgene Chemical to reflect its focus on increasing the number of specialty chemical applications for industrial rapeseed [HEAR – High Erucic Acid Rapeseed] oil.[139] In other words, Calgene decided to exploit traditional rapeseed, the value of which had been all but forgotten in the rush to canola.

Early in 1991, Calgene and Novamont (which is part of the Ferruzzi-Montedison Group which also owns Central Soya, and has an aggregate annual turnover of approximately $30 billion) announced that they would jointly develop and market a family of oleochemical products derived from processing oleic and erucic acids, used primarily in high- performance, specialty lubricants. Novamont was to purchase $3 million worth of Calgene stock. Salquist described the move as, "Another step in our strategy to become a vertically integrated oleochemical company."[140]

> Ferruzzi is a mammoth private Italian company currently named the Ferruzzi-Montedison Group. Late in 1991 all of the agro-industrial operations of the group were merged into a single holding company to be named Eridania/Beghin-Say. Six subsidiaries were to be brought together in this company: Ceresucre, in sugar and alcohol; Cerestar in starch and starch derivatives; Cereol, European oilseed crushing and refining; Central Soya, in oilseed crushing and refining and animal feed in the U.S.; Medeol, in consumer products; and Provimi, in animal feed. The Financial Times top European 500 companies for 1991 included six identifiable Ferruzzi companies with total turnover (sales) of nearly $48 billion.[141]

Three months later, Calgene appointed two new directors, one from Novamont (who worked with W.R. Grace and Cargill before joining Ferruzzi as coordinator of international oilseed activities) and one from the Campbell Enterprises Division of Campbell Soup Company (who was formerly a senior v.p. of Nestlé).[142]

Calgene also began to restructure its operating businesses in order to focus on its three core crops of tomato, cotton and canola. The company decided to sell its alfalfa and corn businesses and planned to downsize its PGK potato joint venture with Kirin Brewery Company.

In mid-1991 Calgene's subsidiary, Ameri-Can Pedigreed Seed Company, requested USDA approval for field trials of genetically engineered canola in southern Georgia. "The varieties to be tested have been genetically engineered to produce a novel oil with dramatically increased levels of stearic acid, making them suitable for margarine and confectionery markets", according to the press release. Ameri-Can announced that it hoped to have genetically modified oils on the market by the mid-90s. Canola production in the state of Georgia increased from 5000 acres in 1989 to 20,000 in 1990 and was projected at 40-60,000 acres for 1991. This projection probably formed the basis of the short-lived Calgene-Central Soya venture in canola processing.[143]

An indication of the speed with which Calgene moves to integrate and consolidate in its chosen fields of activity was its purchase in mid-1992 of Hodag Chemical Corporation of Chicago,[144] and its deal with Mobil Oil Corporation two months later to become Mobil's exclusive supplier of vegetable oil based Environmental Awareness Lubricants. These products, according to Calgene, are functionally equivalent to petro-chemical based lubricants, but because of their rapeseed oil base they are fully biodegradable. Calgene will use the Hodag facility to produce these products for Mobil. Calgene now boasts that it is conducting "the world's largest vegetable oil genetic engineering program aimed at developing a portfolio of new products for the food, oleochemical and industrial lubricant markets."[145]

About the same time, Calgene announced that its principal scientist had cloned the gene for the essential enzyme (lauroyl-ACP thioesterase) in the formation of lauric acid in plants. This gene regulates fatty acid chain length, which in turn determines functional properties of vegetable oils. Laurate is used in the production of detergents, soaps, lubricants, etc., according to Calgene, which describes its achievement as, "the first step toward the production of lauric acid in domestic crops such as canola."[146]

Soon after, Calgene announced it had succeeded in developing rapeseed varieties that produce oil containing lauric acid, stating that this was the first reported development of an oilseed plant producing a fatty acid not naturally present in the seed.

> Calgene has genetically engineered canola plants to produce laurate (C-12, lauric acid), a key raw material for the soap, detergent, oleochemical, personal care and food industries. Commercial sources of laurate are currently limited to coconut and palm kernel oils imported from Southeast Asia. Current U.S. imports of coconut and palm kernel oil are about 1 billion pounds annually.

> The performance of detergents and other products containing laurate cannot be duplicated with other plant fatty acids from commonly available oils such as corn or soybean nor can such crops be modified to produce laurate by conventional plant breeding.

The transformation of canola into a producer of laurate is regarded as a major achievement. Our results clearly demonstrate that the insertion of a single thioesterase (chain length modification) gene can dramatically alter the fatty acid chain length profile in a useful manner.

A Calgene patent application covering all plant thioesterase genes for producing medium chain fatty acids (C6-C14) was published in Europe in October 1991.[147]

After all the effort, public and private, that has gone into creating and developing canola, it seems the original rapeseed does have a high-tech role after all. Calgene has targeted certain oils from plants that are not grown in the U.S., such as palm and coconut, for replication via rapeseed. As of early 1992, again according to their 1992 prospectus, they were working on the following:

Cocoa Butter Equivalents and substitutes, as low-cost chocolate ingredients; non-hydrogenated margarine oil, for non-chemically processed margarine oil; medium chain fatty acids, for high performance synthetic lubricants; medium chain triglycerides, as a high energy nutritional supplement; long chain liquid waxes, as specialty lubricants and cosmetic ingredients; and, Proctor & Gamble sponsored programs for ingredients for consumer products.

Calgene reported in its 1992 prospectus that it had, so far, received 25 U.S. utility patents and 37 foreign patents, with over 175 pending patent applications in the U.S. and abroad. It also stated its intention to strengthen its intellectual property position by licensing technology developed at universities and other corporations. In some instances, it claims, such licenses are necessary to enable the practice of fundamental DNA technology. In other instances, licenses are used to obtain a competitive or proprietary position or to enhance Calgene's technology. In addition to patents, the Company seeks to protect its proprietary know-how [referred to elsewhere as "intellectual properties"] as trade secrets.

Allelix

Allelix Crop Technologies, a subsidiary of Pioneer Hi-Bred International, is one of the major players in the development of canola hybrids. More importantly, perhaps, it is a key player in the contract development of specialty canola seed which produces characteristics in the oil that are specified by food companies such as Proctor & Gamble and Frito Lay.

In 1982 the directors of John Labatt Ltd, the venerable Canadian beer, dairy and sports conglomerate, decided they should take a serious look at genetic engineering. It was a logical step, given their corporate experience in fermentation (beer) and bacterial cultures (cheese/yogurt). The U.S. seemed to be way ahead, and there appeared to be no Canadian biotech company to buy, so Labatts recruited the support of the Canadian Development Corporation and the Ontario Development Corporation to create a new Canadian biotech company.

In 1983 Allelix Inc. was created, with $90 million in capital, by John Labatt Ltd. (30%), the Canada Development Corp. (50%), and the Ontario government (later the Ontario Development Corporation) (20%), with Labatts holding the majority of the seats on the board of directors. John Evans, a past-president of the University of Toronto, became the first chairman and c.e.o., and Graham Strachan, from Labatt, became commercial director. (CDC's stake was actually held by Polysar Energy and Chemical Corp., which was subsequently acquired by Nova Corp., an Alberta-based energy company.) The strategy at that time was to apply biotech to forestry, mining and agriculture (plant biology).

Mining and forestry were dropped out of the Allelix strategy in 1984, to be replaced by specialty chemicals and fermentation. A group of 15 plant biologists, under the leadership of Jim Sheppard, was brought up from Kansas State University to constitute the agricultural division. The Sheppard team had been working on potatoes and corn in Kansas, and they intended to continue to work on these, but when they tried to form commercial partnerships with Canadian processors they discovered the situation was very different from the U.S. In the U.S., as Allelix technology director Roger Kemble put it, "it's all run by McDonald's and everyone grows Russett Burbanks [actually 60% of the commercial crop]. Up here there are several different varieties and the potato companies really don't want to spend money on research. At that time we had never even heard of canola but we knew we had to look for other opportunities."[148]

When the Sheppard team was hired, the intent had been to improve chipping potato stock and to become *the* potato supplier to the chipping industry, where the biggest margin is for contract production of potatoes, according to marketing manager Bruce Magee. Allelix hoped to do this by developing systems for synthetically reproducing seed potatoes, but once the potential of canola and canola hybrid systems were realized the potato research quickly gave way to canola.

Wallace Beversdorf, now head of Crop Science at the University of Guelph, was one of the people Allelix consulted about what they should be doing. Beversdorf suggested they look into canola, partly because it was a model plant biology species to work on and partly because the U.S. was about to put canola on the GRAS (Generally Recognized As Safe) list, which would open the door to unrestricted marketing of canola oil in the U.S.

Feeling they had mastered the technology of tissue culture and cell culture (molecular biology) in their work on potatoes, the Sheppard team wondered if they could simply apply the same technology to canola. When Beversdorf decided, at the end of '84, that rather than take the usual sabbatical he would make arrangements to go to Allelix half-time to work with their biologists on canola, it was clear whose strategy had prevailed and it was not long before Sheppard left, taking his potatoes with him.

> The main goal was to make canola a hybrid crop rather than an inbred crop. We thought we could do that. We were able to isolate protoplasts and regenerate plants from them and then fuse protoplasts. So we were bringing cytoplasmic and male sterile cytoplasms from other brassica species into canola to give us a male sterile plant. For some we had restorer genes and for others we did not. The ones we had restorer genes for we carried all the way through the breeding program into field tests, but they really did not show a significant level of heterosis and increased seed yield. The improved inbred lines that we and others were developing were as good as or better than our hybrids.
>
> Since the cytoplasmic male sterility (CMS) system did not work out for us, we switched to a self-incompatibility system, which is the current system of choice and it is showing a high level of heterosis.[149]

Once Beversdorf was with them, and they were clearly committed to canola, Allelix recruited Dr. Larry Sernyk, a young rapeseed breeder who had been working with Baldur Stefansson at the University of Manitoba. Sernyk had been working on the CMS hybridization system imported from China and Allelix purchased that technology from the University when they hired Sernyk. (Plant breeding in China is discussed briefly in the next chapter.) As Beversdorf remembers, "They worked hard to evaluate it for a number of years, but I don't think Allelix has generated any hybrids using that system, although ICI has. I think Allelix decided, five years later, that there had to be a better system."[150]

According to Baldur Stefansson, the cytoplasm that Allelix acquired from him was so defective that the 40% improvement in yield that he and Sernyk were getting with hand breeding in the lab almost totally disappeared in their field trials, but at the time Allelix did not know this.

Instead of resuming work at Guelph at the end of his sabbatical year, Beversdorf decided to spend four days a week with Allelix and one day at Guelph. Since Sheppard had left, Beversdorf was made director of plant biology. At the beginning of 1988 he moved back to the university full time. It is interesting to note four years later that Beversdorf still identifies with Allelix, as indicated by his use of the term "we" when referring to Allelix (though he interprets this as the collective "we" of canola breeders):

> In '86 we started moving more commercially in order to have some products to sell to keep the research going. We also knew then that eventually we would have to form independent companies in order to attract investors, so the agricultural division became Allelix Crop Technologies in 1988 and was refinanced by the existing pool of shareholders.

One of the fields Allelix had been dabbling in was plant microbials, but by 1987 they had recognized that they did not have the money to bring these to market, so they put that piece of their work on the market. It was eventually bought by Esso to complement their fertilizer and nutrients products. "That left a very competitive program in canola", as Beversdorf put it, "but then the question was, how do you develop global markets without the marketing organization? So they were looking for investors, and the match that they eventually got was the match they had had their eye on for several years."

Allelix c.e.o. John Evans set the tone of Allelix's agricultural strategy in conventional terms, saying, in 1986, that agriculture had to be competitive in world markets and that that could only happen through more efficient and cheaper food production. Evans suggested that biotechnology could help by developing pesticide and herbicide resistance, higher yields from hybrid crops, plant growth regulators and better adaptability, and he called on the government to pass plant variety protection acts and patent laws in order to protect investment in such research.[151]

Earlier that same year, Evans had talked about how Allelix would "help the farmers be very much more productive", and work for "the competitive survival of our primary producers."[152]

While ACT was developing its focus, other Allelix interests were also developing theirs. The diagnostics division had become focused on human health diagnostics using monoclonal antibodies and the specialty chemicals division had decided they wanted to get into pharmaceuticals. The result was that by late 1986 Allelix Inc. had been restructured into three separate corporate units: Biopharmaceuticals, Diagnostics, and Crop Technologies. At that time Allelix had staff of 220 at its $20 million laboratory in Mississauga, with Evans as chairman and Strachan president and c.e.o. A company profile described Allelix Inc. as "privately held by management, employees and corporate shareholders." [153]

By 1988, Allelix Biopharmaceuticals had research agreements with Glaxo, Rhône-Poulenc Pharma, Continental Pharma Cryosan, DDI Pharmaceuticals, Hypercube, and "confidential" others.

Subsequently the senior management of Allelix Biopharmaceuticals bought out Polysar's and Labatt's interests for $30 million, and became an independent company in 1990. At the end of 1991 Strachan took the company public and raised $24 million in share capital.

The Ontario Development Corp. retained its 20% interest in Allelix, which in effect meant that they continued to own the building and facilities used by all three divisions or companies. ODC continues to own the building.

By late 1988 Allelix Crop Technologies was the only Allelix company with its original shareholders: Nova Corp. of Alberta, John Labatt Ltd., and the Ontario Development Corp. In early 1989 these original shareholders were still committed enough to provide financing for another three years, but a year and a half later Nova Corp. ran into trouble, changed strategy and decided to sell off everything not directly connected with the petro-chemical industry.

Labatts had also changed their strategy, having had much less success with their dairy and food businesses in the US. than expected, and Allelix Crop Technologies no longer fit into their plans. As a result, ACT had to look at the alternatives of going public, doing contract research, shutting down the company and selling it off, or selling to another company as a going operation. ACT decided to sell out and Kraft, DuPont, Ciba-Geigy and Pioneer were all interested buyers (according to Magee), with Pioneer winning out in November, 1990:

> Since then we have been integrating into Pioneer. We are very happy to be in that home and they are pleased. There has been some give and take, some adjustments, but that is true in any marriage. Sometimes the bigger partner gets the final vote, but that's o.k. if it's best for the business and the business strategy.[154]

By 1991 the research group had been reduced to 13 people and was to be relocated to the research farm in Georgetown, Ontario, to concentrate on applied research and production and reduce the duplication of work being done by Pioneer's 100 biotech research people in Iowa.

Pioneer's director of canola research worldwide, Ian Grant, describes Pioneer's research organization as "highly centralized, so all the research conducted in the world for each crop has a research director for those activities worldwide." This ensures that their research investment is maximized and that "genetics and crops move across geographic boundaries. . . A decentralized structure could be an obstacle to this."[155] The agenda for research in each crop is set by a management committee, according to Magee, but is focused on the needs of the marketplace: improved yield, disease resistance, and specialty oils in response to the end-user "who comes to us and asks us to produce such and such an oil, and we expect them to share the development costs and we will jointly own the product."

Pioneer's official description of its acquisition of Allelix Crop Technologies was "a superb fit for our Special Plant Products division. SPP is a new division of Pioneer engaged in developing, producing and marketing crops that have valuable traits to end-users and processors."[156]

Pioneer Hi-Bred International, Inc. is the world's largest seed company, with total sales in fiscal 1991 of $1.125 billion. Its operating profit for that year was $233 million. Pioneer operates in 65 countries with 87 research stations, 47 of them in North America, and its products are sold in about 120 different countries.

In 1991 corn accounted for more than three quarters of Pioneer's worldwide sales "Corn is the engine which drives the research train", says Grant. Corn is so profitable that Pioneer can spend $25-30 million per year on corn research and still afford to do research in much less profitable lines such as soybeans (second in sales after corn), sorghum, sunflower, winter wheat, alfalfa and canola.

In mid-1992 Pioneer restructured Allelix, discontinuing the sale of canola seed in the U.S. and concentrating on developing varieties and hybrids for Canada and Europe, along with specialty oils.

Pioneer's 1992 canola research is carried out in four locations with a combined budget of $2,925,000, broken down as follows:

Biotechnica, Edmonton	3 staff,	$290,000
Georgetown, Ontario	29 staff,	$2,029,000
Frouville, France	3 staff,	$430,000
Buxtehude, Germany	2 staff,	$176,000

Edmonton is working on *campestris*, Buxtehude and Frouville on winter *napus*, and Georgetown on spring and winter *napus* and SCV (specialty canola varieties) with modified fatty acid profiles.

Pioneer first got into canola with the purchase of Biotechnica which was then located in Calgary. At about the same time they set up the research facility in France. They were involved in India, where the mustard/rapeseed crop is very large, "but it is very difficult to extract hard currency out of that country, so the future of that research is uncertain."[157]

Pioneer's 1990 Annual Report described how it intended to capture the benefits of tailor-made, "identity-preserved" "seed products", which is where ACT and canola fit in:

> Our Specialty Plant Products (SPP) have been in contact with a number of processors with special needs. Our research people are developing hybrids that will produce grain with those unusual traits. Obviously, the identities of these special grains must be preserved so that they will be funnelled to the processors who need them. The SPP group is structured to facilitate this process. Our people contract with processors to provide them the special grains, then contract with farmers to grow the special Pioneer seed products. We arrange for the delivery of the grain to the processor.

In its 1991 Annual Report, Pioneer added to the above: "By sharing the risk and profit with farmer-partners, Pioneer can justify the expense of the research and development involved."

Grant, speaking for Allelix before it was acquired by Pioneer, described their research activities:

> We have breeding programs in place in every market that we target for development, but since we don't have the resources available to do a lot of the basic work to develop a variety, we have to go the other way and put our resources into what Frito-Lay, or someone else, will pay for. But if we think a particular type of basic technology is needed and is not being worked on, then we will do it ourselves, in house.

> For our Frito-Lay program, we will produce the seed that farmers will grow under contract. They will be paid a premium to grow this crop to certain standards. Then it has to be maintained under an identity-preserved program through the crushing and refining process, because you don't want it contaminated with regular canola. The seed company hopefully benefits because they sell planting seeds, the contract farmers benefit because they are growing a crop at a premium, there is additional work for the crushing industry and the refiners, and Frito-Lay sells more chips, I guess, through they have such a huge market share that their interest is in preservation, not growth. If Pepsi converted all of their processes over to this specialized oil, they would require 750,000 acres of production of this particular seed.

Maintaining identity is one of the challenges. You have to have a growing area of sufficient size to maintain a crushing plant to handle just this one commodity. The farmer is growing this under a contract that states what he should do and that he should deliver it to this elevator at this particular time and he shouldn't mix it with any other canola, etc. You cannot allow a crop's pollination by other varieties because that would degrade its characteristics.[158]

Allelix's canola research for Pepsi Frito-Lay actually began three years before Pioneer bought Allelix. In 1987 Frito-Lay, of Dallas, Texas, commissioned ACT to develop a genetically modified canola plant that would yield an oil with an altered fatty acid profile. Frito-Lay was interested in using an oil in its frying processes that had more than 80% oleic acid and less than 3% gamma-linolenic acid. In addition, it wanted the 6% saturated fat level of canola retained in the new oil. Beside the purported health benefits of this oil composition, the reduction in gamma-linolenic acid would render the oil more oxidatively stable, hence increasing the shelf-life of products fried in it. "According to nutritionists surveyed by Frito-Lay, the high-oleic/low linolenic acid (HOLL) canola oil was considered to be ideal for human consumption", said Grant. Of course, it would all depend on which nutritionists Frito lay surveyed and probably on who they worked for. As Joyce Beare Rogers pointed out (Chapter 4), there are a lot of claims made for marketing, not nutritional purposes, because "we simply do not know."

Grant's description of the technical process used to achieve this nutritional wonder is certainly enough to impress the uninitiated, who would feel that such a process must be good precisely because such a technical description is given:

> Starting with existing spring and winter canola varieties, Allelix used mutagenesis technology to produce individual plants whose seed oil exhibited the desired high oleic acid trait. The mutagenesis event had incapacitated enzymes responsible for the desaturation of oleic acid to linoleic acid, resulting in an accumulation of oleic acid. Similarly, low linolenic acid mutants were developed. Through a subsequent hybridization phase followed by stabilization via self-pollination and haploidy, true-breeding HOLL lines were recovered that had 85% oleic and 3% linolenic acids. . . Worldwide use of the HOLL could require several hundred thousand acres of contract seed production. . . Worldwide this could represent annual seed sales in excess of U.S.$20 million.[159]

If the manipulations of the seed are complicated, and perhaps even mystified a bit, so are the corporate relations of the seed and its oil.

PepsiCo Inc. is headquartered in Purchase, New York. Its subsidiaries include Frito-Lay, Pizza Hut, Kentucky Fried Chicken, and Taco Bell. Its global operations take a variety of forms. In Japan, it shares ownership of Kentucky Fried Chicken with Mitsubishi Corp. as well as public shareholders. Early in 1992 it bought 95 Mexican fast food restaurants in the southern U.S. from W. R. Grace & Co. Also in early 1992, PepsiCo Foods International, its international snack food division, bought Evercrisp, a snack food processor in Chile with 40% of the market. This is in addition to already being the leading snack food producer in Mexico, Brazil and Puerto Rico. In 1990 Frito-Lay had $5 billion in snack food sales and nearly $1 billion in profits.

In Canada, PepsiCo and Kraft General Foods formed a joint snack food company under the name Hostess Frito-Lay Co. in 1988. This partnership was dissolved in mid-1992 when Kraft sold its interests in the venture to Pepsi, saying it wanted to focus on its packaged food businesses.

The attractiveness of such a customer for canola oil is obvious. But the leverage a company like PepsiCo could exercise over the entire canola industry should also be obvious. Once again we have to wonder about who sets the research agenda and how, and to whom the benefits will accrue. The purported health benefits of a modified canola oil might pale into insignificance in comparison with the marketing and profit advantages to be achieved as a result of the reduced oxidation and hence prolonged use-life of the oil and shelf life of the product. The farmer growing the specialty canola under contract might also find that situation somewhat less than ideal given the disparity in bargaining power between an individual farmer and PepsiCo.

Manipulating canola to produce specialty oils under contract is a strategy that seems to be simply a matter of money and applied technology. The development of hybrids is another, offering its own unique advantages: "Hybrids offer a built-in proprietary protection because they are designed to fall apart if they are propagated beyond the F1 stage."[160] But the creation of hybrid canola has not been as easy as the researchers thought it would be, as we have already seen, with the result that nearly two years later, when asked when hybrids would be on the market, Grant responded: "Hybrids are always five years away."

When people got into hybrids, they thought it would be easy –
just apply technology, the genetics looks simple. . . 1989 was to

be the first year of hybrids on the market. The hybridization systems were not as straightforward as they seem. Our philosophy is that we won't go out with a hybrid until it is substantially better – 1995 is now our target.[161]

Grant's sardonic comment about hybrids has a definite history. Two years earlier I had asked him what his/Allelix's biggest mistake or failure had been.

Our biggest mistake was trying to get hybrids out too quickly, hybrids that were not ready to be sold. We were involved in that for a while but we withdrew. Now we are not going forward with a hybrid product until it is worthy of the name hybrid, which means a 15% yield increase and quality characteristics that are not going to be damaging.

An open-pollinated variety can be 1% better than existing varieties and be a saleable product, but you would not want to go forward with a hybrid that was only 1% better and ask for five times the price for it – it just doesn't wash.[162]

Grant's goal of a 15% improvement is somewhat less than the 40% which is the hypothetical advantage of hybridization, as we have already discussed.

In this same interview, I asked Grant the question I have asked others: If the same sort of resources that have gone into developing hybrids were to go into open-pollinated varieties, would it be possible to get the same results?

That's a good question and the answer is unknown. The genetic gains to be achieved in self-pollinating varieties are unknown because the crop has not been around long enough and the work has not been done. We don't know what the answer to your question is, and we won't know until these hybrids are grown on a million acres and we can compare the results.[163]

The problem with Grant's answer, of course, is that if the resources continue to be devoted to hybrids on a scale eventually permitting them to be grown on millions of acres, we never will know what the real answer to my question is.

Allelix, like other seed companies, pursues many routes to financial success, including cross-licensing agreements with other companies, like Weibulls AB of Sweden, as already mentioned in connection with UGG. In 1986, while a subsidiary of Volvo, Weibulls agreed to supply Allelix with their germplasm in return for Allelix's hybridization system, with the royalties for either to be traded. Since then, Pioneer has bought out the public rights of that agreement, so Pioneer can market without owing any royalties to Weibulls.

In 1990 Allelix announced that it had a licensing agreement with Plant Breeding International Cambridge (PBIC) whereby PBIC would supply winter canola varieties which Allelix Crop Technologies will multiply for seed sales in North America. (PBI had been a publicly-owned world-reknowned plant research centre until purchased by Unilever during Margaret Thatcher's privatization frenzy.)

In 1987 Allelix had also entered into another agreement, this one with Cyanamid Canada Inc., to develop a new strain of canola resistant to Cyanamid's imidazolinone herbicides (trade names: Pursuit, Assert, Sceptre). This line of research is particularly significant because the introduction of genes for resistance to this family of herbicides does not produce what is classed for regulatory purposes as a transgenic plant. That is, no genes have been introduced from a foreign species, the canola plant has simply been manipulated within the Brassica family to get the desired results, producing what is called a "transformation plant" rather than a "transgenic plant." The glyphosate tolerant plant that Monsanto is pushing is, on the other hand, a transgenic and is thus under somewhat stricter regulatory control. We will return to this issue in Chapter 11.

Allelix reported in 1987 that licensing tests of a canola strain resistant to an herbicide were to begin later that year, with the marketing of a hybrid spring canola developed with United Grain Growers to follow in 1988. However, it was not until Nov. 1989 that UGG reported that after five years of working with Allelix Crop Technologies, the first new variety, Delta, would be on the market in 1990. UGG also announced that the partnership would have a hybrid canola on the market in 1993 or 1994.

Bruce Magee, with Allelix at the time, described the dilemma created by the logic being pursued:

> As genetic suppliers, our research agenda is to focus on yield, disease resistance, and quality. The chemical company's specific agenda is weed control and selling the most chemicals they can possibly sell. The two come together because the chemical companies have found out that through certain biotechnical practices we can find resistance to chemicals, hence giving the chemicals broader spectrum. Once they discovered that, the chemical companies either developed their own biotech or teamed up with a biotech boutique to develop the resistance, i.e., us and American Cyanamid back in 1987. DuPont has developed resistance for some of their chemicals, and so have Monsanto and Hoechst.
>
> Now they want to get their material into as many different seed lines as possible. So, for instance, Monsanto has approached every canola breeder in N. America and said, how would you

like, on a non-exclusive basis, this inbred line for your canola development program? So Monsanto owns the line and licenses it out to every breeder in the country. What alternative do you have but take it?[164]

The recurring questions about who sets the agenda of the seed, and why, and to what end, often do not get the kind of answers one might expect or hope for from researchers and scientists. Very often the simple answer is "capital" and "more capital." This is reflected in a comment by Grant: "Pioneer has now invested so much money in canola that I doubt that there is a better breeding effort anywhere in the world. Given that, we expect to be the leader in developing the best varieties in the marketplace." In other words, the quality of science is a function of money, and progress is a function of technology, which is also a function of money, although whose technology does not seem to be an issue considered: "Canola is a crop you can really put a lot of technology into."

1991 Annual Report, Pioneer Hi-Bred International Inc.:

The business of Pioneer Hi-Bred International, Inc., is the broad application of the science of genetics. Pioneer was founded in 1926 to apply newly discovered genetic techniques to hybridize corn. . . Hybrids, crosses of two or more unrelated inbred lines, can be reproduced only by crossing their parent lines. . . Varietal crops, such as wheat and soybeans, will reproduce themselves with little or no genetic variation. . .

In 1991, Pioneer seed corn held a market share of 37% in North America. The Company's closest competitor held approximately 9%. . . 23 of our hybrids . . . accounted for about 3/4 of the total sales in North America.

Pioneer believes it possesses the largest single proprietary pool of germplasm in the world. . .

A 20% return on ending equity over time . . . rests on our ability to increase the performance advantages of our products – and our ability to sell them at prices which reflect those advantages.

Our intent is to price our products based on their productive advantages. Ultimately our customers would pay us an extra dollar for every three extra dollars they receive in additional productivity. . .

To increase productivity, growers will count more on genetics in the future. We are in the genetics business.

The utilization of public money has not come to an end just because canola has been substantially privatized. While the funding would appear to be largely corporate these days, and while the public rhetoric is heavy on the free enterprise line, corporate research has been able to count on a fair degree of public support at strategic points.

"Allelix has certainly benefitted from government program money", Beversdorf told me. In 1986 Allelix received an $800,000 grant from the National Research Council's Industrial Research and Assistance Program to develop a new "cybrid" (mixed cytoplasm) strain of canola containing both male sterility and herbicide tolerance. Allelix projected $16 million in annual sales of the seed to farmers once it got onto the market. Apparently it has not made it yet.

Allelix was also involved in a project with Agriculture Canada and Laval University in 1988 to genetically engineer a canola cultivar resistant to herbicide and pathogenic fungi. The project was supported by a National Research Council grant of $4 million for three years. Allelix expected to achieve a marketable product in seven years.

In addition to federal funding there has been significant provincial support for research such as the cooperative breeding program between Allelix and Guelph for the development of winter canola. While the Ontario Ministry of Agriculture and Food (OMAF) is interested in canola varieties for Ontario, Allelix is interested in the potential of the global market for canola. So Guelph produces inbred seed lines which Allelix then carries into hybrids and tests all over the world. If anything commercial results, Allelix pays OMAF a royalty.

Cultivars and patents developed over the past decade by the University of Guelph's department of crop science had generated over $1 million in royalties by late 1991, with 3/4 of the total coming from royalties on plant cultivars and 1/4 from patents on hybridization processes.[165]

Note: In June, 1987, Allelix president John Evans became the first Canadian chairman of the board of the Rockefeller Foundation. According to Evans, the Foundation "has been a pioneer in applying science to human problems."[166] Prior to its role as global colonizer with the Green Revolution, the Rockefeller Foundation was noted for its propagation abroad of American style capital-intensive medical care. For Evans, the move from Allelix to the Rockefeller Foundation was a natural one since Allelix seems to operate with the same particular understanding of science that has guided the work of the Rockefeller, and other, Foundations.

A Question of Control

It is a safe bet that transnational corporations like Pioneer Hi-Bred International and ICI exert more influence over industry and public policy in a country like Canada than do small independent regional seed companies. It is also a reasonable bet that those who are concerned about corporate pensions or their academic career will not be the ones to consider critically the structures of the industry and who controls them.

Control is exercised through explicit structures, but it is also exercised through the terms of discourse, by means of the particular rhetoric used to direct people's thinking. Thus non-scientific words like "productivity", "progress", "competitive" are used as if they had some scientific or factual merit.

A good example of this is a more or less objective description followed by a statement of philosophy, i.e., the attachment of a very particular idea of productivity to a statement about a political-economic process. There is only an ideological connection between the two:

> So what you will see in the future is a closed system of agriculture where a large user of oil, like Proctor & Gamble, would say to a seed company, like Pioneer, we need so many tonnes of seed, or oil. Then Pioneer will create the seed and go out and contract with farmers to grow it. With each step along the way, from commodity to proprietary to specialty, you're allowing increased farmer productivity. [167]

When he said this, Bruce Magee was working for Pioneer Hi-Bred, a company in a position to assert a fair amount of control over the canola industry as a whole. The goals it chooses to pursue and the investments it decides to make will have a lasting influence on the future of canola, and a lot of farmers, unless countered by other interests and approaches.

Magee recognizes that the structures being created in canola are increasingly similar to those already existing in the poultry industry, particularly in the U.S., where the industry is highly integrated and controlled by the end-user or near end-user, i.e., either by Tyson or ConAgra or McDonald's or Kentucky Fried Chicken (KFC). Magee also recognizes that there is a definite trade-off, just as there has been with hybrid corn, and that there is a real issue of control:

> Absolutely. With hybrid seed corn, instead of open-pollinated varieties, because of the tremendous yield advantage, growers have to go back to those researchers who have provided the most productive seed for that area and those conditions, so the grower is under total control to go back and purchase new hybrid seed.

Magee, along with many, many others, accepts willingly and without question the benefit, in terms of productivity, of that trade-off in control: "the quantum leaps in yield provided by that controlled system" far outweigh the social implications of that control in his mind.

Roger Kemble came to Allelix with Sheppard back in 1984, so it may be perfectly natural for him to share Magee's outlook. I asked Kemble the question about hybrids vs. open-pollinated varieties and resources expended in their development, and got the standard declaration of faith:

> In the near term, our inbred open-pollinated varieties have been yielding and performing as well as or better than our hybrids. Some companies are already selling hybrids that are very poor yielders and have a lot of other problems.

> Canola is following the pattern of corn quite closely. We are still in the early stages of crop development: canola as we know it was rapeseed, a weed, 15 years ago [sic]. Canola germplasm is still plastic enough that you can find some heterosis in it through traditional breeding of inbred lines. But undoubtedly that tops out, and if you want to get better performance and increased yields after that, you have to add different genes into your germplasm, and the simplest way to do that is by hybridization.

> In about 1989 we had the technology to the level where we could start applying it, routinely inserting foreign genes into canola. We don't do protoplast fusion any more, but we can isolate pollen grains and routinely generate plants from them which are double haploids, and they immediately become an inbred line which you can use in a breeding program. We can use RFLP – restriction fragment length polymorphism – techniques to genetically fingerprint all our lines. This gives breeders a good marker so they are able to follow a trait through their breeding schemes and it also gives us some legal protection because we can molecularly identify our lines.

> All these developments come from somewhere, and what they come from is just giving people some money and saying, here, it's a good idea, try it.[168]

One of the reasons the issue of control does not seem important to many people is an underlying belief in biological determinism and/or social Darwinism. The direction the industry took is regarded as simply a matter of evolution, of the universe unfolding as it should. That there is a profound contradiction between such a philosophy and the deliberate actions of corporate boards of directors does not seem to be noticed by many people, let alone to be of concern.

When I asked Grant about the consequences of corporate concentration and privatization, for example, he replied that there would be concern if there were only one player, but there are many - at least six - compared to the situation that used to exist in the west where there was only one research establishment and one seed producer, Agriculture Canada, and it was very paternalistic: we know what is best and which variety you will grow. Twenty years ago there were no options.

Such an attitude, of course, invites the question, what role do farmers play in setting the research agenda of the corporations, or for that matter, of Agriculture Canada?

Grant's fellow Allelix employee, Kemble, expressed that same attitude about what might be referred to as "freedom of choice":

> If there is just public breeding, the farmers are going to have only a few choices. With the private sector, what the farmer will get is a lot more choices, and of varieties which have come from a world-wide germplasm base. And they are going to outperform the inbred lines. The farmer will have more choice and better varieties than from just the public system. What is in vogue today will not be tomorrow, so there will be continual changes.[169]

More choice of canola varieties to choose between is not necessarily either good or meaningful. Being in vogue is hardly an adequate criterion for choosing a variety of seed, except perhaps in ornamental flowers. Much more to the point is for the farmer to have a variety that is bred to perform well in his or her local conditions, including weather, diseases, and farming systems, i.e., rotations and management practices. The choice between 15 hybrids, all of which are engineered to be resistant to Monsanto's glyphosate herbicide, or which are Blackleg resistant because they are all derived from Tobin, is hardly a meaningful choice.

The issue of public and private, and the relationship between the two, is always present, though too often unidentified. As we have already seen, the issue surfaces over and over again. There are times when I think the private researchers are more aware of the issue than the public researchers.

> Canola is an incredibly good example of absolutely fantastic publicly funded research. Without publicly funded research, Canada wouldn't have canola - the world wouldn't have canola.[170]

So I asked Magee one of my two favourite questions, the one about whether canola would exist today if the research situation had been, in 1960, what it is today? His response? "No, it wouldn't. Absolutely."

Magee's answer to my second question, are we not cutting our own throats then? was equally blunt:

I hear what you are saying. The end users, like P & G or McDonald's, are only going to start to move when they see something tangible in front of them in a very short time frame. They are never going to commit to technology development out of their own facilities. Nor do they have the facilities or staff.

I am on the advisory board of a couple of federally funded research institutes, and speaking personally, if you want another canola developed, if you want more speculative research to take place, then you have to think of a different way of measuring peoples' careers and career progressions than in terms of scientific publications. For the life of me I do not understand why people in federal research institutions should have the same pressures applied to them, to publish or perish, as university professors. What happens is that scientists in federal institutes do the kind of research that they can do and that they can get a publication out of. So you have everyone working at the same level on canola, all doing the stuff we can do. Nobody can afford to step back and say, I'm not going to get a publication out of this for six years but I want the money to do this work. They won't get it.

If all this is so obvious to Magee, while the destruction of publicly funded speculative research by the federal government proceeds (with all due neo-liberal intent), then the future of science in the public interest is indeed in doubt. What remains surprising, however, is that Magee, and others like him, still seem to think reasonable the split between publicly funded basic research and corporate applied research that aims to capture the benefits of the public work.

Leaning against the wall of Magee's office were a bunch of overlay maps which I could not help noticing. He explained that these showed different areas of production, or potential production, of canola. He pointed out that there are 11 million acres of spring wheat grown in Kansas alone that could be growing canola, though there is not a variety suitable for that area available yet. But, Magee commented, there was a time 45 years ago when they could not grow winter wheat there either.

Our strategy is to go where we can capture the margin and profit of the technology that we have developed, and if it isn't in Canada, it has to be somewhere else. Our strategy and our focus right now is on spring material for western Canada and winter material for Europe. As Allelix, before Pioneer bought us, we spent a significant amount of time and money focusing on the U.S. The problem with that market is that no Canadian or U.S. producer can effectively compete against the EC oil and EC canola coming into the U.S. market. Even if GATT did go through, tomorrow, you'd still only be looking at a 35% decrease in EC subsidies over 6 years. And that's a significant roadblock to an oilseed industry developing in the U.S.

Now, if Calgene and other seed interests and canola processors in the U.S. decide to work to have a countervailing tariff put in place and succeed, in the short term you would see acres pop really quick. But I don't foresee that because P & G and Frito-Lay and Kraft and everybody else are getting good deals for EC oil and they don't want that to stop. A tariff on imported oil is not going to happen because the voice you are hearing at the Canola Association is that of the processor that wants the least cost oil of the highest possible quality, and he doesn't care where it comes from.

Which explains why CanAmera Foods, a partnership of Central Soya (Ferruzzi) and CSP Foods, the latter really owned by Canadian farmers through the Prairie Pools, from time to time imports European canola seed in order to keep their Hamilton, Ontario, plant operating and to satisfy their customers.

Chapter 10

CROSSING THE LINES

Development Assistance

Canada's International Development Research Centre (IDRC) has been involved in two rapeseed/canola projects for several years, one with India, the other with China. They provide a different perspective on the development of canola.

Rapeseed has been cultivated in China for nearly 2000 years and is China's most important oilseed crop. China is also the world's largest rapeseed producer, accounting for 25-30% of world production, according to IDRC. The Chinese were the first to successfully hybridize *B.napus* rapeseed and now, according to Downey, they grow some 500,000 ha. of hybrid rapeseed produced by the CMS system.

China also grows a lot of Chinese cabbage, which is actually a subspecies of *B.campestris*, according to Beversdorf, as well as another rapeseed variety which is eaten as greens. This testimony to the diversity of the Brassicas also suggests that a different intent on the part of Canadian crop scientists might have led to widespread production of edible greens on the Prairies rather than just wheat and canola.

Reliable statistics for a country the size of China are bound to be difficult to obtain and variable, but it is probably safe to say that China grows around 5-6 million hectares of rape, yielding 7-7.5 million tonnes of seed. Rape is grown as a winter crop in rotation with rice in a double or even triple cropping system. Until very recently, China grew only the traditional high-glucosinolate high-erucic acid rape.

Chinese researchers initiated development of low erucic acid and low glucosinolate varieties of rapeseed in 1978, and IDRC has been supporting this work under the leadership of Keith Downey since 1983.

The IDRC-supported work has focused on the use of Canadian varieties of canola both as parent stock and for direct introduction. Canada has also helped with methods of chemical analysis, a memorial, one might say, to the work of Burton Craig three decades earlier. Subsequently, support has been given to research in spring rapeseed, improved breeding techniques, utilization of oil and meal, and the "dissemination and popularization of technologies and improved germ plasm" previously developed with IDRC support.

The IDRC Project Summary points out that the project has been mutually beneficial, with Canada learning from China's experiences and obtaining "valuable knowledge and . . . useful indigenous germ plasm", particularly traits of Chinese germplasm such as disease resistance, while the Chinese gain assistance in popularizing the variety improvements achieved so far and replacing local varieties which have "anti-nutritional factors [which] negatively affect human and animal nutrition." Higher quality (that is, varieties approaching canola quality) rapeseed, according to this project summary, will also allow the meal to be used as animal feed "instead of being wasted or used as an organic fertilizer."[171] There is, as one might expect, however, a trade-off: yields of traditional Chinese rape are significantly higher than the "improved" canola varieties. The use of the words "improved" and "higher quality" needs itself to be noted, of course, since neither are scientific terms.

The project summary contains two other interesting notes: one, that there is an "excellent integration of female researchers into the project"; and, two, that the development of rapeseed quality and production in China "does not influence the world market because of the high domestic demand."

In light of the process of privatization that has been taking place in agriculture in general and rapeseed/canola in particular, it is interesting to find explicitly articulated in this IDRC report that one of the objectives of the project has been "to facilitate information and germplasm exchange." What is not stated is whether the recipients of this information (germplasm and otherwise) are committed to maintaining the information in the public domain since the work is publicly financed.

Although the general objective of the last phase of this project is to popularize and disseminate the "improved" varieties released in the first phases of the project, the IDRC recognizes as the project "succeeds" and the improved varieties take over, "to avoid the loss of valuable rapeseed resources, collection expeditions need to be quickly organized." This collection, at least in Guizhou Province which has a very complex ecology and is a major centre of *B.juncea* germplasm, will take about three years to complete and then each accession will be evaluated for "disease resistance, quality, insect resistance, hardiness and drought resistance."

Finally, a highly significant part of this project will be the exchange of researchers between China and Canada so that researchers can work side by side on common projects. Obviously this is more than simple information exchange; it is also genuine technology transfer. To what extent it is also cultural transfer is not addressed in the project summaries. The assumption would appear to be that science is science, and that the culture and social agenda of the Chinese is no different than that of their Canadian advisors. If, however, the scientists involved ever discuss politics and culture, one might expect some interesting meetings. A companion sociological study might be more interesting than the plant biology.

IDRC's India project started out very similarly to the China project, except that China has been self-sufficient in oil, or at least chose not to import oil, while India has been a major importer of both fuel and edible oils, at a cost it could not afford. According to *Oil World*, India's average annual production of rape and mustard between 1981-90 was only 2.98 million tonnes, so the overall aim of the project was to increase India's oil production and decrease its oil imports. Specifically, the initial goals of the project were to achieve improved disease-resistant varieties of rapeseed, increased and more stable yields utilizing heterosis, and improved oil and meal quality.

Given the fact that average yields of rapeseed grown under the dryland, rainfed production conditions of small farms in India was only 650 kg per hectare, the objective of doubling production and increasing rural processing by 1991 seemed only reasonable.

Just as the Chinese chose to take the hybrid route, so did India, and IDRC accepted that choice. While it is beyond the scope of this study to examine the education and training of the Chinese and Indian scientists, it is probably a safe guess that at least the Indian scientists were trained in British schools and strongly influenced by the culture of British science, so whether the decision to go the hybrid route was theirs as Indians, or theirs as British scientists strongly influenced by the conventional wisdom of plant breeding, we can only surmise.

The IDRC project accepted the view that "the incorporation of disease resistance into high-yielding varieties can be achieved in a relatively short time without any increase in cost to the farmer", while "the pooling of knowledge and resources should make possible the development of high yielding hybrids in a reasonable time frame."

> This project is expected to result in varieties of rapeseed and mustard available to the farmers which have higher and more stable yields, and better returns. The improved oil quality will result in improved utilization in the diet while improved meal quality will provide a higher quality non-toxic livestock feed. Increased rural processing will result from an increase in oilseed

production. Since 80% of rapeseed/mustard production is likely to be by small farmers without irrigation, the smaller farmers are likely to be the greatest beneficiary.[172]

It must be noted again here that the word "improved" is used with excessive frequency, particularly in the absence of a culturally defined description of what is meant by improvement.

As with the China project, the exchange and training of scientists has been a major dimension of the India project. "A succession of Indian scientists to the same institution should ensure continuity of the research, and enable each scientist so trained to carry on the research as soon as he/she returns to India." The project thus called for the explicit exchange of information and the transfer of technology via the persons trained in its use.

This type of technology transfer, which is also a transfer of the culture of the technology (the values and social organization it expresses), has been common in the dissemination of industrial agriculture. In their examination of the work of the International Rice Research Institute, Anderson et. al. concluded that,

> values and models of research and social organization have been transferred along with agricultural technology. . . Marketing and image-building was a natural feature of the world which most of IRRI's research staff inhabited; it was an essential part of the commercial agriculture to which IRRI was committed. The axiom of these concepts and models was and is that the life of the user-customer shall be transformed by the purchase or adoption of the "product."[173]

What is meant here, as Anderson et. al. make clear elsewhere in their study, is that the culture of the recipient will itself be transformed by the process of adopting the new technology.

The IDRC project report also mentions that, as with China, the exchange of "breeding materials and germ plasm" will benefit Canadian as well as Indian breeding programs. In fact, the project report emphasizes that "seed materials necessary for the execution of this project will be freely exchanged."

It is interesting to note the contradictory aspects of this project. On the one hand it supports the development of hybrids, while on the other it advocates the free exchange of information. Surely consistency would demand the development of open-pollinated varieties because the free exchange of information is exactly what characterizes the social relations of open-pollinated plants, to the benefit of both the farmer and genetic diversity.

In addition to the issue of freedom of information, there is the fact that hybrids determine, by their nature, certain social and economic structures. By determine I mean that they require, for their use, certain economic and institutional arrangements, the most obvious being a reliable distribution system for the seed and an adequate economic climate to permit the grower to pay for the seed with cash as well as to purchase the fertilizer and chemicals required by the demands bred into the seed. Hybrids are, by definition, high-response varieties, not simply high-yielding ones.

The latest aspect of this IDRC project is a push by the National Dairy Development Board of India to speed up the introduction of canola quality rapeseed so that the meal left after crushing could be used as a protein supplement in the feed of dairy cattle. The NDDB is already involved in oil refining for the production of dairy products and margarines, etc. My sceptical mind wonders if an increase in demand for protein for feed is anticipated because recombinant Bovine Growth Hormone is going to be introduced by U.S. drug companies eager to develop a market, having been excluded, so far, from Europe and North America. This may seem far-fetched, but in 1992 Monsanto announced that it would donate 100,000 doses of slow release RBGH to the Russian Academy of Agricultural Sciences for distribution to Russian dairy farms. Freely stating that of course this was a case of market development, Monsanto also pointed out that this gift was made only after the U.S. government had extended credit to the C.I.S. for the purchase of feed grains. Without the necessary increase in protein intake, the administration of rBGH would not only be a failure, it would be a disaster for the cows since it would literally burn them out.

The mentality that opts for the development of hybrid rapeseed is the same mentality that would choose to increase milk production through the administration of synthetic hormones. Both have the direct and almost irreversible effect of making the primary producers increasingly dependent on input suppliers, i.e., seed, fertilizer and chemical companies. In choosing to develop canola-quality hybrids rather than open pollinated varieties, India, like China, is making an ideological or political choice, not a practical or scientific choice. Up to now, China's traditional open-pollinated rapeseed varieties are considerably more productive than the canola-quality varieties replacing them.

One also has to wonder what effect the introduction of canola will do to the traditional production of rapeseed cultivars as edible greens. Might the IDRC support a project that worked on the development of such a crop for the Canadian Prairies, utilizing Chinese expertise?

A Different Route: Processing

It seems to have been an unquestioned assumption from the very beginning that the route to a useable rapeseed oil was through the seed. It was not until my research was nearly complete that I got around to visiting Leon Rubin, retired head of Canada Packers research lab, who is now Professor of Food Engineering at the University of Toronto. Rubin and L.L. Diosady constitute the Food Engineering Group at the University.

The role that Canada Packers' research lab, under Rubin's direction, played in the development of canola, particularly in the person of its head chemist, Bart Teasdale, was discussed in Chapter 4. The breeders and the major processor were both working to develop a high quality edible oil, and it seems to have been taken for granted all along that the one and only way to achieve that goal was through the transformation of the seed.

Rubin, however, was an engineer, not a chemist, so he did not quite share the perspective of the breeders or even of chemist Bart Teasdale, though he supported their work, as we have seen. When Rubin retired from Canada Packers in 1979 he moved to the University of Toronto, where he continues, as an engineer, to develop a processing system that will do for rapeseed oil what the plant breeders have done for it by altering the seed. In other words, what the breeders did in changing the agenda of the seed Rubin and his colleagues are trying to do by means of processing technology without reprogramming the seed. If Rubin succeeds, we might well wonder why such an alternative was not given as much attention in the beginning as was the transformation of the seed itself.

The Food Engineering Group is focusing on rapeseed as a staple food, and thus on its high protein content, rather than on its oil content, trying to "produce products essentially free of glucosinolates and fibre, and low in polyphenols and phytate."[174]

> Rapeseed/canola contains glucosinolates and phytate (phytin) and has a high fibre content in the hull (30% of the meal). The phytin contains a lot of phosphate groups which the plant uses as a source of phosphate for its growth, but it is an anti-nutritional element in that it interferes with the absorption of essential elements like iron and zinc.

> The glucosinolates were the first problem to be tackled because they are toxic and goiterogenic, interfering with the action of the goiter in the absorption of iodine. These anti-thyroid factors are very important, but the presence of phytate should not be underestimated. In addition, rapeseed is high in polyphenols which give canola oil a dark or green colour.

So our aim was to develop a process which would specifically treat rapeseed/canola and remove the disadvantages which are built into it. As engineers, this is a more natural thing for us to do.[175]

Traditional rapeseed crushing technology is simply adapted soybean crushing technology, as Rubin described it, with pieces added – pre-pressing, refining, etc. – to deal with particular canola characteristics. So most processing plants have been gradually rebuilt completely from their origins as soybean facilities. For example, CP's CVOP plant in Hamilton was built to process only soybeans and only recently was it rebuilt so that canola could be processed as well.

Rubin and his colleagues started from the beginning, rather than trying to adapt a technology designed for another purpose. Clearly, as an engineer, Rubin sees processing from a radically different perspective than the crop scientists.

To achieve their objective, Rubin and colleagues have developed a two- phase solvent system in which a methanol-ammonia system for treating defatted canola meal was combined with the usual oil extraction solvent hexane to produce canola-quality oil and a meal that is essentially free of glucosinolates and contains significantly reduced levels of polyphenols.

A U.S. patent was obtained on this part of the process in 1984. A second patent was obtained, in 1989, on the oil-extraction part of the process, and a third patent has been obtained on an ultrafiltration process that yields protein isolates. The whole process now involves a single extraction step followed by two stages of ultra-filtration.[176]

The Canola Council paid for Rubin's initial work, but since then most of it has been paid for by the Natural Science and Engineering Research Council. They have gotten as far as developing a semi-pilot process with a ton of material, but it will require $1-1½ million to build a continuous-process pilot project. If someone would pay for it, such a process could be done with the Protein Oil and Starch (POS) plant in Saskatoon, says Rubin.

What Rubin and Diosady have achieved is an improved meal that contains 50% protein instead of the 38% protein now available in commercial canola meal, which makes the meal comparable to soybean meal. It is also low in polyphenols, but still has the hulls in it. The second stage is the development of two protein isolates which are over 90% protein, which is as good or better than soybean protein. Their three patents cover the basic process of a two-phase solvent system, the second covers the column extraction process, and the third the protein isolates. The university actually owns the patents, but Food Biotech Corp., the company of which Rubin and Diosady are the owners, licenses the patents from the university.

As Rubin tells the story, he embarked on the development of this process shortly before he left Canada Packers when a news item in a journal triggered a thought. While the idea seemed to show some promise, they never did anything with it at CP. When he came to the University of Toronto he started working on the idea and by 1984 they had the basic lab process sorted out and patented, though it took a few more years to really get it all going. While a number of processors are now interested, Rubin and Diosady are also talking with the manufacturers that supply oilseed processing equipment to plants around the world. Currently, however, the whole industry is in such bad shape that no one is interested in picking up anything. Given the investment that CanAmera (Central Soya) and the others already have in processing facilities, it would seem unlikely that they would want to invest in a technology that might make their existing plants obsolete. One can also imagine the seed companies throwing up a lot of opposition.

While the IDRC is trying to help China transform their rapeseed into canola through now-traditional breeding, Rubin sees China as the most promising area for his processing technology because of the size of their rapeseed industry and the fact that they cannot utilize the meal except as fertilizer. If the meal can be improved so that it is a valuable animal feed, it could be worth $180 per tonne instead of $15 per tonne. The potential value of the high-protein meal in human nutrition is also high on Rubin's mind.

The Chinese would like someone to build a pilot plant utilizing Rubin's process, which would seem to be a sound strategy. To be practical, such a plant would have to process at least 100 tonnes per day. Canadian plants crush about 600 tonnes per day, but that is too big for China because if does not have the transportation and storage infrastructure, says Rubin.

Just as Downey and others have had Chinese students working with them on the plant breeding side, Rubin has had a student from China working with him for a year, learning about what they are doing in processing technology. Half jokingly, I asked Rubin if they had spent a year teaching a Chinese student all their trade secrets: "You could say he was here in a very expensive way doing industrial espionage. But we do have a Chinese patent and hopefully we will be able to protect ourselves with it."

THE AGENDA OF THE SEED

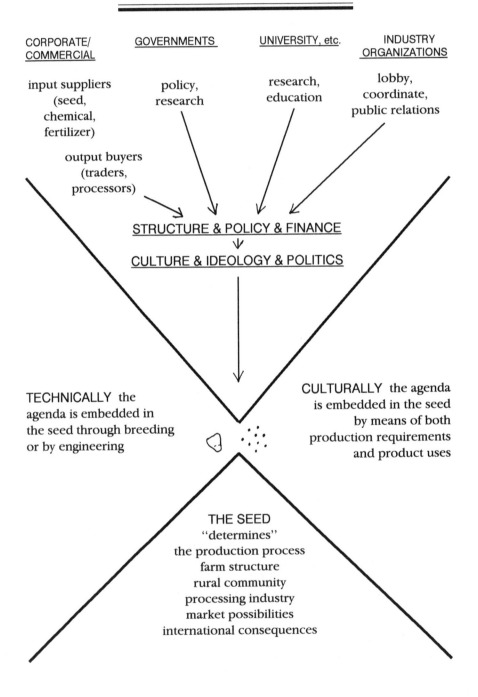

CORPORATE/
COMMERCIAL

GOVERNMENTS

UNIVERSITY, etc.

INDUSTRY
ORGANIZATIONS

input suppliers
(seed,
chemical,
fertilizer)

policy,
research

research,
education

lobby,
coordinate,
public relations

output buyers
(traders,
processors)

STRUCTURE & POLICY & FINANCE

CULTURE & IDEOLOGY & POLITICS

TECHNICALLY the
agenda is embedded in
the seed through breeding
or by engineering

CULTURALLY the agenda
is embedded in the seed
by means of both
production requirements
and product uses

THE SEED
"determines"
the production process
farm structure
rural community
processing industry
market possibilities
international consequences

Chapter 11
A CLASS STRUCTURE FOR THE SEED

> All scientific knowledge is always, in every re-
> spect, socially situated. Neither knowers nor
> the knowledge they produce are or could be
> impartial, disinterested, value-neutral,
> Archimedean. *Sandra Harding*[177]

The application of social concepts to scientific matters is apt to be considered bad science by those who follow the reductionist belief that
there is such a thing as objective fact without context. Yet the decision
to invest time and money in plant research, like the decision on how to
conserve genetic information, is more a social, economic or political
choice than a matter of science.

The stubborn and costly pursuit of hybrid canola is a good example.
Virtually every plant breeder will insist that hybrids will always outper-
form open pollinated varieties, ignoring the equation between input and
output. As German canola breeder G. Röbbelen says, "Every comparison
to a considerable degree will always reflect the attention and input previously granted to the crop by breeders and agronomists."

Röbbelen goes on to explain that the economic advantage of an F1
hybrid over the best conventional open pollinated varieties is still an
open question because "the heterotic gain in the performance of F1 hybrid varieties may not be sufficient to balance the additional cost of hybrid seed production." In fact, says Röbbelen, the "satisfying performance of present hybrids may not be much more than merely
accidental."[178]

Even with my belief that science and its projects embody social con-
structs, I was startled when a seed production manager at Pioneer Hi-
Bred commented that "corn is a bourgeois crop." The more I have
delved into this business of canola, the more that comment has haunted
me.

In defining "bourgeois", Langdon Winner cites the work of Jacques
Ellul and writes:

A bourgeois is above all else someone who has mastered technique. The bourgeoisie first developed financial and commercial techniques and went on to originate the factory system, the rational administration of the state, technical schools, and so forth. They were truly people suited to their times – marginal, atomized individuals, obsessed by special interest, fascinated by science, and convinced that reason must be made active in every corner of social and material existence.[179]

The current status of canola, and particularly the efforts to hybridize it, are often compared, as we have noted, to corn in the 1930s. The assumption seems to be that canola is no different than corn, and that canola can be programmed to reproduce the same industrial methods and class structure as was built into hybrid corn.

While modernized hybrid corn fits Winner's definition of bourgeois well, traditional corn expressed a very different culture. For centuries peasants have cultivated a multitude of varieties of corn, usually in combination with beans, squash, or some other complementary (companion) crop. (The Museum of Anthropology in Mexico City is a good place to see this.) Seeds for the next crop were selected from the current crop each year for agronomic, religious and nutritional reasons. Being open-pollinated, selected seed would reproduce its own characteristics with some genetic variation depending on other varieties nearby. If one seed was considered better than another, it was only for a specific purpose, not because it was ontologically superior (superior in its Being). There was no class identity imposed on the seed, only a practical or vocational differentiation. And what might not be considered useful was probably still grown off in a corner because it might be useful next year or the year after.

In his lyrical and reverent book about plant selection and seed saving in the Indian cultures of the North American southwest, *Enduring Seeds*, Gary Nabhan cites ethnobotanist Janis Alcorn's description of the unwritten "scripts" that guided seed selection and kept agricultural practices relatively consistent from generation to generation:

> Each individual farmer might edit this script to fit her or his peculiar farming conditions, but the general scheme is passed on to the farmer's descendants. Thus the crop traits emerging through natural selection in a given locality are retained or elaborated by recurrent cultural selection.[180]

From his own observations, Nabhan points out that where Indian farming has persisted, families frequently grow four or five different kinds of beans every year, and it is still possible to find villages that harbour ten to eighteen "land races" or locally-adapted bean variants, most of which have been passed from generation to generation for no less than a century.

Joachim Voss, director of the sustainable production systems program which is responsible for the canola projects of the IDRC in China and India, told me another little story about beans which not only illustrates the problem with western Science and Technology, but also its domination over differing social systems:

> I worked at International Centre of Tropical Agriculture (CIAT) for five years, and their big success the year I arrived was the black bean variety that took over Cuba, or that Cuba took over. With its system of state farms, Cuba declared it the best bean variety and just covered the country with it. The year that I left disease resistance in those beans had broken down and they were desperately looking for a solution to this disaster. But during these same years someone was looking at genetic mixtures of beans and coming up with very interesting data: you get both more stable and higher yields by putting together the right kind of mixtures. You get synergistic effects and synergistic disease resistance with nowhere near the same problem of the breakdown of resistance.[181]

The restructuring of corn in the 1930s has been described by Jack Kloppenburg as, "The historical transformation of the seed from a public good produced and reproduced by farmers into a commodity that is a mechanism for the accumulation of capital."[182] The consequence was not only that the farmer had to return to the breeder each year for seed, but also that the seed was not necessarily adapted to the specific conditions of the farm on which it was to be grown, apart from the heat units required for it to mature. The process of creating dependency was underway: if the seed was better suited to the accumulation process of the seed company than to the natural conditions on a particular farm, the farm conditions could be changed to suit the seed – and its maker – by the addition of agro-toxins (chemicals) and synthetic fertilizers and the use of specialized, costly machinery (the mechanical harvester and then the precision planter) – all of which are generally referred to as progressive, if not benign, "technologies."

The social history of plant breeding in the 20th century, says Kloppenburg, is essentially a chronicle of the efforts of private industry to circumvent the twin obstacles of the reproducibility of the seed by the farmer, that made every farmer a potential competitor of the seed company, and public breeding and commercialization programs that made the state a competitor to the private seed company as well. The canola story illustrates this well. As I have shown, the private companies are making heroic efforts to hybridize canola or to breed into it special characteristics that will effectively put the growers under contract while at the same time applying increasing pressure to force the state out of any commercialization activity.

In addition, the social history of the seed reflects what are often considered the more "objective" cultural values of those directing the breeding programs, whether at the universities or in the corporations. The standard of success is Productivity is measured by yield and a narrow conception of quality. If increased yield requires increased fertilizer, this is simply a cost required for progress. If the trade-off for increased yield is reduced disease and stress tolerance, then the additional chemicals required to counter the consequences are also counted as no more than the price of progress. The same thing will be said of irrigation. Agro-toxins and synthetic fertilizer come to be considered "good" since they increase yield and manageability, at least in the short term. This reflects capitalist accounting, which has long focused only on the immediate project, ignoring the system as a whole. Costs such as degradation of the land, pollution of groundwater, consumption of non-renewable energy, and erosion of genetic diversity, if they are recognized at all, are deliberately, if unconsciously, externalized.

We have already seen how the transformation of rapeseed started with traditional selection and reproduction, and how this traditional method of plant "improvement" is being overtaken by genetic engineering and the teleological manipulation of genetic information. As canola is increasingly made to resemble the model of hybrid monocultural corn, the genetically profligate rapeseed is transformed into a capital intensive, high-class, high-return crop.

This process might be paraphrased this way: a small portion of the proletarian genetic population of rapeseed has been streamed (picked up and rather quickly transformed) into the upper class. This elite requires a special infrastructure or support system (agricultural "inputs") including adequate amounts of water, fertilizers and "crop protection agents" (the military guard) as well as moderate weather (heating and air conditioning).

As I have already pointed out, the agents of this elite, the breeders, recognize what they are doing, and their choice is not necessarily as much a matter of science as a matter of politics. Hybridization is pursued because it is in the corporate interest to maximize profit. Hybrid seed does not breed true, it degenerates, (the managerial elite does too when it gets too small), thus requiring the farmer to purchase new seed from the corporation for every crop rather than using seed saved from the previous crop.

In other words, the seed is being - or in the case of corn, has been - recruited into the class structure of the society and given a class identity, which becomes embedded in the seed. And just as the upper class of society depends upon and consumes far more than its share of global resources and human labour, so does upper-class hybrid seed.

The farmers growing hybrid seed become agents of a class structure they can only marginally participate in. They perform as members of the feudal household, spending the squire's money on seeds, fertilizers, chemicals, machinery and irrigation, to produce a crop that yields a particularly healthful edible oil available to those with the disposable income to afford it. At the same time, this hybrid and/or specialty crop, because of the cash return it brings in the market, tends to drive out proletarian subsistence food production along the way.

Thus, public funds are siphoned off into esoteric research to further refine the "health" and/or processing characteristics of this upper class oil, while basic research into sustainable, low input food production falls by the wayside, or, more accurately, is starved out.

At the same time, the *belief* that canola can and should be turned into the same kind of capital intensive "bourgeois" crop as corn is so strong - as previously noted - that it appears that the energies and ingenuity being applied to the selection of open pollinated canola are only for the purposes of producing a marketable hybrid.

This is not accidental. As Kloppenburg points out, "It was neither chance nor an immanent and ineluctable technical logic that produced the development of hybrid corn. "

> In the 1920s there were several possible paths to corn improvement. At least one of these, population improvement, may well have been as productive as hybridization. That hybridization was the route that was pursued was determined not by strictly scientific considerations but by the provision of funding incentives and the manner in which political power was wielded within the U.S. Department of Agriculture.[183]

Carefully applied research funding by transnational corporations can provide the leverage required to shape the political agenda without a public political base. The public sector may continue to fund the majority of basic research in agriculture, but the research agenda will be shaped and its fruits harvested by private interests.

One might argue that it would be in the corporate interest to consider a broader market with the development of low input open-pollinated varieties, but this would go against the ideology of the class that makes the decisions about "resource allocation", i.e., investment of corporate funds and exploitation of public and natural resources in the interests of capital accumulation. It all comes back to the issue of control because control is essential to the accumulation of capital.

———————

Just as science and technology are expressions of the culture from which they arise, so is the canola they "create." Science provides the understanding, however partial or inexact, of the natural, material world as experienced and observed by a culture. Technology constitutes the specific tools by which the culture expresses (embeds) its values in the material world.

Science and technology are the means by which a society recreates its values and structures and pursues its goals in the material world. Thus it is only logical that the material world created by a capitalist culture presumes the availability of capital and the necessity of its accumulation. High Response Varieties (HRVs) that are highly dependent on capital intensive inputs (chemicals, fertilizers, water) are created to displace the naturally adapted varieties that utilize both the elements already present in a particular environment and the effects of symbiosis. Competitive capitalist monoculture drives out socially oriented diversity and interdependence.

Anderson, Levy and Morrison, in their study of the International Rice Research Institute (IRRI), state that the IRRI's underlying conception of science and its applications is based on the assumption that "new science and technology would lead inevitably to increases in aggregate rice production. Knowledge from the lab and plot would diffuse out to the progressive cultivator who would overcome conservative traditions to adopt the new technology."[184] Thus IRRI workers advised the Bangladesh government "to ignore the slow-adopting farmers or non-adopting farmers and to concentrate entirely on fast adopters."[185]

This centre-out diffusionist approach has been the guiding principle of the U.S. land grant colleges and the U.S. agricultural extension system for more than a century as well as the principal model of Canadian agricultural extension work.

A culture that believes in progress and development (themselves linear concepts) will describe what it sees in the natural world in the words of "progress" and "development." The discovery of rapeseed with desired characteristics creates an "improved" rapeseed. Plant evolution is described as "development" – which may be true in a very particular genetic sense – as if it were fulfilling a particular goal or following a desirable direction.

This concept of development is also expressed in the "human potential" movement wherein people are counselled to devote their energies to fulfilling their individual potential within the given social context, rather than counselling that they seek to both heal individual trauma and alter the social context. This is, of course, nothing but neo-Darwinist determinism – or Calvinist predestination, if you prefer. It certainly is not biology.

But each "improvement" in agricultural crops like canola has brought with it a multitude of demands and compromises. What is an improvement to some is a liability to others, and the farmers who are considered progressive or "early adopters" today may well be the casualties of tomorrow when their hybrid monoculture fails because there is no money to import fertilizer or chemicals, or because of drought or irrigation system failure due to the absence of spare parts for the pumps.

The problem with the notion of progress is that it fosters the idea that we can get something for nothing (an idea also fostered by a stock-market mentality), but in the long run nature does not work that way. For everything that looks like a gain, we should be asking, what is the price, and who or what is paying it? The trade-off for increased yield may be, as we have seen with canola, increased disease susceptibility and increased sensitivity to stress under adverse weather conditions. The trade-off for the bourgeois affluence, of course, is the impoverishment of others whose deprivation is, at least in part, the source of this accumulated wealth.

The "development" of a high-yielding cassava (manioc) by the International Institute of Tropical Agriculture in Nigeria, reported the Financial Times of London,[186] has caused researchers to be "cautiously optimistic that the new varieties will give Africa a long-overdue breakthrough to higher food output." Claiming that the new varieties can double or triple the farmers' crop, the report gives no indication whatsoever of any downside effects or any trade-offs. Although this may only reflect the enthusiasm of the reporter, it is probably an unfortunate reflection of the attitudes of the researchers. I find it hard to imagine improving on a crop, such as cassava, which produces, in poor soils, a tuber resembling a large potato while not requiring chemical fertilizer and rain or irrigation. According to the FT report, the plant's long roots tap moisture deep in the ground; when drought strikes, cassava has a "defensive mechanism" which causes its leaves to drop while the tubers survive. This has led to the claim: "Where there is cassava there is no hunger." Cassava also has the advantage that it can be stored in the ground for a year, giving farmers the freedom to eat it or sell it when the need arises. This gives local farmers control over the disposition of their crop and some freedom from The Market.

It is even harder, however, to imagine that doubling or tripling the yield will not have its costs. Given the record of the Green Revolution, one must be extremely naive to believe there are no trade-offs, such as requiring commercial fertilizers and agro-toxins in order to produce the increased yield, or, more subtly, drawing down the water table when yield is doubled.

However, scientists and technicians are taught, expected, and paid to work on quite narrowly defined problems without examining either significant alternatives or the assumptions – cultural, social or political – on the basis of which they carry on their work. In other words, the researchers are to stick closely to their text, paying little attention to their context. Given their sociological uniformity, it would, perhaps, be unreasonable to expect anything else. This is not to fault them, because in sticking to their text they are simply acting "normally", that is, like people of their class and profession are supposed to act.

It was Frank Scott-Pearse of King Agro who described for me the complex and wonderful character of the Brassica family and got me to thinking about how a social construct like class structure, and not simply the corporate agenda, can get embedded in the seed.

Actually, I had read a text book on rapeseed oils[187] early in my research, but at that point I did not know enough about the subject to see any significance in the structure of the Brassica family. It is possible that no one attached any real significance to this structure until efforts at hybridization became serious in the late 1980s. The book describes certain essential characteristics of the Brassicas, but Self Incompatibility is not mentioned as such and there is no discussion of the significance of the differences between the three monogenomic or basic species *(B.nigra, B.campestris and B.oleracea)* and the three secondary amphidiploids *(B.napus, B.carinata and B.juncea)*.

To identify these in more familiar language, cabbage, kale, cauliflower, broccoli and the other cole vegetables belong to the *B.oleracea* family, while "Argentine" rape and rutabaga belongs to the *B.napus* family and "Polish" rape and turnips belong to *B.campestris*. Varieties of mustards make up *B.carinata, B.juncea* and *B.nigra*.

The variation, or discrepancy, in the use of words such as "variety" and "line" reflects the breakdown in reductionist classification that tries, according to Linnaean principles, to develop a tidy definition of everything. Increasing knowledge of natural diversity and fluidity makes all neat categories suspect, to say nothing of what genetic engineering does to tidy botanical classifications.

As Downey expressed it in his contribution to Kramer et al, "Since early botanists attempted to separate plant groups on the basis of morphological characteristics, the occurrence of similar or identical plant forms in more than one Brassica species resulted in much confusion." The taxonomists, however, continue in their quest for the perfect classification and have put forward a new name, *B.rapa*, for *B.campestris*.

B.nigra, *B.oleracea* and *B.campestris* are the primary Brassica species and they are self-incompatible, meaning that they will not accept their own pollen, even though they make perfect flowers (complete with male and female parts). This characteristic forces them to cross-pollinate, that is, to breed with other plants of the same species, and it is this natural necessity of out-crossing that makes these plants natural hybrids. They are haploids, meaning that the maintain the basic number of Brassica chromosomes, about 18.

B.juncea, *B.napus* and *B.carinata* are the secondary species of the Brassicas and they are highly unusual in being what Scott-Pearse refers to as "mergers" with about 36 chromosomes. Ordinary crossbreds (diploids) are the result of the crossing of two lines, producing a new line with a new combination, but the same number, of chromosomes. A merger, or amphidiploid, is the joining of two lines and a doubling of the number of chromosomes, since the merger retains the original chromosomes of both lines that come together. A normal tetraploid, like red clover, also has double chromosomes, but they are a doubling of the same chromosomes. *B.juncea* is a merger of *B.nigra* and *B.campestris*; *B.carinata* is a merger of *B.nigra* and *B.oleracea*; and *B.napus* is a merger of *B.oleracea* and *B.campestris*. (Triticale, the laboratory synthesis of rye and wheat, is also an amphidiploid.)

> Nature took thousands of years to create these three amphidiploids, and certainly failed millions and millions of times along the way, but now we can get them to merge quite easily by means of cell biology [i.e., embryo rescue – the process of generating whole plants from a bit of plant tissue by just floating it in the proper medium].[188]

Napus, *juncea* and *carinata* are not self-incompatible, which means that they can breed themselves as well as interbreeding. It also means that it is easy to develop pure lines of these plants simply by ensuring that they breed only themselves.

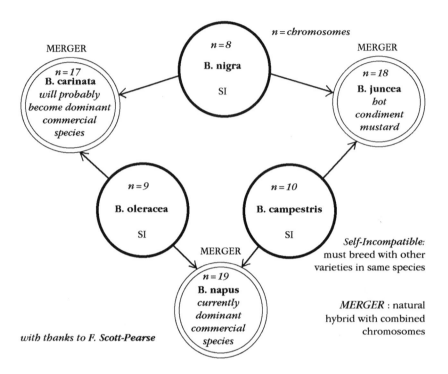

n = chromosomes

MERGER

n = 8
B. nigra
SI

MERGER

n = 17
B. carinata
*will probably
become dominant
commercial
species*

n = 18
B. juncea
*hot
condiment
mustard*

n = 9
B. oleracea
SI

n = 10
B. campestris
SI

MERGER

n = 19
B. napus
*currently
dominant
commercial
species*

Self-Incompatible:
must breed with other
varieties in same species

MERGER : natural
hybrid with combined
chromosomes

with thanks to F. Scott-Pearse

Only 10% of biotechnology may be transgenics, that is, moving genes between species in a way that does not happen in nature, but, as Scott-Pearse puts it, transferring genes around "the way nature does, only doing it a lot more efficiently, more quickly", is not "just following nature." Nature only transfers genes slowly. Transferring genetic information rapidly is not the same-thing-only-more-so, except in the logic of reductionist science which does not place much importance on the symbiosis between seed and environment. Rapid genetic transference does not allow time for this symbiosis to function, though as Scott-Pearse notes, current industrial breeding subjects far larger numbers of plants at one time to this environmental interaction.

What is the consequent relationship of transformed plants to their environment when they do not go through the slow natural process of evolution together? Scott-Pearse says that this "speeding up" of natural processes does not get out of sync with the larger environment because the minute the plant is taken out of the lab or the greenhouse the environment starts acting on it. If the new plant, or certain of its new characteristics, are not acceptable to its environment, nature will quickly intervene to correct the mistakes, or simply to kill the plant, "as nature has been doing for thousands and thousands of years", I was assured. But how does he know this for sure? We do know of many examples of human intervention that have, unnoticed until later, subtly transformed environments. (See Wm. Cronon, *Changes in the Land*.)

I do not find the assurances so reassuring, not because I know more science than the scientists, but because I trust my common sense and the questions it asks. If deceit and conceit are common in human relations, why can't they occur in our relations to the environment?

Take the preservation of genetic diversity, for example. It is today widely recognized that there has been a rapid erosion – or destruction – of genetic diversity as a result of industrialization and the advance of capital-intensive agriculture.

The reductionist response to genetic erosion has been to establish *ex situ* seed banks. These are refrigerated vaults where seed collections can be maintained in perpetuity, almost invariably located in wealthy northern countries. While the seeds may have to be grown out and replaced periodically to maintain their viability, this is done under conditions that ensure that the seed remains pure, or the same is it was when originally collected (in theory, anyway). Who is to be sure that there has not been some interior changes in the genetics *(mutagensis)* that are unknown to their keepers, and which might only be discovered if the seed was grown out under conditions similar to those from which it was collected in the first place?

But *ex situ* conservation is not natural, and if the seed is re- inserted at a later date into the environment from which it was taken, there is no guarantee that the plant will be adapted to this environment or even viable because the environment will have been evolving while the seed stood still. A distance between the seed and its apparent natural environment will have been established.

The realization of this has led more recently to recognition that *in situ* conservation is also required so that the seed continues to evolve with its environment. This directly challenges the virtual monopoly control of germplasm that can be achieved with *ex situ* seed banks.

In situ germplasm conservation means the conservation of seeds by their deliberate continuing propagation and replanting year after year in their native habitat so that the seeds continue to evolve with their environment. Practically, this is best done by the small farmers who have traditionally done this as part of their culture, not as a business enterprise. But such labour-intensive forms of conservation (production and reproduction) has always been hard for capital to control, particularly in contrast to the ease with which control can be exercised over centrally located refrigerated seed banks where one can always threaten to pull the plug.

So we have here two models of conservation: a reductionist capital intensive monopoly form and a holistic, low cost, labour intensive democratic form.

Leask's wave theory of crop development (Chapter 8) – and here the term "development" is deliberately used to reflect the cultural-ideological bias of Leask's typology – is a good description of what has happened with the imposition of a class structure in the seed. Historically, changes in the seed came about as a result of farmer selection, and while this selection might be for a wide variety of reasons, all of the reasons would be those of the farmer and/or his or her community. Because the plants were all open-pollinated of necessity, and were grown, selected and stored locally, each seed evolved in a dialectic between the constantly changing environment and the choices of the farmers selecting the seed for the next crop. Diversity and proximity were the norms for this highly democratic form of plant selection or breeding.

The development of commodity production – whenever that occurred for a particular crop – demanded commodity seed, that is, seed that was visually uniform and clean and healthy. This "first wave" of industrial seed development was followed in the 30s and 40s by a "second wave" in which the goals set for the seed are narrowed considerably and the breeding moves from the farm to the research laboratory.

At this point the "improvement" process begins. Up to this point this lineal concept was not really present since it was seed function and exterior quality that were the dominant criteria, not the selection of one or two varieties that were better in principle than others. The introduction of the idea of improvement was fundamental to the corporate program of taking the selection and breeding of seeds out of the hands of farmers. The corporations – Pioneer, Funk, DeKalb, etc. – were not interested in producing a different seed for every little bio-region and every possible use. On the contrary, industrial agriculture called for industrial seed, seed that could, like Ford cars, be marketed all over the country and even around the world, as long as there were the prescribed number of heat units. All the rest of the micro-environment could be added or subtracted by means of agricultural inputs.

To preclude any questioning of the whole enterprise, it was labelled Progress. And it was Modernization and Progress that were sold to the farmers. The retailers of this ideology, the ag schools and the agricultural extension agents, had their work cut out for them – at home and abroad.

The Green Revolution, as it came to be known, was simply an adaptation and extension of this logic, as discussed earlier in this chapter. Promoting the development and dispersion of High Yielding Varieties, as they were called by those who promoted them, or High Response Varieties by those more explicit about their characteristics, "favoured the mercantile structure of the business class", according to Anderson et al. For example, in Bangladesh, "These wholesale agents [for the seeds, fertilizers and chemicals], procurement specialists, importers-exporters, were part of a whole mentality of doing business by trading but not by manufacturing or producing anything."[189]

Leask's second wave introduces the concept of class into the seed and amongst those who grow it. Where there was, historically, only one (peasant) class of farmers, two now appear: the old-fashioned and the modern, the slow-adopters and the early-adopters. The old-fashioned are those stigmatized as subsistence farmers, that is, looking after themselves and not producing primarily for the market, while the modern are those fully integrated into industrial production for the market.

With the third wave, another class is added on top of the previous two. For a premium price – supposedly – the best farmers will identify themselves by moving into contract production of specialty seeds for the corporate elite, thereby joining, by association, the elite of society.

But look at what has happened: "Merit has traditionally been defined by the needs of farmers such as yield improvements and disease resistance. . . The third wave means that merit will be determined by the crop's utility further down the chain of production."[190]

In this movement from first to third wave two things have happened: control has shifted from the farmer through the seed company to the processor, or from the rural sector to the urban; and, the production process has become increasingly capital intensive because that has been the understanding of progress that has been embedded in the seed. Indeed, it has been the drive to develop the means of capital accumulation that has marked the development of modern urban industrial agriculture. The first wave was rural, with the characteristics of a decentralized, local, self-reliant and diversified economy implied in the term.

The third wave, with control shifted from farmer to corporation, is urban not only because that is where the decisions are made, but because the culture that makes the decisions *is* an urban culture. Progress is an urban concept, and the "development" of canola or the "improvement" of the seed is its urbanization. To be modern is to be urban. Development, on whatever scale, means inclusion into (or enclosure by) the urban culture and economy.

So we might say that rapeseed was a rural crop while its improved form, canola, is an urban crop. This is reflected in methods of production, uses of the crop, and the dependency of the crop.

When Peter McVetty told me that with hybrids "its always a matter of how deep a hole you want to dig before you start building a ladder to get back out again", I asked him if the whole exercise is really worthwhile from the farmer's point of view? In the short run, no, he replied, but there is promise of improved agronomic performance. "The problem is to take that improvement from small plots in a limited number of beautifully manicured in-house trials and translate it into commercial advantage on a couple million acres."

The breeders will keep trying, in part because of the sheer challenge of the task, in part because it is the kind of research that the private sector – and a market-mentality government – will pay for.

But even if hybridization is achieved, and the yield is significantly better – remember, the breeders told me when I began researching canola that a 40% gain is what to expect, though they have now toned that down to 15% – the plant varieties would still better be described as high response rather than high yielding. McVetty himself is unequivocal about this:

> If you want to grow a hybrid that yields 50% more than an open variety, I guess you had better be prepared to use more fertilizer, at least. And it won't be worth a darn in a drought year and it could be even worse than a conventional crop because the hybrids we have at the present time are, in large part, very vegetatively vigorous producers of plant material and absorb a lot of water before they flower. You have to have water, you have to put on the fertilizer, you probably have to routinely spray a fungicide on – you have an investment and you want to protect it.[191]

To my suggestion that the whole exercise is an upper-class project, McVetty agreed, and added:

> You pay more for the seed, more for the inputs. It is the good growers that will go this way; their risk is not as high, because they have the management ability to do everything right. They will get the genetic potential they paid for.

> There will be conventional varieties on the recommended list for another twenty-five years. They will be lower cost, less risk, lower performing: for the marginal farmers or the in-and-outs. But I think there will also be some spectacular hybrids in the next decade or so – the Rolls Royce varieties for the boys that do everything right – and it will pay off.

But how many of "the boys" will be able to do everything right, and can they count on nature and the weather to do their part? Not likely.

McVetty's career has been in a public institution and Scott-Pearse has been in business. That doesn't mean they think differently. Hybrids, Scott-Pearse assured me, "ultimately out-yield any open pollinated or any line which you can develop." But, he agreed, only with the kind of inputs which have been applied to corn.

There is a choice, and we can be quite sure that we have not yet observed, much less figured out, the wonderful possibilities that nature might already have come up with, such as the Brassica amphidiploids.

Kloppenburg relates how workers in the land-grant universities became interested in natural forms of out-crossing and hybridization in the 1890s as an adjunct to the selection breeding they were doing. "It is important to understand that during this period hybridization simply meant the cross-breeding or sexual combination of two varieties of plant or animal." It was not until the mid-30s that the term "hybridization" was given a much narrower meaning "in reference to a combination of two inbred lines, as in corn."[192] The difference was that the latter – and what is now accepted as *the* definition of hybrid – was the product of two deliberate *inbred* pure lines.

The emphasis on hybrids and commercially exploitable characteristics has, in the view of Joachim Voss and others, had a detrimental effect on the science of plant breeding itself. "The whole system of incentives – publish or perish, both research papers and seeds – is such that the young, upcoming breeders make their names by coming out with the magic bullets, the ultimate variety that takes over Cuba, for example. You don't make your name by coming up with the best mixture of varieties for Cuba, with the result that the breeders I have worked with in the Third World are like the newly converted in their zeal. Sowing hybrids in rows is modern."

But, Voss said, not only do we have to consider inter-cropping and companion crops, we also have to consider what combinations of food people eat. Crops grown together have often been eaten together, providing a balanced diet for traditional peoples who have understood the continuity between what they grow and how they grow it and what they eat. Such complexity overwhelms reductionist science.

Every once in a while someone lets their imagination wander off the beaten path and suggests a different way of viewing "reality" that reveals just how limited our thinking is much of the time. Frank Scott-Pearse suggests (and he is not alone) that there could well be a connection between the insect-repellant characteristics of glucosinolates (or rather the isothiocyanates that are derived from them) in the soil during and following the growth of rapeseed and other Brassicas and the use of hot mustard on foods in tropical climates.

It seems that the condiment mustards, high in glucosinolates, might render food edible that would otherwise make people sick. He got to thinking about this because there are soil fumigants on the market in which the active ingredient is an isothiocyanate and he knew that *B.juncea* is hot precisely because of the glucosinolates in it. In fact, onions and garlic are also members of the genus *Cruciferae* and share these fascinating health characteristics with the Brassicas. Altogether there seem to be some 90 known glucosinolates.

According to Röbbelen, "Discussions have been raised in Europe on the desirability of keeping the glucosinolate content of the green plant high for reasons of plant disease or pest resistance or even for securing its full vigor."

Does this suggest that we may see plant breeding come full circle, with characteristics removed from plants in the name of productivity being restored in the name of ecology? Will we decide that erucic acid in small amounts is harmless, and that the adverse properties of rapeseed should be dealt with by means of processing technology rather than biotechnology? Time will tell.

EVOLUTIONARY

NATURAL SELECTION,
TRADITIONAL BREEDING,
GENETIC RESOURCES
TO BE CONSERVED,
ENVIRONMENT
TO BE CARED FOR

TELEOLOGICAL

MANAGEMENT BY OBJECTIVES
GENETIC RESOURCES
TO BE MINED,
ENVIRONMENT TO BE CREATED,
TO ACHIEVE GOAL OF
CORPORATE CONTROL
AND ACCUMULATION

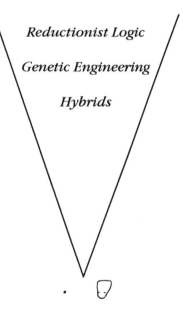

Reductionist Logic

Genetic Engineering

Hybrids

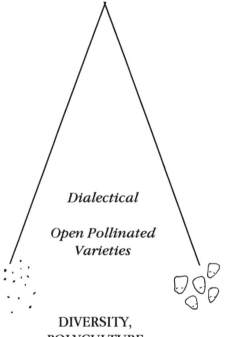

Dialectical

*Open Pollinated
Varieties*

DIVERSITY,
POLYCULTURE
SUSTAINABILITY
LOCALIZATION

MONOCULTURE,
SPECIALIZATION
DEPENDENCY
CONCENTRATION,
CONTROL

Selection and Diversity

Chapter 12

PROCESS AND PRODUCT: REGULATION

Biotechnology is the use of living organisms, or parts thereof, for the production of goods and services. . .

Biology has moved from an observation-based science to an interventionist science.

National Biotechnology Advisory Committee

These two simple sentences, from a single document, together describe the transformation that has taken place in biology in the past decade. From observing and trying to understand what has been observed, biology, with the aid of the tools of genetic engineering, has become a means to determining what organisms will do for the benefit of corporate profit. In the simplistic and profoundly biased words of the Canadian Government's "User's Guide to Bio-tech Regulation", biotechnology is simply another means "to improve the quality of life."

Other sciences have been interventionist for a long time, most notably chemistry. Goals, usually corporate, have been established and resources allocated to meet these goals. Nowhere is this more evident than in the field of agricultural chemicals and human drugs. Forty years ago, "Better living through chemistry" was a popular corporate (DuPont) slogan in the 1950s and the products could not be generated fast enough. Any problems were attributed to carelessness rather than to any inherent possible fault in the process or product of chemistry.

Biotechnology and canola today seem to be where industrial chemistry and corn were half a century years ago. In the meantime, however, the pace and power of science have increased dramatically, and so have unresolved regulatory issues.

The clear blue skies of chemistry have given way to thunderstorms of concern and protest over the consequences of the chemical industry's arrogance, while regulation and litigation have become huge legal and financial burdens on the industry itself. This really should not have surprised the corporate chemists. It's just that, as Langdon Winner expresses it,

> Unintended consequences are not *not* intended. This means that there is seldom anything in the original plan that aimed at preventing them. Until recently, the idea that any precautions should be taken when a new technology entered social practice was virtually unheard of.[193]

People in the biotech industry seem to be hoping that they can head off the problems of unintended consequences by shaping the rules of the game to absolve them of responsibility before the public can intervene. In biotechnology in general and molecular biology in particular, this reshaping is being focused on the issue of what to regulate: product or process. The industry and its adherents are endeavouring to cast biotechnology in the role of an environmentally benign gateway to a sustainable future, playing down the fact that the biotech companies and the chemical companies are in many cases one and the same.

Bruce Magee and Dave Sippell, of Allelix, gave me the corporate argument about regulating biotechnology:

> Initially the seed directorate wanted to regulate both the product and the process, and we finally have them regulating only the product now. However, they wish to include everyone and their great uncle in regulating the product, including the ministries of Environment and Health and Welfare, to ensure that our consumers are not going to get a toxic oil.

> In the case of mutagenesis [plant transformation], where there is no foreign genetic material being introduced, you don't need to regulate either product or process. It's the same mutagenizing process that breeders have been using on open-pollinated varieties for years. It is just transgenics (a plant which you have modified through molecular biology by inserting foreign genes or some piece of DNA that then regulates or inhibits another gene) that should be regulated, and then just in terms of product, not the process by which it was made.[194]

The ideology of productivity has shaped science as an expression of western industrial culture, with little more than utilitarian concern for the process whereby results are achieved. Utilizing new technology to bomb Hiroshima and "end the war" was more important than what might happen to the victims of that process, just as "feeding the hungry" is more important than any "unintended consequences" of the process employed to achieve that end (if, indeed, it is achieved at all).

Similarly, hybridizing plants and getting new chemicals and novel "foods" on the market is more important than what might turn out to be insidious consequences of the process of getting those products to market and using them. With pride in its ability to predict and control both the results of its interventions and their possible consequences, science has seen little reason to be concerned about process. It is product that counts. It is product that can be accumulated.

> Industry research will only drift southward if regulatory affairs don't provide opportunities for commercialization of products that are being developed in shops like ours. If regulatory affairs are going to constrain us to the extent that we can get to the market faster in other areas around the world, we'd be fools not to go there.[195]

The pressures to get a product to market will, of course, have some bearing on the willingness of the corporation to tolerate lengthy regulatory inquiries. The industry would regard it as a step in the right direction if the process were simplified by a declaration that only products and not processes will be regulated. If product regulation can then be limited to transgenic plants, so much the better.

The demand for product-only regulation is reasonable, however, only within the context of the reductionist notions of its proponents. If food, or a plant, is nothing more than the sum of its parts (its chemical components), and its purpose were only to be purchased and put into storage, then such an approach might be reasonable. But when the product is a food intended for human or other complex-organism consumption, then a mere chemical analysis, or a declaration of purity from the standpoint of detectable toxins, is hardly adequate. Such analyses will reveal nothing about the interaction of the consuming organism with that food and its component parts.

No lab experiment can prove a plant or a food safe, any more than a plant breeder who is able to produce a hybrid in the sanctity of his or her lab can guarantee that the hybrid can be produced outside and in great numbers, with or without known consequences, for better or for worse, resulting from the interaction between plant and environment.

It would be much wiser to proceed slowly, acknowledging that the process by which a product is produced may give us more indication of its character than a reductionist analysis of the product alone. What goes in must come out. If a high dose of some agro-toxin is essential to commercial production, then residue testing for some arbitrary limit is simply dishonest. One may be able to describe what one *knows* to be there or not be there, but what one does not know, and therefore cannot look for, cannot therefore be discovered by end-product analysis only. This is why those practising organic agriculture have insisted that it is the process that counts, not the analysis for pesticide residues in the product, and have campaigned for standards based on the practices and processes of organic agriculture, not on product characteristics or lack thereof.

This is not a new issue, as Anderson et. al. point out:

Since the seventeenth century science has advanced by employing the two-part strategy of "reduction" followed by divide-and-conquer. The reductive step consists in casting problems narrowly. In methodological terms the divide-and- conquer approach involves treating portions of the real world as isolated systems, systems whose "external" connections can be ignored.[196]

It is obviously in the interests of private seed companies to weaken regulations so that they can pursue their marketing strategies with as little hindrance as possible. As Magee stated it, "The issue right now for Canada is to create a regulatory system that does not inhibit or slow the commercialization of new products in the canola industry."

This sounds quite reasonable until you put it in context. As we have seen, there are substantive issues lying between the purposes of public and private plant breeding. While there is apparent consensus on the need for public involvement in and financing of basic research, there are opposing principles involved in the second, or commercialization stage.

If public agencies could be stopped from taking their varieties all the way to market, "private firms with research capabilities would not only dominate their weaker competitors who depend on publicly produced varieties [like SeCan in Canada] but also, by virtue of their structural position, would be able to determine public research agendas, because basic research has no [market] value unless it can be used in applied work."[197] In the case of canola, we have seen exactly this demonstrated by the steady erosion of public research and the ascendency of private corporate research.

However, having to prove through cooperative trials that a variety is at least as good as the check variety, *and* offers distinct advantages, is a real obstacle to the proliferation of proprietary seed varieties. Seed that is to be sold in Canada, whether developed in Canada or not, and whether public or private, must be entered in co-operative trials for evaluation against check varieties whose attributes and characteristics are well known and accepted. Canadian standards have held that being simply *as good as* the check variety is not sufficient to warrant registration. A new variety has to be *better than*. Simply being different has not been enough up until very recently. The purpose of the Canadian system, of course, is to enable the farmer to make an informed choice among different varieties all of which will provide some difference or "improvement" of significance. Choice for choice's sake is not enough. (In the U.S., by contrast, the Plant Variety Protection Act permits the differentiation of products to provide farmers with "choices" – as in the supermarket – without necessarily offering any comparative benefits.)

The private seed companies have lobbied hard and now largely won their way with the registration of plant varieties: the regulations for canola registration in Canada, for example, now require that new varieties be merely equal to the mean of three *B.napus* designated checks or two *B.campestris* checks.

New obstacles arise, however, over the question of transgenic plants. Should the regulatory agencies make a distinction between the products of genetic engineering and the products of traditional breeding techniques and regulate differently? The answer lies partly in the question, "when is *more* different?" At what point does the speed of change break the natural processes of evolution? Does it occur simply by speeding up the process, or by crossing lines that nature refuses to cross?

The corporate attitude, all too often, is simply not to worry, as Allelix spokesman Magee well articulates:

> Plants have a remarkable tendency to clean themselves up. In a lot of the protoplast fusion work that we are doing, and in some of the transgenic plants we produce, the original plant we grow out looks like a dog, but if you can get it to cross, or self, it will really clean itself up, and a lot of the stuff that the plant doesn't really want to carry around will get kicked out. So just in the normal process a plant will clean itself up. And if it doesn't, it won't live anyway.[198]

Part of the problem faced by companies like Allelix is that they want to create seeds that will produce the specialty oils that other companies, like Proctor & Gamble or Frito Lay, are willing to pay for. Because the seeds capable of providing these specialty oils are created by means of molecular biology, even though they may contain no foreign genetic material, the Canadian government considers them transgenic and thus under regulation. (The working definition of a transgenic plant provided by the Animal and Plant Health Directorate of Agriculture Canada is, "an organism that is obtained by *in vitro* alteration of genetic material including, recombinant DNA, nuclear and organelle transplantation.")[199] Plants modified by traditional breeding or mutagenesis are not subjected to the same regulations.

As long as the seed is still in the laboratory regulation is not an issue, but when it comes time for field trials, permission is required from Agriculture Canada and information as to the location of and conditions surrounding the trial plots must be provided.

If the exceptional plant makes it past these initial field trials, another problem arises. All seed sold in Canada must be entered in public trials. Allelix, and others, claim that they cannot put their specialty oil seeds into these trials without, in effect, giving away their trade secrets. So they argue that Canada must develop a special regulatory procedure for testing, registering and reproducing these seeds so that they can be licensed for production under contract without going through public trials. Leask, speaking for the trade, argues that "registration and entry in trials gives away trade secrets, and this is not acceptable."[200]

At the same time, of course, the same companies are pushing hard for much less regulation of any sort. In August 1992 the Canadian Seed Trade Association (CSTA) argued in a brief that there should simply be a system of minimum standards that would apply only to specific characteristics like disease resistance and oil quality, with all varieties that meet these standards being registered. Although this approach does do away with the older notion of Progress, it substitutes the newer fetish of "choice." How the farmer will be able to make an informed choice is another question, particularly when the CSTA claims that "the disclosure provisions of the registration system can be excessive." Nevertheless, the CSTA argues that farmers "deserve to be given choices about their business practices."[201]

The CSTA represents the companies selling seed, some of whom also grow seed. The Canadian Seed Growers Association (CSGA) represents about 5000 seed growers, most of which are individual farmers growing seed for sale either directly to other farmers or through SeCan or a private company. CSGA does not entirely share the perspective of CSTA, judging by these remarks made by the 1st v.p. of CSGA to the annual meeting of their Alberta branch:

> Expect a proliferation of new varieties . . . The annual model change holds some marketing allure for seed, too, just like selling cars. Under the Canadian system [now revised], a new variety must show some advantage to existing ones to get the nod, but if an applicant is willing to spend enough time to gather enough data, he is eventually bound to be able to prove some advantage in some area, however obscure.

> The customer who calls on May 10 might find his pet variety is gone and we'll have to learn to switch him into something he really doesn't want and that we don't really think he should have, but business is business.[202]

A Dutch seed trade journal provides a succinct summary of this issue from the corporate perspective:

The emphasis has shifted from catering to the farmers' agronomic needs to catering to the specific needs of the food producers and industrialists. . .

Ironically, the Seeds Act, which is one of the major legal foundations of the industry, is now being looked upon as an impediment . . . as its objectives are to serve agriculture in the traditional sense. Contract growing of "identity preserved" varieties, which have been developed in co- operation with processors, is a concept that doesn't always match the requirements of the Seeds Act, where the agronomic merit is emphasized. Furthermore, the registration process requires extensive testing and disclosure of relevant information, whereas the processor often needs quick action and protection of "trade secrets."[203]

The real reason why the processor needs to act with such haste, of course, has to do with marketing, not agriculture or nutrition. This applies to "trade secrets" as well, since these are often little more than marketing strategies.

The importance, and difficulty, of the issue of product or process differentiation is illustrated by the act of breastfeeding. Is a woman nursing her baby simply providing milk (delivering a product) containing certain amounts of vitamins, minerals, proteins and fats to her baby? The milk itself is the product of a process that goes on in the woman's body – but the woman is more than a milk factory. The process of suckling is much more than the transmittal of nutritional components, because her milk is also providing antibodies and thus passing on to the baby the means for thriving in the environment that it actually inhabits. The intimate relationship involved in the act of nursing is also providing the infant with a social context of security and love, and there are physiological, sensual and emotional elements for the mother as well.

Exactly which, or what, are product or process in this case? Would it be adequate to regulate the content of mother's milk while paying no regard to the context or the process of the delivery of that milk? Or would one want to regulate what the mother ate? Or would one test the health of the baby?

The product of the process of nursing is obviously more than milk and its delivery to an infant. Yet such a reductionist paradigm is what the infant formula industry pursues and wants us to believe, because if that is all breastfeeding is, then why not use a bottle?

It is an illusion that we can make a tidy distinction between product and process even at the best of times. The distinction is more idealistic than scientific. Take the example of a canola plant that fertilizes itself and produces a seed which subsequently grows into another plant.

From its own point of view, the seed might understand itself as the product of the biological processes of the plant, the expression of the plant's purpose, the culmination of its Being. To the plant, the seed is the process by which the plant reproduces itself.

From the human perspective, the plant is little more than the means of producing the seed, itself a little oil factory, a means of or process for producing an edible oil. The oil, in turn is only the means, a process, for providing human nourishment or corporate profit. In other words, from the human point of view, the product is either human nutrition or corporate profit, or sometimes both, and the rest is all process.

For every text there is at least one context. The current debate about the regulation of the processes and products of biotechnology is taking place in a specific and immediate cultural/political context. For biotechnology in Canada, the documentation of this context seems to begin in 1980 with the publication of *Biotechnology in Canada - Promises and Concerns* by the Science Council of Canada and the Institute for Research on Public Policy.

The foreword to this brief report states that, "Canada has a unique opportunity to compete with other countries in the development of biotechnologies", thus establishing international competitiveness as the *context* of biotechnology regulation. Social responsibility is treated as one means to this goal of being competitive, not a value in its own right: "At this early stage . . . we have the opportunity to incorporate social responsibility into a national industrial strategy."

W.A. Cochrane, currently on the National Biotechnology Advisory Committee (NBAC) and a participant in the workshop reported on in this publication, said that while licensing and regulatory requirements were yet to be defined, "Generally accepted guidelines have been established with regard to recombinant research. *Hopefully* they are being followed by organizations dealing with such technology." [emphasis added]

Stuart Ryan, Prof, of Law, Queen's Univ., wrote a highly critical statement of concern which is appended to the document, in which he said: "As a result of my experience and examination of available evidence, I am more than concerned - I am frightened - when I contemplate the growing activity of the private sector in the field of biotechnology."

In commenting on this workshop report, the authors of *Regulating the Regulators* (Science Council of Canada, 1982) recognized that, "Even at this gathering . . . the call for industrial strategies far outweighed technology assessment."

The environment or culture in which the regulation of biotechnology was discussed in the 1980s is captured in these breathless opening sentences of another Science Council report issued in 1985:

> Biotechnology may generate the last major technological revolution of the 20th century. The promise is already turning to profit; the pace is rapid; the potential is vast and exciting.

> The Science Council believes that Canadians must grasp the opportunities offered by biotechnology if Canada is to improve its competitive position on world markets.[204]

More specifically addressing plant agriculture, this same report proclaims that, "Biotechnology offers a wonderful opportunity to remove what to date have been considered inherent geographical barriers to production and to tackle environmental issues."[205]

It is little wonder that Prof. Ryan regarded as frightening what was happening in biotechnology. When the advisors to the regulators behave like a public relations agency, what confidence can the public have in their deliberations and recommendations?

With the first goal of biotechnology research and regulation being to make Canada more "competitive", the role of the regulators is defined in terms of risk assessment. Since Canadian regulators make frequent reference to practices and documents in the United States, it is reasonable to seek direction from these documents in trying to understand the development of Canadian policy. (It is also helpful when trying to understand the negotiations of various trade agreements around the issues of non-tariff trade barriers and intellectual property rights.)

The U.S. Council for Agricultural Science and Technology (CAST) issued a report in 1986 that stated the context of regulatory policy with great simplicity:

> Application of any new technology requires caution and prudence until the pitfalls are understood and thus become avoidable. Nothing is without risk. Thus it is important to weigh objectively the expected risks and benefits before taking action.[206]

The focus on "risk" is not casual. Over the past decade the notion of "risk assessment" has been taken up by the practitioners of corporate science and by the regulators as a way of reducing the issues of safety and regulation to a manageable scale. It is a traditional process of redefining the problem to fit the solution at hand.

Of course nothing is without risk, but so what? The point is that by reducing the issue of regulation to a process of risk assessment, the larger issues such as: Who wins and who loses? Who is in control? What is their agenda? and, Is there another way of doing this that is more environmentally friendly? get pushed aside, or buried. "As compared to other varieties of moral and political argument, risk assessment seeks a very narrow consensus", in the words of Langdon Winner.[207]

Current Canadian regulatory policy development was summed up in a presentation to a Symposium on the Regulation of Biotechnology in 1989, (prepared jointly by the ministries of Agriculture, Environment, and Health and Welfare) by Jean Hollebone, current director of the Issues, Planning and Priorities Division of the Pesticide Directorate of Agriculture Canada:

> Federal activity in biotechnology began in 1980 with the establishment of a private sector taskforce to advise the government on how to proceed with biotechnology.

> The federal government established the National Biotechnology Strategy in 1983 on the basis of the recommendations of this task force. At this time it also established the National Biotechnology Advisory Committee (NBAC).

> In 1987 three regulatory departments – Agriculture, Environment, and Health and Welfare – agreed on several working principles, among them: to build on existing legislation; to regulate the product as opposed to the process; to build on internationally developed guidelines; to use risk assessment principles.[208]

According to Sheila Forsyth, also of the Pesticides Directorate, "Agriculture Canada early on decided that the existing legislation was broad enough in scope to cover most products of biotechnology." In other words, Agriculture Canada had decided that there is nothing really new under the sun – or at least that there is nothing novel about the ability to intervene directly in the shaping of life forms. This position is a logical consequence of a belief in a historic, material continuity that precludes novelty. There is nothing but Progress. All one can do is ask, in a highly relativistic fashion, Do we like what we have done?

Forsyth continued,

> Emphasis is placed on the intended use and traits of the product rather than the technique to make the product. While examination of the genetic construction and transformation is an intrinsic part of the review process, nevertheless, it is the whole product which will be released for sale... Hence, its total properties, safety and environmental impact are considered in the risk assessment process.[209]

On this same occasion, T. C. McIntyre of Environment Canada, which is not part of the agricultural establishment, pointed out that,

> There is a groundswell of public concern in a number of industrialized countries over questions of government accountability

and objectivity and its ability to assess a technology that it is promoting so resolutely!

McIntyre went on to indicate various potential areas of environmental concern about the manipulation of micro-organisms, which are: microscopic in size; capable of mutation, reproduction and persistence; opportunistic; extremely mobile; and, respect no political borders.

McIntyre also asked a number of questions about the socio-economic impacts of biotechnology, questions which the European Community is insisting on as relevant to the regulation of biotechnology: Will biotechnology products exacerbate current overproduction in key areas, e.g., synthetic chemicals, food production? Will biotechnology exacerbate current problems of agricultural surplus? What will the effect be on developing Third World economies? Will patenting of organisms lead to a monopoly on husbandry by major chemical, pharmaceutical and biotechnology companies?

He also referred to the historical experience of technology development, pointing out that "in many instances technology has exhibited untoward and unanticipated side effects" and that "these effects have escaped detection or were unknown when the original assessment was undertaken."

Such concerns were certainly not shared by the spokesman from Health and Welfare Canada, who simply stated that, "In general, it is not felt that new legislation is required to deal with biotechnology." With a risk-based approach, he said, "the need for notification and assessment is dependent on the potential hazard. This may have a certain element of putting the 'cart before the horse'. Nevertheless, a risk-based approach would be desirable if appropriate criteria could be determined."[210]

Against this background, it is hardly surprising that when the government actually stated, in "Bio-Tech Regulations: A User's Guide, 1991", how it intended to interpret and apply the existing legislation in regard to regulating biotechnology, it came out sounding a bit like a youthful cheerleader unburdened by the responsibilities of adult living.

> Biotechnology is the application of science and engineering to the direct or indirect use of living organisms, and their parts or products, in their natural or modified forms, to provide goods and services.

> Biotechnological processes have been used to improve the quality of life for thousands of years . . .

> The recent development of biotechnological techniques such as recombinant DNA and cell fusion to manipulate cells or their

genetic materials has created exciting new dimensions in our potential to improve human life. With this potential has come the responsibility to ensure that the new products under development or soon to be developed will be used under conditions that will minimize the possibility of accidents and maximize safety.[211]

A phrase like "exciting new dimensions in our potential to improve human life" is strikingly out of place in a regulatory guidebook, unless, of course, the regulations are not to be taken seriously or are there only to mollify public apprehension without actually regulating the industry.

Twelve years after the opening exchange, little has changed. There have been no known disasters, but not enough time has elapsed for us to discover the consequences of what has been so blithely initiated. There has been, however, sufficient increase in the occurrence of allergies, asthmas, cancers, immune system disorders and similar illnesses, for which there is no adequate explanation, to give us good cause to doubt the assurances about the safety of scientific endeavours in general and biotechnology in particular.

Biotechnology remains firmly entrenched in the service of national competitiveness, and the industry is as clear as ever that ethical issues, public concerns, and government regulation must not be permitted to stand in the way of corporate progress. "Canada cannot afford to fall behind its major international trading partners in the development and commercialization of new crop varieties, improvements to animal products and advances in food technology", warns the National Biotechnology Advisory Committee, calling for a balance to be struck, "between regulation and promotion, equity and efficiency, protection of the public and the environment, as well as the furtherance of private interests and economic growth. "

Governments must maintain a business climate which is attractive for innovation and foreign investment, and act to remove the barriers within their jurisdictions, that are inhibiting the commercialization of biotechnology research.[212]

The more detailed recommendations of the Business Strategy (that refers to "the biotechnology community") deal specifically with the question of process and product:

New products based on the use of biological organisms and/or processes [should] be regulated on the basis of the category of risk the product might pose to humans and the environment, rather than on an assumption that every biologically-based product or process automatically poses a risk. . . .

The adverse economic and social consequences for Canada of not using biotechnology for the development of a wide range of commercially competitive advanced crop varieties tailored specifically to Canada's climatic conditions, will be severe.[213]

In August, 1992, with a variety of genetically engineered foods, or foods produced by means of new biotechnological processes, about to come onto the market, the Health Protection Branch of Health and Welfare Canada finally issued an Information Letter on the subject of Novel Foods and Food Processes. The letter points out that "non-traditional foods and food processes are being introduced into the Canadian marketplace" and that "these products and processes often do not explicitly fall within the existing regulatory framework."

According to this letter, controls on food additives were first introduced in 1964 by means of a "pre-market clearance mechanism." Subsequently this approach has been taken with food irradiation, maximum limits for agricultural chemical residues and for the ingredients of infant formula, which the Letter refers to as "human milk substitutes."

The Branch also believes that novel substances, that could be used as replacements for conventional ingredients, should be reviewed prior to sale because these substances could affect the health, safety and nutritional status of consumers using such products. . .

A novel food may be defined as any food that has not been previously used to any significant degree for human consumption in Canada. This definition includes the use of existing foods for roles in which the food has not been previously used, and existing foods that are produced by a novel process. Examples would include . . . genetically modified plants and animals. . .

A novel food process may be defined as a process that has not been previously used for the manufacture of food sold in Canada. A modification of an existing technology would also be considered a novel process.[214]

Clearly it is not possible, on the basis of the argument of this Letter, to maintain a distinction between product and process. Although the Pesticide Directorate may claim that it is quite sufficient to examine the products of biotechnology only, when it comes to food that humans eat directly product and process *seem* to be indivisible. Herbicide resistant canola may or may not have any human health impact, but Health and Welfare should probably not make any reductionist guesses about that. Nor should we simply accept the Health of Animals Branch claim that it is adequate to test the milk from a cow treated with recombinant Bovine Growth Hormone without doing any clinical studies of the possible effects of this milk on humans.

Health and Welfare does say that it must be notified of each new food or food process before it is put on the market, and this notification must include a "statement of the nature of the novel food, its process of manufacture, intended uses and history of consumption . . . the name and nature of the novel food process [and] data to establish the safety of the novel food and/or process [and] the possible displacement of existing foods and the nutritional impact thereof."

This would seem to indicate that Health and Welfare accepts the impossibility of distinguishing between process and product and recognizes the importance of considering both in whatever semblance of a regulatory process there might be.

The relative clarity of the H & W position is unfortunately obscured by other Federal Government policy statements.

The "Principles for a Federal Framework in Biotechnology" (1992) states that the objective of the "federal framework" is "To protect the safety of human health and the environment by minimizing risks associated with products produced by biotechnology, thus fostering competitiveness and marketability of Canadian products." To achieve this goal, the federal framework is to be, among other things, "accountable and predictable;" to use "science-based risk assessments and risk management principles;" to build "on existing legislative elements where possible;" and, to "regulate on a product basis (while considering the process used)."[215]

In a letter to me, Jean Hollebone of Agriculture Canada adds that, "The federal approach to the regulation of biotechnology is *product-based*. . . because federal legislation is primarily set up to deal with products."[216]

The logic of Hollebone's argument is both interesting and alarming, because it definitely puts the cart before the horse while arguing that this is the proper place for the cart to be because it has always been there. She explains that "the expensive and slow process of building a new act" has been avoided by "allowing the government to build on existing legislation." It also means that administrative guidelines can be used to set requirements.

As might be expected, there is increasing demand from industry that regulations be simplified so that only the product is regulated and only certain products at that. Industry argues that *how* the product is created is not significant. Besides which, they usually say, there is nothing new about biotechnology: people have been making beer for millennia and soya sauce, and wine, and cheese and yogurt, and all of these are created by microbial action, so what is so special about biotechnology?

The choice to utilize existing legislation, conceived in an era when biotechnology was the stuff of science fiction, is much more than a matter of efficiency. Such a choice virtually ignores the realities of molecular biology and the changes in our understanding of life and our ability to manipulate life that it has brought about. It is the same as saying that nuclear power is no different than solar power, or an oil- fired boiler, because they all derive their energy in one way or another from the sun.

More insidious than the assertion that there is nothing novel in genetic engineering, however, is the fact that regulation by means of administrative guidelines ensures that the public, and public discussion, is effectively, if not deliberately, excluded. It is not cynical to suggest that the resulting governance by means of the regulatory process will be a matter of plea-bargaining between the transnational corporations' lawyers and the government "regulators."

If the argument for utilizing existing legislation to deal with a matter for which the legislation could not have been intended is not already twisted enough, Hollebone next confuses the issue of "product-based" regulation even more:

> The approach to regulation is also risk-based, and takes the process by which genetically-modified organisms are derived into account. The concept of *familiarity* is being used to define categories of risk. . . This means that products derived from genetic engineering are initially treated in a category of risk until sufficient experience and knowledge is gained to reduce their risk category. . . Regardless of the process of construction, mutagenesis or genetic engineering, products are evaluated on the basis of the risk posed to humans and the environment. The process of making the genetic construction is considered [as well as] . . . the process by which the product is made. . .[217]

One is tempted to say that the casuistry (the rationalization or justification of behaviour for a price) of the medieval church has nothing on the casuistry of what are supposed to be the agencies protecting public interest.

Canadian biotech strategy also calls for "harmonization of regulatory requirements, evaluation procedures and the mutual recognition of approval systems with those of the U.S. and Europe" and the harmonization of Canadian patent laws "with those of other developed countries." Since it has become normative, under the Conservative government, for Canada to slavishly follow the line of the U.S. administration, we would expect this to hold for biotech policy as well, but harmonization with the

U.S. will remain a challenge given the conflicting positions of various government agencies at this time. How this morass will be negotiated will depend, at least to some extent, on how much vested interests and corporations engaged in biotechnology are willing to invest in skilled lobbying. There is certainly a challenge here to initiate a long-overdue public debate on the subject and thus force the regulators to be at least more sympathetic to public scepticism.

I have already noted the dominance of the ideology of "competitiveness" as the context for Canadian policy, so it is no surprise that the policy of the U.S. Food and Drug Administration (FDA) on the regulation of genetically engineered foods was announced by the U.S. President's Council on Competitiveness, chaired by v.p. Dan Quayle, in May, 1992.

Essentially the policy states that new or modified products developed by biotechnology companies will be accepted under the same standards as all other foods. The FDA will not require pre-market review if the food constituents in a new plant variety are "the same or substantially similar to substances currently found in other foods, such as proteins, fats, oils and carbohydrates."

The Council's own press release described the policy as one of "streamlining federal regulations." Health and Human Services Secretary Sullivan explained that, "These new technologies will benefit all Americans by providing foods that are tastier, more varied, more wholesome and that can be produced more efficiently. The policy we are announcing today will ensure the safety of these foods while facilitating their availability as quickly as possible."

The new "regulatory" approach advocates three principles: first, regulation of biotechnology should be based on the risk posed by the final product rather than on the production process; second, regulatory oversight is unnecessary unless a product presents *unreasonable* risk; and third, more stringent regulations should not be applied to altered organisms than those that apply to parent strains when the new product does not possess new traits known to be more dangerous than the parent strains. The second principle is particularly significant because it places the burden of showing evidence of a hazard on the regulator rather than placing on the producer of the new organism (or food) the burden of proving safety and efficacy. In other words, "regulation" is based on the principle of "safe until proven otherwise".

This approach has already been applied in the case of Calgene's tomatoes.

Perhaps the most amazing aspect of this "regulatory" approach is that it leaves it up to industry itself to decide when a new product presents sufficient risk to require federal oversight. In addition, the Food and Drug Administration approach does not require labelling to inform the consumer or notification to inform the agency (FDA) that a new product is the result of genetic manipulation, even though the manipulation might involve insertion of a gene from a plant to which some people are allergic.

The White House Council on Competitiveness has already advocate that this approach be applied to the release of novel organisms into the environment, calling for "oversight and regulation to be limited to only those microorganisms that could be proven *a priori* to cause harm to humans or the environment." In other words, the burden of proof on the safety of novel foods or novel organisms of any kind is on citizens as individuals, not on the corporate producers of these novelties, and for a new product to come under regulation, the public must prove *a priori*, i.e., before it has been tested, that it is unsafe!

The sole criterion of value in this approach is productivity/product. But production is not enough, either to feed people or to have an economy that works. We have a growing number of food banks and hungry people in North America, but a shortage of food (food production) is not the problem. In fact, greater productivity seems to make the matter worse by bankrupting more farmers. This would, one might think, point to a problem in the *process* of food production, understood as the production of well-nourished people.

The process of food production cannot be evaluated by the criterion of food safety, which would ask how well the food in the grocery store stacks up against some reductionist list of ingredients on the label, because that is only one aspect of the product of the food system. Just as the whey from the cheese plant is not a by-product to be disposed of, but a valuable food for the hogs on a nearby farm, so the women and children in the food bank line-up are not by-products of an otherwise successful food system, but persons who are denied access to the resources to feed themselves by a distorted and malfunctioning food system. Biotechnology, if viewed as simply one more tool in the production and accumulation process, will only aggravate existing injustice and environmental abuse.

Chapter 13

OWNING AND KNOWING:
KNOWLEDGE AS COMMODITY

Science . . . succeeded first as a way of knowing
and as a vision of the world. Only later, as scientific technology, did it triumph as a means of
control and manipulation.

Langdon Winner [218]

I was taught in school that Christopher Columbus "discovered" America.
While I recognize the need to demythologize this "discovery" and describe it more honestly as a mission of imperial conquest, I also recognize
that from his own cultural perspective Columbus did indeed discover
America. In fact, had the current American rules of international trade
and intellectual property rights been in place 500 years ago, Columbus
would have been able to obtain a patent on his discovery on the grounds
that he was entitled to a return on his (actually, Queen Isabella's) investment. Once the U.S. was free of Britain, as Vine Deloria puts it in *Custer
Died For Your Sins*, "the U.S. adopted the doctrine of discovery that gave
the U.S. exclusive right to extinguish Indian title of occupancy either by
purchase or conquest."

This same mentality is reported in this recent description of the
claiming of the territory of Canada:

Legally, European nations based their right to declare
sovereignty on the right of discovery, a right granted by themselves and the Pope, who initially sanctioned the dividing of the
New World between Spain and Portugal. Despite refinements, to
this day the legal foundation of Canada's sovereignty over the
land and over native people is founded on that same right of
discovery, and on a unilateral declaration by European nations
that only they could exercise sovereignty. [219]

The ownership claim made by Columbus and others could be recognized because those who make up the rules decided that if someone from

the dominant civilization (i.e., the one with the most soldiers) discovers something "out there" previously unknown to the dominant civilization, it can claim ownership, regardless of the actual status of what has been "discovered". That the land "discovered" by Columbus was already inhabited and was known to and by its inhabitants has no bearing on the legitimacy of its "discovery". What is valued is what is known by the dominant civilization. There simply is no other knowledge.[220]

The analogue in contemporary biology is obvious. If I "discover" a gene, or sequence a specific bit of DNA, I can establish an ownership claim (patent) over my "discovery." No matter that I did not engage in an inventive step, or that the material, the gene or genetic information, had and continues to have an existence quite independent of my "discovery". In other words, there was no creative action, however much expense or labour might have gone into the "discovery."

This view is bolstered by those corporate lawyers who claim that what has not been discovered does not, to all intents and purposes, exist. This line has been most cogently argued as follows:

> It is not the role of the patent system to create exclusive rights in ideas or theories of any kind, and any person is free to make use of these ideas in his *thinking* (but *not* necessarily in his *application*). On the other hand, a "product of nature" is always a tangible thing, a thing which falls squarely within the statutory categories of invention, e.g., enumerated in the U.S. patent law. . . Therefore. . . nothing is taken away from the public. . .

> "Products of nature" which are unknown to mankind are no more useful than are inventions that have not yet been made. If researchers cannot patent their newly discovered "products of nature", they may be encouraged to keep their existence a trade secret or, alternatively, society may not see fit in the first place to invest the capital necessary to discover them. . .

> The basic tenet of patent law is that subject matter is in the public domain only if it is *both* old (lacks novelty) *and* obvious (lacks inventive step). *Only* if it is in the public domain should it remain free for all to use. . .

> The patentability requirements of novelty and inventive step are sufficient to preclude the patenting of any products which are already reasonably available to man . . . the public remains free to do anything that it could have done prior to the inventor's discovery of the so-called "product of nature." In other words, the *actual* "product of nature" can never be patented and does remain free for all.[221]

The claim in this position is that nothing exists until it is discovered (or "invented") and that which is discovered is private until it is made public by the "inventor." Even if something is known to exist, it is private until it is publicly available, and it is only made publicly available through the efforts exerted by individuals (or corporations) who, in this way of thinking, can claim a reward for discovering, or what is then referred to as "inventing", what is referred to as subject matter that is "useful." Since the public benefits, by definition, it is perfectly reasonable for the state, on behalf of the people, to grant a license for monopoly rights to the "inventor."

The proponents of this philosophy also put forth the argument that since the public cannot benefit by the subject matter until it is "discovered", it can't miss what it was not aware of. This amounts to claiming that there simply is no such thing as public property. Creation then is, of necessity, ontologically (by its nature) private. Whether this means that it is owned by God or The Creator, or only becomes real at the point that it is privatized (i.e. discovered) remains unclear.

This is an extreme expression of commodification. The implication is that unless something can be bought and sold, it cannot exist. It cannot be bought or sold before it has been discovered. Therefore it does not exist in any state other than that of a commodity.

It is perfectly reasonable, and indeed it can be quite wonderful, for people to discover things, whether it be a new friend, a new sensation, or a wart-hog at the bottom of the garden. Such a discovery has nothing to do with ownership and nothing to do with invention. It is simply discovery.

There is, perhaps deliberately, the same kind of confusion surrounding the notions of discovery and invention as there is about the broader subjects of science and technology, and indeed about knowledge itself.

Science . . . has become the direct generator of economic, political, and social accumulation and control. Now we can see that the hope to "dominate nature" for the betterment of the species has become the effort to gain unequal access to nature's resources for the purposes of social domination.[222]

The scientific attitude of curiosity and the willingness, or determination, to allow that curiosity to overcome all sorts of deterrents and discouragements is the generator of discovery. The purposes of the endeavour, and its utilization, are another matter. This is not to claim that all discovery is science. Certainly Columbus' discovery was not science, and in a sense we might even say that the discovery of low-erucic acid rapeseed was not science, though achieved by scientific method.

Science, besides facilitating discovery, provides an analytical framework within which to organize and identify experience, but invention itself is often the work of technology. Beversdorf puts a slightly different twist on this:

Technology is really tools, and science is the discovery of knowledge. They tend to evolve together. Useful technologies usually evolve from a need: you have a question, and current tools are not useful, so you develop a new tool. On the other hand, when you have a new technology then all of a sudden it is applicable to a whole bunch of things you hadn't thought about, so a whole bunch of new discoveries emerge from the tools.[223]

Prairie plant breeders did not invent double-low rapeseed forty years ago. Nor, really, did they create it. What they did do was discover its constituents and then recombine them. The building blocks had been there all the time, for millennia, in fact, before they were identified or recognized for what they were. Part of the problem lay in the fact that neither the scientists – nor anyone else – had the means to observe or recognize what was already there. They lacked the ability to see what was before their eyes, and what they invented was the technology with which to see what was there. What they gained was knowledge. What science now seeks, in canola and even in the human genome, is not knowledge but intellectual property, information that can be sold and bought. This definition of what is there to discover is essential to the project of capital accumulation.

Recent developments in biotechnology provide more than sufficient cause to reconsider the notion of private property and the nature of knowledge. The context of this consideration must include the fact that biotechnology now offers the means to identify and commodify genetic material (information), including that of the human genome. Capital, meanwhile, is in the process of consolidating and centralizing its hold on the global economy through an increasingly limited number of transnational corporations. And governments, sometimes seen as the defenders of public interest and common good, increasingly play the role of licensors of corporate domination and of tax collectors for corporate treasuries.

European culture spawned both industrial capitalism and socialism, and both opted for the idolatry of technology as an expression of historical determinism. In other words, both accepted technology as the means of industrialization and industrialization as the means of Progress. Biotechnology, in this culture, is just one more technology.

With the collapse of the purportedly socialist economies in eastern Europe and the former Soviet Union (FSU), we see the rapid expansion in breadth and depth of transnational capital, whose resources, planning abilities, and effective range of control far surpass those of most states.

At the same time, developments in the production, organization and privatization of knowledge have exceeded the expectations of even the most enthusiastic free-marketers.

These tendencies do not bode well for the majority of humankind or the nurture of Creation. They further the polarization of wealth and power, and for the marginalized and dispossessed this can only mean a harsher and shorter life. Nowhere is this clearer than in the functioning of the global food system which is being continuously refined as a vehicle of capital accumulation and technological domination. For all the stock-salesman hyperbole that has accompanied the birth of biotechnology, as it is currently being applied it is just one more capitalist technology. Whether it could be anything else remains a moot point.

The most recent articulation of the uncritical culture of science and technology is the idea of *sustainable development*, which itself has given a boost to biotechnology as an acceptable and even morally superior technological implement for Development.

Since, however, Development really means incorporation into or enclosure by the dominant market economy of capital, biotechnology is no more moral than any other technology created by and intended to serve the interests of accumulation. While biotechnology may give the appearance of being clean and green, it cannot be a means of achieving justice if it is just one more tool of the structures of capitalist development. Nor can it make any special claims as science.

Progress, like Development has, in western culture, become synonymous with urbanization, and urbanization has become synonymous with civilization. The biblical story of the Battle of Jericho (Joshua 6) describes an heroic assault on the pride of "civilization", the City. While the Bible provides no commentary on the character of the city at that point, the attack by the people on the fortified city, with God's blessing, contradicts the pervasive idolatry that the Hebrew deity is a god of the temple of urban civilization – The Golden Calf of Capital – rather than the tent-dwelling God of nomadic peoples. In fact, the city of Jericho is symbolic of a self-satisfied, hugely demanding and costly "civilization" brought low by the God of the desert.

The walls of the city might be thought of as all of the legal and political devices put in place to protect the property structure that is the heart of every city. Intellectual Property Rights are simply another of these protective devices that serve to exclude the nomads, the farmers, the peasants and fisherfolk – the marginalized and increasingly dispossessed – from the fruits of their labour and the gifts of creation which are expropriated by the project of Development. The fortifications of the city were not brought down by force of arms or an army of patent lawyers, but by the united voice of the peasants and artisans after they had marched around the city seven times, refusing to be impressed with the technological and civil might of the city or the power of its ideology.

Utilizing the mythology of this biblical story, we can put another gloss on the suggestion, in Chapter 11, that rapeseed has historically been a rural crop, a traditional, widely dispersed and very genetically diverse species that was processed and utilized locally, that is, within a village economy. As rapeseed was "developed" into an industrial crop it was captured by the city and its dominant powers. Canola, as a result, can be seen as the product of European culture and practice (science and technology) and thus an urban crop. (The efforts being made by both China and India to transform their rapeseed production into canola production, and simultaneously to hybridize the crop, are a poignant example of this urbanization since rapeseed has been an essential rural crop for thousands of years in those countries.)

> Genetic and cultural information has been produced and reproduced over the millennia by peasants and indigenous people. Yet, like the unwaged labour of women, the fruits of this work are given no value despite their recognized utility.[224]

Commodification and packaging are both ideological terms; ideas given the power to define or redefine experience. In modern market terminology, the problem (described above by Jack Kloppenburg) lies in the inadequacy of packaging, that is, the product has been poorly packaged and is hence of negligible market value; it is not "value-added". "Value-added" infers, of course, that things have little inherent or use value, only an exchange or market value which depends largely on packaging, or marketing. Carrots, for example, are considered as nothing more than raw material until they have been washed and packaged, or until they have been engineered into "baby carrots" which, after scrubbing and packaging, can be marketed as an up-scale food product.

Thus a proponent of intellectual property rights can describe human or any other DNA sequences as of little value in their natural state "but of immense worth when packaged correctly." The point is that DNA – genetic information – is of little apparent value unless one knows what its function is, what it does. This attitude is reflected in the term "junk DNA" which is applied to all the extra bits of DNA that appear to the researcher to serve no useful purpose.

That we have little idea what most genetic material is "good for" does not seem to interfere with this evaluation, nor does the fact that the organism containing the genetic information may itself "know" what the information is or may be "good for." It is the same with herbal extracts used in traditional healing: the village elder or wise woman knows where the substance comes from, how to prepare it and what it is "good for". To the foreigner, or corporate scavenger, the information in the substance itself is of little obvious value since he knows neither how it is produced or how to apply it, but he collects it in the hope that some profitable product can be created out of the raw genetic information.

Traditional foods can be considered in a similar fashion, of course. To counter this, the agro-toxin industry, bent on protecting its control and its profits, insists that what is safe to eat is a matter for reductionist science to decide, not cultural wisdom. Residue testing by a corporation takes the place of experience shared within a community, and this is supported by public regulators as we have seen. The fact that human diets vary drastically from place to place, and that the human organism can and does adapt to a wide variety of environments, and in turn alters its environment – text and context oscillate, as it were – finds little recognition in capitalist science and its production monoculture. This should not surprise us since the centralized control required to accumulate capital requires a high degree of cultural uniformity – one could say, "monoculture".

The uniformity required by the market economy is even more understandable when the seed is considered as currency. A unit of currency of a particular value has to be interchangeable with every other similar unit for the currency (seed) to be useful, to be of "value" and accumulated.

What is at issue is the nature and value of knowledge and the social relations of knowledge. Knowledge does not – in fact, cannot – exist as an extract, an essence. It exists only as a cultural project or as cultural wisdom. In that sense, it *is* the packaging that establishes the value. Without the knowledge of what the information is good for, it is good for very little. The text without a context is only information. A television journalist commented that "TV has a problem with context." It is good at motion, at close-ups, but it does not even have the ability of print to provide the context. Violence and war make good TV news, but the reasons for the violence do not, unless it is more violence, such as pictures of starving children or earthquake victims.

But then the question arises, can knowledge be extracted from the culture that knows what it is good for and repackaged for the market? If culture is not neutral, can the information extracted from it be considered neutral (or value-free, if value is considered to be added in the packaging and marketing) and thus owned and traded as a commodity such as corn flakes? This is, after all, what is being done by corporate seed breeders and plant geneticists.

> Nature-as-an-object-of-knowledge simulates culture, and science is part of the cultural activity that continually produces nature-as-an-object-of-knowledge in culturally specific forms.[225]

Traditionally, genetic information has consisted of the knowledge of the characteristics of seeds, that is, how the genes are expressed. This is not abstract or Platonic knowledge, but "environmental" knowledge. This knowledge/information could be concerned with where the seeds grow best, how much water they need or how much drought they can tolerate, when and how they are to be planted, how the crop is to be cared for, harvested, prepared for use as food or fibre, and finally, how the seeds from one harvest are to be conserved for the next planting. One could describe all of this information as cultural, which it is, but it can also be described as genetic, since it is the external expression in a particular time and place – a particular culture – of the information contained in the seed's genes.

The ambiguous relationship between contemporary science and traditional culture is well articulated by canola researcher Beversdorf, who says he still believes that the disclosure of new information that evolves through patents is worthwhile. For example, he says, "if nobody goes to the medicine man and finds out that something works, and then tears it apart to find out why it works and what elements in it work, then there is no knowledge, other than the general knowledge that some extract works sometimes and alleviates some pain, or whatever."[226]

The value of the knowledge gained, says Beversdorf, "in the long term depends on many factors beyond its inherent value. It depends on how much capital you have to leverage an economic advantage within the time limit of exclusivity of the patent." Beversdorf does not deny that this offers a distinct advantage to the corporations that either have or can leverage capital and can afford the tax lawyers and accountants to make the system work for the corporation. Private individuals or peasants or even crop scientists on their own do not have this possibility open to them.

In genetics, it is as important to know if and how a gene expresses itself in the organism (publishes itself) as it is to know the make-up of the gene itself. I use the word "express" intentionally in at least two ways and I also use the word "public" because the choice is between the gene keeping its information to itself or making it public (making it known, or publishing it).

The issue now facing us is: can or should this public expression of genetic information be captured for private use? The historic answer is no, it cannot be, because it is cultural information, that is, information essential to the culture as a means of healing, nourishment, and the ordering of social life. It is, therefore, inherently social in character.

But the dominant culture has changed, and now it contends that all value can be marketed – indeed, that value exists only if it can be marketed – and that any and all information can be privatized and owned. It even contends that information has to be owned or there can be no Progress because Progress is defined as the accumulation of capital. Public cultural information does not permit the accumulation of private capital but only social "capital" in the form of the functional wisdom of elders and in the community as a whole.

> What is called "knowledge" cannot be defined without understanding what *gaining* knowledge means. In other words, "knowledge" is not something that could be described by itself or by opposition to "ignorance" or to "belief", but only by considering a whole cycle of accumulation: how to bring things back to a place for someone else to see it for the first time so that others might be sent again to bring other things back.[227]

Bruno Latour is not talking here simply of the accumulation of ideas or "facts". He asks, "Will we call knowledge what is accumulated at the centre? . . . Will we call it power? . . . Maybe we should speak of money or more abstractly of profit since this is what the cycle adds up to. . . We could of course talk of capital, that is, something (money, knowledge, credit, power) that has no other function but to be instantly reinvested into another cycle of accumulation."[228]

The immediate link between the notion of intellectual property and capital becomes obvious.

This whole discussion, despite the appearance of being very modern, is indeed very ancient. The relationships between knowledge/wisdom and culture are the subjects of every cultural tradition, including the Judeo-Christian. In the Biblical canon the discussion starts with the first chapter of the first book and revolves around the question of faithfulness and the appropriation of knowledge. Faithfulness is the issue rather than faith because, as with the gene, it is the *expression* of faith that counts, not the doctrine.

The primacy of faithfulness – of expression – over "objective" knowledge reflects the inability of creature to fully know Creation, and establishes the primary relationship of the faithful to knowledge as a recognition that our knowledge is, at best, imperfect or incomplete, and consequently we can never fully predict or control the consequences of our actions. Chaos, as science now tells us, is not necessarily the total absence of order. It has more to do with our inability to perceive than with objectivity. Thus the inability to either completely predict or control the consequences of our actions does not contradict the possibility of a fundamental unity of all Creation. It simply expresses what we experience as diversity. If we cannot perceive the unity in the face of apparent and real diversity, that does not mean it does not and cannot exist.

The tradition of the Enlightenment, however, has been that of seeking to eliminate mystery, diversity and uncontrollable power by asserting and imposing the rationality of the currently dominant interests: we will force the world to conform to our understanding of reality. This practice of domination has always been contested by those who assign ultimate power and authority to God; and when faithfulness has required vigorous dissent, the temporal powers have frequently not hesitated to eliminate such perceived assaults on their authority. Darwinism offered a more genteel solution than the stake or the guillotine. As biologist Steven Rose has written, "The dominant class de-throned God and replaced him with science. The social order was still to be seen as fixed by forces outside humanity, but now these forces were natural rather than deistic."[229]

In addressing the question of how we know the world, in both unity and diversity, Rose describes the first principle of his science as "ontological unity and epistemological [interpretive] diversity. "

> I insist (contrary to some philosophers) that there is one material world out there, and that it is possible to obtain knowledge about that world. Within our knowledge of that world there must be an epistemological diversity because there are many ways we can understand what is going on in the world. I am not privileging scientific knowledge over the knowledge of the poet, artist, or writer. I do insist, however, that we are all talking about the same world.[230]

Such an attitude invites both science and faith to recognize the validity and truth of diversity while also seeking to understand the unity that might lie beyond or beneath apparent antagonisms. In other words, the antagonistic contradiction itself becomes an invitation to further analysis and a caution against using force to impose a false unity. Such a unity is not merely mystical. It is material and historical.

While there have, from the beginning, been relentless efforts to interpret the Hebrew Yahweh as a transcendental God, Yahweh nevertheless remains a God realized in the material forces of unity that make the chaos of Creation meaningful.

Although Mendel, Lamarck and Darwin all came a long time later, the authors of Genesis, and their sources, saw fit to record in detail, at the beginning of their story of creation, that God said, "Let the earth produce vegetation: seed-bearing plants, and fruit trees bearing fruit with their seed inside." (Genesis 1:11)

The significance – and power – of the seed, of course, lies in its ability to reproduce itself when fertilized. This power to both produce and reproduce is indeed miraculous, a form of immortality that provokes a jealous response by reductionist science seeking to dominate the process either by controlling the fertilization (through hybridization), or by controlling, through ownership, the seeds themselves. Feminists point out the parallels in the historic attack on the reproductive power of women, from burning midwives as witches to the contemporary efforts in reproductive technology.

The notion of owning the means of natural reproduction – the genes with their information as to what to reproduce and how and under what conditions – is, of course, a proclamation of idolatry. Many cultures and native religions recognize seeds as sacred and can not conceive of owning, and thereby controlling, the gods of fertility. This same relationship to Creation is expressed in the aboriginal cultures which cannot conceive of land, as Mother Earth, the wellspring of life, as private property.

It is but a short step, in a sense, from the accumulation of offspring and heirs – the expression of fertility and wealth – to the accumulation of wealth in the capitalist culture through the ownership of the means of production and now also the means of reproduction; seeds and their genetic information, from plant cell to animal embryo to human genome.

In a capitalist economy, where only that which can be commodified is valued and value is, at least theoretically, directly related to scarcity, knowledge must be made scarce, by one mechanism or another, in order to be valued.

In the case of seeds, which are little more than particular configurations of (genetic) knowledge in the reductionist tradition, there are various mechanisms to create scarcity in places where abundance is nature's choice, among them hybridization and patenting.

In rendering seeds effectively sterile, and in claiming ownership of seeds, that is, in asserting control over self-reproducing organisms, we are also laying a peculiar claim to immortality. The reproduction of life becomes dependent on the creator, in this case a transnational corporation.

As we have already seen in the case of canola, capital and its culture make a variety of extreme claims for Intellectual Property Rights, or patenting. The ideology of patenting – or any other form of intellectual property protection – is that the granting of a patent (an exclusionary right - the enclosure of the patented object or idea) will encourage innovation by providing an incentive – a reward – to the inventor in the form of royalties or fees. That is the theory; but since a rapidly increasing number of scientists and researchers work for large corporations, or universities which function as corporations, the theory breaks down because the researcher is a salaried employee and the rewards – if not the prestige – go largely to the employer. Yet the researchers go on working.

Another of the traditional rationalizations for Intellectual Property Rights (IPR) is that inventors, researchers, artists, writers, and now computer programmers, deserve compensation for their labour and require rewards of sufficient magnitude to ensure their continued productivity. Of course this is true, but the same concern should be expressed for all cultural workers.

The real issue, then, is not personal but social; not whether a society should compensate its cultural workers, but how? Canada, among other countries, has a very significant history of publicly supported cultural work (the Canadian Broadcasting Corporation and the National Film Board, for example) as well as agricultural research, including the breeding and development of major Canadian crops such as wheat and canola. Without any sort of intellectual property protection, many scientists have spent their entire working lives in the public sphere producing variety after variety of crops. Their compensation has been in the form of salaries and public recognition, rather than in royalties. Their work has been based, until very recently, on the fullest possible sharing of information in every form, from genetic to agronomic and production information. The development of canola is an outstanding example of this.

As we have seen, however, public research is now being squeezed out of any independent existence by the corporate (private) sector that feels it now has the power, with the support of government, to assume full control. The public sector is assigned the role of carrying out the basic long-term research that cannot provide an economic return. This process is replicated in the plant as the corporate sector strives to drive out open-pollinated crop varieties that make it possible for primary producers to retain some control over their production processes.

For the culture of capital the real function of Intellectual Property Rights (IPR) is to achieve and maintain control of the development of technology. By means of patents, capital can ensure that only certain technologies are developed and used while others are not. As Andre Gorz expressed it,

Capitalism develops only those technologies which correspond to its logic and which are compatible with its continued domination. It eliminates those technologies which do not strengthen prevailing social relations, even where they are more rational with respect to stated objectives. Capitalist relations of production and exchange are already inscribed in the technologies which capitalism bequeaths to us.

Taking the logic one step further, not only can the desired technology be protected and, due to assured long-term monopoly profitability, drive alternative technologies out of the market, but the technology itself can be designed to determine both the product and the process of producing it. This becomes obvious when we look at the application of biotechnology, or just traditional plant breeding in the hands of capital, to microorganisms and plants. Plants can be designed to require irrigation, insecticides, fungicides, etc.. One need not go so far as to suggest, as many have, that a Monsanto or an ICI would produce seeds requiring, i.e., having a tolerance for, their own herbicide, but we have seen that Monsanto will create and disseminate a technology, like glyphosate resistance, for inclusion in every canola seed produced by every corporation.

The crucial issue is the relationship between labour and capital. Since the onset of the industrial revolution, progress has been defined as the substitution of capital for labour. While the obvious reason for this is to increase the return on capital – to capture a larger percentage of the return – there is also a second reason, and that is to increase control over the production process itself. One only needs to look at the development of agriculture in North America to see this. In the past forty years, the period of most rapid industrialization of agriculture, the production process in agriculture has been capitalized and the labour component of primary production radically diminished.

Within the larger framework of the whole food system, the overall labour component, however, has not been reduced: it has been shifted from the farm family to reappear as migrant labour; it has been shifted into the production of agricultural inputs and into processing, packaging and distributing; and it has been shifted to the Third World where the labour of subsistence agriculture is displaced with production for export. One result is that the total labour component of the food system (as a percentage of population) remains about the same, but because it now utilizes a lot of capital, the net result is considered modern. Another consequence is that labour that once supported communities in traditional and sustainable self-provisioning agriculture has now become a dependency in a system determined and controlled by capital.

The concurrent rise in the level of malnutrition and starvation, domestic and worldwide, indicates that the purpose of capitalization was not to increase the level of wellbeing of the public, and not even to actually increase productivity, but to increase control and the rate of return on capital. Now the return on capital is coming not so much from food production itself, but from agricultural inputs and from the transformation ("value-added") and distribution of agricultural product.[231]

Patenting, hybridization and other forms of ownership claimed and asserted over "intellectual property" are simply the latest means of extending monopoly control.

Chapter 14

THE SOCIAL CONSTRUCTION
OF SCIENCE AND TECHNOLOGY

> Since the beginning, Western science has been
> conceived as a way to harness nature for use.
> But it is true that much of the science that is
> produced at present is for accumulation and ex-
> change, not for use. . . Although science has
> developed historically as an adjunct to capital-
> ism and has incorporated the capitalist ideology
> implicitly and usually without question, this ide-
> ology need not be part of science.
>
> *Ruth Hubbard* [232]

I started to write the story of canola as an "objective" history of the
privatization of science and its product. That led to a critical examination
of the structures of the scientific undertaking and its uses of technology.
Now we need to move to the broader role and understanding of science
and technology.

The story of canola illustrates how science has become a project of
capital, designed to serve not the quest for understanding or public
good, but the further accumulation of capital and with it, control. If
there is, as Ruth Hubbard says, no science, only scientists, then it is perfectly reasonable to ask who they work for and what specific culture they
represent.

The researchers who created canola were white, male, Prairie-raised
and university-trained. Each of these categories left its imprint on their
science and on the product of both their science and technology. Their
successors continue the project, though in recent years the culture shaping the science has been more urban than Prairie and more deliberately
interested in the mechanisms of capital accumulation than farm welfare
and knowledge.

This description is not intended to denigrate the men who worked honestly and openly in their fields of interest to achieve the very significant transformation of rapeseed into canola. But the fact is that they themselves were mono-cultural and the science they practiced was regraded as the only science. Canada was white European, science was reductionist and positivist, and progress was measured by industrialization, advanced through the application of technology and capital. If there were any other world views contending for the name of science, they were successfully suppressed. For all practical purposes there was one culture, one science and one concept of technology. The native peoples, and whatever culture and knowledge they might have had in the eyes of the colonialists, had been successfully externalized or eliminated. The culture of industrial Europe and the science and knowledge of the Enlightenment were the definition of civilization and its ways of knowing.

The understanding of history that both gave rise to the power of this culture, and rationalized its excesses, was linear and progressive. The line of progress was perceived to be sloping relentlessly upward ("up", in this culture, being synonymous with "good"). When taken as an act of faith, this perspective leaves little room for discussion about alternatives. Monoculture takes the form of necessity and progress becomes technological determinism.

A critical perspective was, therefore, simply excluded. One does not question what is considered a normative and universal civilization any more than one goes to the doctor complaining that one has two arms and two legs.

The mythology of technological neutrality and historic necessity has been used to deflect all discussion about the culture that the technology actually represents "by employing a narrow, restrictive definition of what counts as technology" and then dismissing any unintended or negative consequences of the use of the technology to "factors external to 'the technology' rather than due to 'the technology' itself."[233] In addition to this technique of externalization, Anderson et. al. describe how the International Rice Research Institute, for example, made its agricultural program acceptable to those it was "helping", by reshaping their consciousness so that IRRI's specific procedures and programs would become perceived as natural and reasonable. "There had to be a transfer of IRRI's cultural norms as well as a transfer of technology." The strategy employed by IRRI was to focus all attention on "the product", that is, on the yields of High Response Varieties of rice, rather than on "the product's underlying relations and assumptions."[243]

This common, if not universal, practice on the part of the salesmen of industrial agriculture and its technology produces a situation in which if one does persist in raising questions about *any* particular technology, one is more apt than not to be accused of being "Luddite" and against *all* technology. Or one is accused of being against Progress, as if Progress was a moral category rather than an ideological term used to describe the continuation of a particular historic process, in this case, the development of technology for productivity enhancement and capital accumulation. As Langdon Winner aptly put it, "While it is widely admitted that the structures and processes of technology now constitute an important part of the human world, the request that this be opened up for political discussion is seen as an attempt to foul the nest."[235]

There is, of course, a certain reasonableness about the suspicion that anyone raising critical questions about particular technologies might also be questioning the whole logic of technology as it has been created by Western industrial culture, but even a fundamental critique does not necessarily imply or require a negative judgement or rejection of the specific technology being questioned. It's just that there ought to be time and space within which to evaluate possible consequences and to consider alternatives. One should be able to make the pragmatic suggestion that if a business monopoly is not in the public interest, perhaps a technological monopoly is not either. That such comment is not allowed or considered reinforces the observation that technological determinism is accepted, and that, in defense of power, ideology is preferred to practicality. How else can we explain the commitment of scientists to hybridization?

It is ironic, Sandra Harding comments, that "natural science, presented as the paradigm of critical, rational thinking, tries to suffocate just the kind of critical, rational thought about its own nature and projects that it insists we must exercise about every other social enterprise."[236]

In formulating a means for responding to this situation, Winner suggests the term "epistemological Luddism" to describe "a method of inquiry" whereby "structures of apparatus, technique, and organization would be, temporarily at least, disconnected and made unworkable in order to provide the opportunity to learn what they are doing for or to mankind."[237]

Critical thinking about science and technology has begun to challenge the dominant monoculture's interpretation of the nature of science and technology and how facts are made. In *The Social Construction of Technological Systems*, Bijker, Hughes & Pinch provide a number of historical examples of the social production of science and technology. Referring to the sociology of scientific knowledge, they offer a three stage explanation of how scientific fact and technology are created. In the first stage, which we can identify in the history of canola as the period during which the plant breeders were discovering the immense diversity of rape-seed and its characteristics, the interpretive flexibility of scientific find-ings is displayed. At this stage scientific findings are open to more than one interpretation, requiring the explanation of scientific developments to be shifted from the natural world to the social world. In other words, a social decision has to be made about which "facts" are to be accepted and whose agenda is to be pursued. In the case of rapeseed, it was a question of which characteristics to focus on and which to ignore (whether by intent or out of ignorance of their existence) and whether to focus on processing technology or seed breeding to achieve similar results.

This flexibility disappears in the second phase and "a scientific con-sensus as to what the 'truth' is in any particular instance usually emerges." "Social mechanisms that limit interpretive flexibility and thus allow scientific controversies to be terminated" come into play. This is the stage when the development of certain agreed upon characteristics was carried forward and "improvement" defined.[238] This phase might be linked to Leask's second wave when certain agronomic characteristics are settled on as desirable because they are compatible with the commit-ment to chemical agriculture. Biologist Ruth Hubbard supplies a differ-ent description of this stage of "fact" creation:

> Scientists do not just hold a mirror up to nature. They use some-thing more like a coarse sieve through which fall all the things they don't notice or take to be irrelevant. The intellectual labour of scientists consists of constructing a coherent picture of the world from what they sift out as noteworthy and significant.[240]

In the third stage these "closure mechanisms" are applied to the wider social-cultural milieu. For example, canola is defined as a means of producing specialty oils and with it comes the rise to dominance of transnational capital.

Using the example of the bicycle, the development of which came to rest for reasons not particularly scientific or technological, Bijker and Hughes point out that,

> Closure in technology involves the stabilization of an artifact and the "disappearance" of problems. To close a technological "controversy" one need not *solve* the problems in the common sense of that word. The key point is whether the relevant social groups *see* the problems as being solved. In technology, adver-tising can play an important role in shaping the meaning that a social group gives to an artifact. Thus, for instance, an attempt was made to "close" the "safety controversy" around the high-wheeler [bicycle] by simply claiming that the artifact was per-fectly safe.[241]

This process has been well illustrated by the presentation of recombinant Bovine Growth Hormone (rBGH), the synthetically produced analogue of a naturally occurring hormone which Monsanto took the lead in creating. In 1986 Monsanto and the contracted researchers at Cornell University claimed that this drug was able to increase milk production per cow by 40% with minimal additional cost and no ill effects on anyone or anything. The claims made for this synthetic Growth Hormone were, in fact, very similar to those that have been made for hybrid canola. And as with canola, the practical results have been in the 15% rather than 40% range and the trade-offs associated with adoption have been substantial.

In the case of rBGH, although no clinical studies have ever been carried out on the possible effects the use of rBGH might have on the consumers of dairy products, the "authorities" ostensibly responsible for food safety have, since 1985, assured everyone that the technology is perfectly safe. Their explanation and justification of FDA procedures, articulated explicitly in an article in *Science* magazine[242], is based on purely theoretical and largely ideological grounds. In addition, the primary author of the article in question, Judith Juskevich, was herself under contract to the U.S. Food and Drug Administration to deal with rBGH and at least one of the articles peer reviewers, Dale Bauman of Cornell, was a primary developer of rBGH under a contract with Monsanto. It is thus hard to accept their evaluation as objective. They can and do, however, speak with "authority" to settle debates as long as no one objects.

Hughes describes this process of settling contentious debates, such as the one over rBGH, as one in which, "over time, technological systems manage increasingly to incorporate environment into the system, thereby eliminating sources of uncertainty."[243] As a consequence, organizations rarely nurture a radical invention, "because radical inventions do not contribute to the growth of existing technological systems, which are presided over by, systematically linked to, and financially supported by larger entities."[244]

The process described by Hughes is also evident in the overall direction of canola research compared to the work of Leon Rubin on rapeseed processing technology, discussed in Chapter 10. The corporate sponsors of canola research and development are sticking to the biotechnology pathway because they have that under control. It is less risky than a radical alternative. They also have a mechanism, in the Canola Council, for exercising this control.

Referring again to the example of rBGH, it is obvious that this technology is the product of a certain form of economic organization just as much as it is the product of a clearly identifiable ideology, in this case the ideology of production agriculture. Thus the new technology, rBGH, is conceived as a means to extend the praxis of control and the ideology of the dominant organizations of production agriculture, among them Monsanto. Those who evaluate the technology and decide on its safety for target animals as well as humans are fully integrated into this structure of ideology and organization. The product is safe because they say so.

Those not sharing an *a priori* commitment to this structure (culture) are dismissed for resisting Progress, or, as David Baltimore expressed it, "This notion that there are things too dangerous to know is fundamentally anti-science and anti-progress. It is not a good representation of what the human spirit wants."[245]

Shortly after making this statement, Baltimore resigned from his job as president of Rockefeller University blaming the "personal toll" resulting from his extended battle against accusations of scientific fraud.[246] Opposition is simply not tolerated on the grounds of what can only be described as social Darwinism. Thus a "system of artifact, social group, and technological frame gains *technological momentum*."[247] [author's emphasis]

Whether we look at the case of rBGH or that of canola, it is clear that, as Bijker puts it, "a technological enterprise is simultaneously a social, an economic, and a political enterprise."[248] This is amply illustrated by the work of the Canola Council of Canada and its predecessor, or the functioning of the National Dairy Promotion and Research Board in the U.S. in its promotion of rBGH.

The purchase and use of any agricultural "technology", as agri-business likes to refer to its products, whether rBGH or a proprietary canola seed, "is mediated by the complex organizations that are required to integrate the knowledge and resources necessary to produce and distribute the artifact or service." Most of the time, however, the individual farmers who make use of such technologies, "do not deal with technological systems in their entirety."[249]

When a farmer buys certified or hybrid seed, such as canola, she is buying the product of 30 years of plant breeding carried out in a variety of separate institutions in a coordinated manner; the farmer is also, in a sense, buying both the system of propagation, which is both social and technical, and the system of distribution. Each of these steps contains elements of technology and structure held together by economic and social relations. But, more importantly, the farmer is buying a highly organized system of technology which expresses the interests and origins of a particular culture, including the very expensive advertising and marketing program of which the farmer is the victim.

Both recombinant Bovine Growth Hormone and low-linolenic or high-stearic acid canolas are technological expressions of a cultural agenda designed to serve the interests of corporate profit and capital accumulation. That does not mean that the culture and interests of Monsanto or Proctor & Gamble are necessarily shared by Canadian farmers – or anyone other than their shareholders and senior management, for that matter. That Calgene or Monsanto claims scientific breakthroughs with their discoveries of how to create specialty oils or herbicide-resistant canola does not give any moral or even scientific authority to these "breakthroughs." Their "construction" and possible adoption remain fundamentally social issues.

The purported neutrality of technology and altruism of science are recruited in the service of a wide variety of political and corporate agendas, international trade negotiations being one of them. The U.S. government is quick to refer to social and environmental concerns as "non-tariff trade barriers" which stand in the way of the free movement of goods, services and information (intellectual property). Concerns are labelled by the so-called free-traders unscientific and therefore unacceptable as restrictions to international commerce.

The European Community (EC) seems to agree with the U.S. on the basic criteria for evaluating new products of biotechnology: 1) efficaciousness; 2) safety for target population; and, 3) human safety. However, the EC is also, apparently, committed to a fourth criterion: social and economic impact, and the addition of this fourth criterion transforms the application of the other three from simple reductionism to a more holistic approach. The U.S., on the other hand, is deeply committed to the reductionist mode and insists that the fourth criterion is nothing but a non-tariff trade barrier – since social and economic issues are unscientific according to its definition of science.

It is interesting, then, that there is now a tendency on the part of the agro-toxin industry, and the regulators and trade negotiators operating on their behalf, to use the phrase "sound science" when they are trying to protect themselves from their critics. By making their distinction between "science" and "sound science", (they do not try to attack the content of the science of their critics), the users of the term "sound science" are, in effect, admitting the arbitrary, or culturally determined, character of scientific knowledge, and thereby destroying its claimed facticity. If there can be science and sound science, then there can also be blue science or green science. The social character of science is unavoidable.

In the case of the EC ban on the use or import of meat produced in any way with synthetic hormones, including milk produced by cows treated with rBGH, the Europeans have said, in effect: We do not want milk produced with rBGH, so why should we have to allow the drug to be available, and why should we have to allow food produced with the aid of synthetic hormones to be imported? We really don't care what you think of your technology. We see no need for it and don't want its product and don't want to be voluntary victims of its possible consequences. Your science does not impress us.

The response of the U.S., and the transnational corporations it represents, is that such obstructions are "non-tariff trade barriers" because they are not based on "sound science."

If one admits the European approach, then the issues of safety and efficaciousness become more complex. If the drug does not make an animal sick but does shorten its working life, is it "safe"? If the use of antibiotics is increased to combat the increased level of mastitis, can the probable residues of increased antibiotic use be ignored and is the product still safe for human consumption? If there are increased levels of Insulin-like Growth Factor (IGF-1) in the milk, is it still safe for human consumption? The reductionist argument may say Yes, while the holistic argument will say No.

In the case of canola, it is conceivable that the EC could say that it will not allow the introduction of glyphosate-tolerant seed because it does not want to encourage the use of such herbicides on the grounds that they encourage monoculture rather than diversified small-scale farming. There could even be an argument against the introduction of hybrid canola seed based on the negative social impact associated with dependency on transnational corporations.

Technological determinism is founded on the assumption, known as reductionism or positivism, that how things are organized is of no significance in understanding what they are. If organization makes no difference in explaining reality, then there is no need to analyze the functioning of organizations and corporations. They can remain invisible. The organization is simply treated as a technology in the same way that rBGH or herbicide resistance is treated as a technology. A corporation, like any other organism, is then analyzed through questions asked not about the functioning whole, but about the bits and pieces that suit the analyst, such as: Is the c.e.o. a nice man? How does the corporation treat its workers? Do its products work? Does it pollute? Questions of structure, power, and control are preempted by what Edward Goldsmith refers to as the Paradigm of Science:

Scientists try to make us believe that the world is made up of a multitude of discrete, mechanistic units, the way they are organized being of no consequence for understanding how they function – hence the inference is that they can be understood in isolation from the system of which they are a part, and at the same time they can be shifted about, changed and transformed at the whim of their human managers.[250]

Goldsmith adds, "The very notion of organization is in effect incompatible with the reductionist approach embodied in the Paradigm of Science", which may explain why the transnational corporations have been so successful in being "invisible."

Thus new technology is received, no questions asked about its source or the situation of those who created it, and then evaluated solely on the terms laid out for its use by its creators and their largely invisible sponsors. Questions about the intentions of the purveyors of the technology, and the potential consequences of being enlisted in its service, are, as described previously, precluded by focusing all attention on "the product" and all energy on its application. Instead of pondering whose agenda they are furthering by planting the canola seed that will yield a specialty oil, farmers are led to focus on obtaining the maximum yield from the crop.

Science, from this point of view, is about fact, which purports to represent a piece of material reality. As such, it is not open to any social interpretation and since this science has no subjectivity, any discussion of morals or values is irrelevant. Science is science, fact is fact. There is only one truth, science is the means to understanding that truth, and technology is the means of applying that understanding. The only social issues are those arising out of the consequences of adopting the new technologies and what to do with those who cannot or will not adopt or adapt.

In the case of rBGH, this means that no questions are asked about the interests of the drug companies developing this drug. No questions are asked about the need for this drug. No questions are asked about the cultural assumptions (gender, class, ethnicity) of the people creating the technology. No questions are asked about the consequences for the industry or the society of using the technology. Yet all of these questions are critical in evaluating the technology and its acceptability (the fourth, social, criterion).

An illusion that everyone has the same interests is also fostered by the reductionist approach. It assumes that there is no organization of significance. Dairy farmers, transnational chemical/drug companies, and the public are all presumed to share identical interests. This is obviously not the case. A corporation is in the dairy business to make money out of milk. The public consumes dairy products primarily for nutritional reasons and secondarily for entertainment, while the farmer wishes to make a living through farming and producing the basic ingredient for dairy products. It is not that the individuals involved in these activities see each other, or should see each other, as enemies; but the drug companies have got to get as much as they can for their drugs, the consumer wants wholesome and inexpensive food, and the farmer wants to make a reasonable living while treating the land and the livestock well. It is not apparent, in the case of rBGH for example, that human nutrition or the quality of milk will be improved, or that cows will live longer and enjoy better health and less stress, or that farmers will benefit in any way from the introduction of this technology. The only sure thing is that the drug companies will benefit through the manufacture and sale of this drug.

In the case of canola, one has to ask who will benefit from hybridization of the plant or its transformation into a producer of the specialty oils desired by transnational corporations like Proctor & Gamble or Pepsi-Cola? One also has to ask if canola with .05% erucic acid is really significantly better than canola with 1% or even 2% erucic acid. Just because something can be done does not mean that it should be done. But it may mean that a special interest wants us to believe that it must be done because progress is brought to us by science and technology. It is simply wise to ask if this is so, and to inquire as to whose special interests or corporate profits will be served by the adoption of this or that technology or its products.

Chapter 15

THE CONSTRUCTION
OF SOCIAL POLICY

Rape is always an exercise of power
and control.

This book has chronicled the changing character of power and control over rapeseed/canola as private interests have captured the public good. This corporate takeover was never the subject of public debate nor was it a deliberate social choice, though it can be described as a consequence of public policy: not policy publicly debated, but policy made by neglect on the one hand and vested interests and ideology on the other.

The policy, and the takeover, were not inevitable, as many would have us believe, but were the clear results of well organized efforts, whether in the area of science policy, research funding, technology transfer, regulation or "intellectual property rights." Behind this lay the ideological monoculture of reductionist, positivist science and a determinist faith in Progress.

Policy is the framework of values that expresses a vision or commitment; thus social policy should be the expression of the shared values of a society. As such, policy can be broad or narrow, and articulated or not, but it is still identifiable through analysis of the collective or public action of the society.

We have been accustomed to considering an elected government as the expression of such commonly held values, with public policy the outcome of organized public debate focused on the legislatures and concluding with legislation and allocation of resources that express the public will. Public confidence in this process is clearly waning, but in any case it never has never been the way agricultural policy has been made, at least in Canada.

There are, I suggest, at least seven elements that contribute to the formation of social (public) policy: the public (legislatures); public sector (government/university bureaucracy, including researchers); industry (corporate and industry-lobby); farmers; the idea of The Market; Science and Technology; and, access to information. As we have seen, each of these seven elements was involved in this history of canola.

In the years following WW II, when rapeseed was being transformed into canola, agricultural policy was basically made by those active in the public service, whether in the universities, public research institutions or government. The researchers related directly to the farmers on the one hand and to the domestic processors on the other.

Farmers' cooperatives, particularly the Saskatchewan Wheat Pool, played a role in the development of canola through their oilseed processing operations, but apparently had little influence on the direction of research. The only prominent corporate presence was Canada Packers (for many years Canada's largest food company), and while it certainly pursued its own interests, Canada Packers nevertheless participated in the development of canola not as a dominant power, but as one of many interested parties. In recent years, however, that corporation has undergone a transformation not unlike that of rapeseed itself. In 1990 Canada Packers was purchased from its Canadian owners by Hillsdown Holdings of Britain. The company that has emerged, Maple Leaf Foods Inc., is still Canada's largest food processor, but the boss is away in England.

If there was neither a dominant government bureaucracy nor a dominant corporation, neither was there any legislatively-arrived-at policy for oilseeds. Indeed, there was no such policy for agriculture in general, apart from the legislation establishing the Canadian Wheat Board and national transportation (i.e. railroad) policy (for example, The Crow).

Oilseeds policy was created, *de facto*, by the decisions of the researchers who were able to function in this way because the work they were doing was supported out of general provincial and federal funding for teaching and agricultural research, and was not dependent on grants for narrowly defined projects. Given the common culture and close relations between the plant breeders and the public they served, this may have added up to a more democratic process than any that might have been achieved through legislation, but the fact remains that there never was any public debate or, apparently, even any critical discussion, of different possibilities and alternatives.

The structures that have funded agricultural (and other) research in Canada have always been elitist and the policy documents from organizations like the Science Council have never emanated from genuinely public discussion. In fact, the public has tended to be regarded as ignorant and unable to understand the issues. The defenders and practitioners of the established process frequently refer with contempt to the "fear, ignorance and lack of knowledge" of the public and anyone who raises a question about science, technology or corporate control. While information may have moved freely amongst the decision-making elite, the public was expected to abide by the results with gratitude, or at least without complaint or question.

Rapeseed, and then canola seed, as well as their production and reproduction, were once completely in the public sphere. The returns on public investment were, like the costs, broadly shared. Consequently the issue of social policy appeared to be relatively unimportant. There were enough players, with enough information, for broader public interests to be reasonably well represented even in the absence of any formal structures or mechanisms for such representation. Without either "plant breeders' rights" or the possibility of patenting biological material, there were no legal reasons to restrict access to or the flow of information. (After 5:00 p.m. every door in the crop science building at the University of Guelph is locked. My faculty escort, as door after door was unlocked so I could retrieve my jacket from the office, explained that this was the consequence of intellectual property rights: a researcher had some seeds "stolen" and was sued for breach of contract by the corporation paying for the research.)

The climate of public effort for public good no longer exists. The current ideology, tersely expressed by Agriculture Canada's assistant deputy minister of research, is that, "A public good is what is not profitable."[251] It has become obvious that if there is to be any publicly determined social policy, other than one dealing with leftovers, it can no longer be left to government, or university and farm organization bureaucrats (the old boys' club). Despite the a.d.m.'s statement, it is simply a lie that "public servants have no decision-making power."[252] It is precisely public servants, acting on behalf of corporate interests on the one hand and neo-liberal Market Economics on the other, who work with elected politicians to make the pragmatic decisions that create public policy.

Unfortunately, farmers, apart from brief periods earlier in this century when there were farmer-labour provincial governments, have been a highly diffused and often confused voice due to individual isolation and the difficulty of making their lobby groups and commodity associations responsive to grass-roots concerns. As a result, farmer representation in the formation of agricultural policy, as opposed to farm-bureaucrat representation, is marginal.

The neo-liberal policy of turning public policy over to the corporate sector was clearly stated by Canada's science minister, speaking at the opening of the new $7.5 million research farm of the Shur-Gain division of Maple Leaf Foods. Mr. McKnight praised this corporate initiative and advised his listeners that the days of predominantly governmental initiatives in agricultural research were over, "Because governments don't know what to do with the research and development, industry does."

In spite of what the Minister says to corporate ears, for appearances' sake the pretence is maintained that public policy is a governmental matter, to be decided if not in the legislature, then at least in consultation with interested parties – as if food were nothing more than a "special interest". However, if anything marks the transformation of the food system and agricultural policy, including that of research, it is the rise of transnational corporations – such as Hillsdown Holdings, Cargill, Philip Morris/Kraft General Foods, Monsanto, etc. – to positions of dominance in every sector of the food system. Legislatures and sectoral-interest organizations like the Canola Council may like to think they are making policy, but they are probably deceiving themselves. It is the representatives of the TNCs who are in the best position to lean heavily on public structures and deputy ministers and their assistants, or to be the actual policy negotiators, as has happened in international trade negotiations. Canada still does have a Parliament, however, and it could be used for determining policy.

It is the myth of the neutrality and non-political character of science coupled with the myth of the inherently progressive character of technology that have made it possible for the transnational corporations to remain invisible as they have risen to positions of dominance.

While it may not be visible to the naked eye, corporate policy is also being embedded in the seed in three ways: in the genetic information that will produce a desired specialty oil; in biotechnology that renders the plant resistant to an herbicide; and in the purported heterosis of hybrid seed. In each instance, it is the transnational corporation that determines the agenda, an agenda subsequently reproduced by the seed itself.

Just as the agenda of capital accumulation gets embedded in the seed, so does the agenda of the science and technology that have created the seed, and thus of the creators of that science and technology. The myth of neutrality thus makes it possible for the seed itself to be referred to as both as a technology and as a means of technology transfer, or policy implementation, as in the following description of the seed as a kind of Trojan Horse: "A new seed variety, which already contains in a single package all the technology, is the best way to transfer technology."[253]

A more recent addition to the team of policy determinants is the idea of The Market as an autonomous force. As The Market has come to be ideologically defined by corporate interests and agricultural economists, social policy is limited to the service of the "invisible hand" guiding the economy. When the researchers began looking for an alternative crop for Prairie farmers, however, they were not operating under the ideological command to make Canada "globally competitive", nor were they looking primarily for an export crop that might improve Canada's balance of payments. Today, however, The Economy is defined in a way that precludes notions of self-sufficiency or at least self-reliance. The desire of Canada Packers for a secure domestic source of edible oil would today be ridiculed, just as would breeding seed for the domestic market alone.

The growing power of the corporation has brought with it a preoccupation with intellectual property rights and the exercise of control over all forms of information. The patenting of genetic material and life forms themselves is simply an extension of the accepted logic that ideas are private property, commodities to be marketed. Just as regulatory legislation is re-interpreted to cover transgenic plants, so patent legislation is extended far beyond the intentions of its initial creators to include the patenting of life forms.

If Monsanto obtains a patent on its glyphosate-resistance genetic material, and succeeds in convincing every seed company to incorporate this "technology" in its canola seed, then Monsanto gains effective control over canola. If Calgene succeeds in obtaining a patent on certain stearic oil characteristics, this will provide even greater return and control, since whatever oilseed plant incorporates these characteristics will be covered by Calgene's patent. In the U.S., the most aggressive jurisdiction in this matter, patents on characteristics such as Calgene's anti-sense technology have already been granted, though they are being challenged by others who claim infringement on their own work.

Two or three years ago Monsanto published an attractive full-colour, full-page ad titled "Farming: A Picture of the Future." The picture over which the language was superimposed was of the sort of farm one seldom sees any more, with sheep, of all creatures, in a paddock in front of a mixture of old and new barns, all in the traditional barn red, with concrete-stave silos out behind. Except for the sheep, I would describe it as a picture of a dairy farm of 20 years ago, the kind of farm one is apt to see abandoned in upper New York state or Wisconsin. Monsanto's text was, like the picture, reassuring: "Biotechnology will revolutionize farming . . . but it won't change the way things look. The products of biotechnology will be based on nature's own methods, making farming more efficient, more reliable, more environmentally friendly . . . Plants will be given the built-in ability to fend off insects and disease, and to resist stress."

We have seen (in Chapter 8) that this promise has not been kept. "The way things look" has already changed due, in no small part, to the efforts of companies like Monsanto. It is not stability in the crop or disease resistance that Monsanto has invested in, but herbicide tolerance, and the result, whether through biotechnology or not, has been to increase "productivity" and stress intolerance.

Monsanto's goal is profit maximization, and the social program it is pursuing is that of creating dependency, the dependency of crops and animals – and hence farmers – on Monsanto products. Ecological agriculture is not on their agenda unless it serves their purposes. Of course Monsanto is not alone; there are also Ciba-Geigy, Rhône Poulenc, ICI, BASF, Cargill and others.

An article published in the June 1992 issue of *Scientific American*, titled "Transgenic Crops", illustrates both the phenomenon of the social construction of science and the context of social policy formation. One of the two authors of the article, Robert T. Fraley, is currently vice president of technology for Monsanto in St. Louis, Missouri. The other author, Charles Gasser, worked with Fraley at Monsanto for five years before moving on to the University of California at Davis.

Their article starts off with the familiar argument that, "Modification of crop plants to improve their suitability for cultivation has persisted for at least 10,000 years. Early farmers produced better crops simply by saving the seeds of desirable plants." The next sentence devalues this historic process by saying that "plant breeding has become more rigorous in its approach." The word "rigorous" implies that what has been done traditionally is poor science, if science at all, as compared to current practices, which the authors then describe:

> By using recombinant DNA techniques, biologists can direct the movement of specific and useful segments of genetic material between unrelated organisms. This approach can add a significant degree of diversity to the total repertoire of traits from which the plant breeder can choose. In the laboratory plants can be made to withstand insects, viruses and herbicides.

The article continues with an unargued statement that, "Although genetic engineering is more complex than traditional plant breeding practices, it is just as safe." To support this claim, what is presumed to be an authoritative voice, the White House, is brought to bear on the matter, again with no empirical foundation:

> This past February the White House stated that genetically engineered products should not be subject to additional federal regulations, because they do not pose any unreasonable risk.

The authors provide, as a conclusion, what they and others consider to be the clincher for biotechnology: we have a moral responsibility to feed the world. This argument, often repeated by those committed to industrial agriculture, conveniently ignores the fact that it is "we" who have caused much of the world hunger problem, through western imperialism, industrial agriculture, and resource exploitation, in the first place.

World food production will have to increase threefold during the next 40 years to meet the needs of an estimated nine billion people. Biotechnology is one of the few new solutions to this problem. Another important advantage of the genetic engineering of plants is that it provides the very latest technology to farmers in a very traditional package – the seed. Even the most impoverished nations will thus have access to the benefits without the need for high-technology supplies or costly materials.[254]

In light of this self-serving rhetoric, it is interesting to note what is actually happening in Canada as reflected in transgenic plant trials.

Agriculture Canada's working definition of a transgenic plant is "an organism that is obtained by *in vitro* alteration of genetic material including, recombinant DNA, nuclear and organelle transplantation."[255] In more common language, transgenic plants are plants that contain, as a result of genetic manipulation, genetic material not normally found in that species.

The following table of transgenic plant field trials, supplied by Agriculture Canada, is described as "perhaps misleading in that it lists the information on who is conducting the trial, and may not accurately reflect the financial sponsorship of the trial. Trial applicants are not obligated to disclose funding sources to us."[256]

Field Trial Details, Canada:	1988	1989	1990	1991	1992
transgenic plant trials	5	19	36	53	205
transgenic canola trials	4	10	21	33	164
corporate sponsored	4	8	16	27	160
university sponsored	0	2	2	3	1
public sponsored	0	0	3	3	3
herbicide resistance	2	8	20	30	159
disease resistance	0	0	0	1	1
specialty oils	0	0	0	0	0
protein alteration	0	1	1	0	1
increased oil	0	0	0	0	1

Analysis of research currently underway around the world:

48% of work undertaken is aimed at the introduction of a gene giving resistance to a herbicide;

13% is aimed at a gene for giving resistance to a virus;

11% at a gene for resistance to insects or disease;

11% is devoted to evaluation of risk;

7% is aimed at creating male sterility;

5% at adapting the plant material to new growing conditions (drought-stress, for example);

5% at the improvement of nutritive value.[257]

It is obviously not disease resistance or genetic variability that is being pursued, whatever the corporate ads and government propaganda say.

As the private sector (primarily transnational corporations) has succeeded in capturing control over every aspect of the food system, the issue of control, and hence of public policy, has gained urgency. There is no means of public appeal to the board of directors of ICI Seeds or Monsanto or to their senior management. With the privatization of information, from trade secrets to patented genetic material, there is no means to determine how the corporate research agenda is to be shaped or implemented. As well, the relationship between costs and benefits is broken, with costs still largely borne by the public while the benefits are captured by private interests.

There are choices, and there are people who make the choices for us privately if we do not make them publicly. It is necessary, then, to create the means through which public policy for science and technology and for agriculture can be made. For public control to be real, and policy to actually be an expression of the public (social) interest, the determination of policy and the structures to implement that policy must be built from the ground up. There is no blueprint for this project. To offer one would be to replicate what I have argued against throughout this book.

The fact is, we don't need to see rapeseed simply as an oilseed plant. We could, for example, see it as a tasty and nutritious green. Nor do we need to see food in terms of corporate-sponsored biotechnology. We could begin to think – and work – in terms of locally-controlled, diversified and sustainable food systems.

ENDNOTES

NOTE: Proper names only with dates refer to interviews by the author, in most cases recorded. To avoid unnecessary annotation, quotes are referenced here when it is unclear in the text who the speaker is or when the statement was made. When numerous conversations were held with the same person, or when the date of the statement is irrelevant, the reference may be to the speaker only (eg. Beversdorf, Scott-Pearse). See Directory of Interviews for complete names and identification.

1. "A Winning Formula. . .", *New Scientist*, 4/7/92
2. Downey, 14/9/92
3. *Canada's Canola*, Canola Council of Canada, rev. 1991
4. Boulter, p.80
5. *Western Producer*, 26/3/92
6. McAnsh, James, "The First Six Years – 1967-1973", Rapeseed Association of Canada, 48pp, no date, p.7
7. ibid, p.14
8. MacGregor, 2/12/87
9. Daun, 28/9/90
10. Beversdorf, 24/3/92
11. *Canada's Canola*
12. Daun, 28/9/90
13. Buttel, Fred, in Goodman, Sorj & Wilkinson, *From Farming to Biotechnology*, Basil Blackwell, 1987 1989, pp. 49-50
14. Forbes, 16/10/89
15. More, 28/9/90
16. ibid.
17. ibid.
18. Daun, 28/9/90
19. More, 28/9/90
20. Broeska,27/9/90
21. Hubbard, Ruth, *The Politics of Women's Biology*, Rutgers, 1990, p.12
22. Downey in Kramer, J.K.G, F.D. Saur, W.J. Pigden, eds., *High and Low Erucic Acid Rapeseed Oils*, Academic Press 1983, p.2
23. *Canola Oil and Meal – Standards and Regulations*, Canola Council, 1990
24. Annual Report, Canola Council of Canada, 1990
25. Stefansson, 17/7/90
26. Craig, letter to the author, 7/2/90
27. Stefansson, 17/7/90

28. quoted by G. S. Boulter in Kramer, p. 67
29. Craig, 30/1/90
30. Downey, 19/7/90
31. Campbell, Wayne, "Rapeseed success story – Rise of a Prairie 'sun' flower", S/D, 1974/4
32. Craig, 30/1/90
33. *The Globe and Mail* 8/9/92
34. Craig, 30/1/90
35. Downey, 19/7/90
36. Stefansson, 17/7/90
37. Craig, 30/1/90
38. Daun, 28/9/90
39. Downey, 19/7/90
40. Rubin, 25/5/92
41. Teasdale, 25/5/92
42. ibid.
43. ibid.
44. ibid.
45. Rubin, 25/5/92
46. Stefansson in Kramer, p.154
47. Beare-Rogers, 15/6/92
48. ibid.
49. ibid.
50. *The Globe and Mail*, 22/1/87
51. Teasdale, 25/5/92
52. Pigden, 31/10/90
53. ibid.
54. Stefansson, 17/7/90
55. ibid.
56. McVetty, 26/9/90
57. McVetty, 24/7/92
58. ibid.
59. McVetty, 26/9/90
60. Arntfield, 26/9/90
61. Forhan, Mark: *Presentation to the Canola Council Annual Convention*, March 1992
62. ibid.
63. ibid.
64. Kennema, 19/11/90
65. McVetty, 24/7/92
66. Hubbard, p.16
67. in Kramer, p.155
68. in Kramer, p.156
69. "Implications", *AgDecision*, June 1990
70. *Research Highlights*, 1990
71. *Milling & Baking News*, (USA, weekly), 20/10/92
72. McVetty, 24/7/92
73. ibid.

74. Glick, 24/7/92
75. Beversdorf, 24/3/92
76. McVetty, 24/7/92
77. *Manitoba Cooperator*, 20/12/90
78. Beversdorf, 20/8/91
79. More, 3/10/91
80. Beversdorf (formal interviews and telephone conversations have been combined)
81. ibid.
82. ibid.
83. Craig, 30/1/90
84. Broeska, 27/8/90
85. *Oils & Fats International*, (England, quarterly), No. 2, 1991
86. Broeska, 17/9/92
87. Hamill, 6/3/92
88. Jaeger, M., "Likely Effect on Ontario Soybean Producers of the Shift in Location of a Soybean Crushing Plant from Toronto to Windsor", Economics Branch, Ontario Ministry of Agriculture and Food, 1979, p.11
89. *Western Producer*, 26/3/92
90. Sommerville, 26/5/92
91. author's notes on a presentation by a Japanese representative at American Oil Chemists Assoc. meeting, Toronto, 1992
92. Hayward, 7/10/91
93. ibid.
94. More, 3/10/91
95. Broeska, 17/9/92
96. Broeska, 3/10/91
97. *Western Producer*, 14/9/89
98. *Milling & Baking News*, 7/5/91, 14/1/92
99. More, 3/10/91
100. Leask, 15/6/92
101. ibid.
102. Leask, presentation summary, 3/92
103. *Research and Technical Information Highlights*, 1991
104. Canola Council, *9th Project Report*
105. Report of work of W.A.Keller, Plant Research Centre, Ottawa, in *Canola Research Summary*, 1986-90, Canola Council, 1990
106. *Western Producer*, 2/4/92
107. Hayward, 7/10/91
108. ibid.
109. "Seeds – Our Vision; Seeds – Our Heritage", ICI Seeds, A business unit of ICI Americas Inc. 1992
110. *Milling & Baking News*, 9/10/90
111. *Cultivar Seed Business*, 6/92
112. Hansen, 4/10/91 – subsequent quotes are from the same interview
113. *Biotechnology and Development Monitor*, (The Netherlands, quarterly), No 11, June 1992
114. Lisieczko, 2/6/92 – subsequent quotes are from the same interview

115. Scott-Pearse, 17/7/92
116. ibid.
117. Kennema, 19/11/90
118. information from SeCan Association, Ottawa
119. Roger Salquist, Calgene, quoted in *Comstock's*, June 1991
120. *ataglance*, Feb. 1992
121. *Comstock's*, June 1991
122. 1992 prospectus
123. prospectus 3/8/89
124. press release, 28/9/89
125. press release, 26/10/89
126. 1992 prospectus
127. press release, 12/8/91
128. press release, 30/8/89
129. press release, 30/7/90
130. press release, 26/11/90
131. press releases, 12/8/91, 15/11/91
132. press release, 22/4/92
133. *New Scientist*, 18/7/92
134. press release, 5/8/92
135. 1990 Annual Report
136. *ataglance*, Feb. 1992
137. 1992 prospectus
138. 1991 Annual Report
139. 1989 Annual Report
140. press release, 6/3/91
141. *Milling & Baking News*, 19/11/91, *Financial Times*, 11/1/91
142. press release, 27/6/91
143. press release, 16/9/91 – Calgene announced, 29/10/92, that it was forming a partnership with Cargill subsidiary Stevens Industries to process specialty canola for Calgene in southern Georgia, U.S.A.
144. press release, 20/7/92
145. press release, 22/9/92
146. press release, 16/5/91
147. press release, 22/1/92
148. Kemble, 22/4/92
149. ibid.
150. Beversdorf, 4/3/92
151. *Western Producer*, 6/11/86
152. "Business World," CBC, 13/2/86
153. 88/11/09
154. Magee, 9/4/92 – Magee has since left Allelix/Pioneer
155. Grant, 29/6/92
156. Pioneer press release, *Manitoba Cooperator*, 8/11/90
157. Grant, 29/6/92
158. Grant, 24/10/90
159. Grant, in *Seed World* (USA, monthly), 9/90
160. Grant, 24/10/90

161. Grant, 29/6/92

162. Grant, 24/10/90

163. ibid.

164. Magee, 9/4/92

165. "Research", Univ. of Guelph, Spring 1992

166. *The Globe and Mail*, 23/6/87

167. Magee, 9/4/92

168. Kemble, 22/4/92

169. ibid.

170. Magee, 9/4/92

171. IDRC Project Summary 91-1037

172. 1988 IDRC Project Summary

173. Anderson, Robert S., Edwin Levy, Barrie Morrison: *Rice Science and Development Politics - IRRI's Strategies and Asian Diversity 1950-1980*, Clarendon Press, Oxford, 1991, p.142

174. Rubin, "Protein Supply in a Divided World," 11/5/92

175. Rubin & Diosady, 25/5/92

176. Rubin, summary, 2/92

177. Harding, Sandra, *Whose Science? Whose Knowledge?*, Cornell, 1991, p.11

178. Robbelen, G., *Rapeseed in a Changing World: Plant Production Potential*, proceedings, GCIRC Congress, Saskatoon, 1991

179. Winner, Langdon, *Autonomous Technology*, MIT Press, 1977, p.125

180. Nabhan, p.75

181. Voss, 15/6/92

182. Kloppenburg, J. R.: *First the Seed - The Political Economy of Plant Biotechnology*, Cambridge Univ. Press, 1988, p.xii

183. Kloppenburg, p.281

184. Anderson, p.121

185. ibid., p.268

186. 4/7/92

187. Kramer

188. Scott-Pearse, 5/10/92

189. Anderson, p.300

190. Leask, "The Third Wave. . ."

191. McVetty, 24/7/92

192. Kloppenburg, p.68

193. Winner, 1977, p.97

194. Magee/Sippell, 9/4/92

195. Magee, 9/4/92

196. Anderson, p.370

197. Kloppenburg, p.135

198. Magee, 9/4/92

199. letter from Louise Duke, Chief, Variety Registration Office, Agriculture Canada, 18/9/92

200. Leask, 15/6/92

201. *Ontario Farmer*, 5/8/92

202. Don Ostergard, Report to Alberta Branch, CSGA, annual meeting, January, 1991

203. *Prophyta*, 6/92
204. *Seeds of Renewal*, Science Council of Canada Report 38, 1985, p.11
205. ibid., p.30
206. *CAST Report #110*, 9/86, "Genetic Engineering in Food and Agriculture"
207. Winner, Langdon, *The Whale and the Reactor*, Chicago, 1986 p.139
208. Hollebone, Jean, speaking to Canbiocon Conference, 19/9/89, transcripts published 5/91
209. Canbiocon 1991
210. Canbiocon 1991
211. Government of Canada, "Bio-Tech Regulations: A User's Guide, 1991"
212. "National Biotechnology Business Strategy: Capturing Competitive Advantage for Canada," 1991, p.3
213. ibid., p.35
214. Health Protection Branch of Health and Welfare Canada, "Information Letter: Novel Foods and Food Processes," 8/92
215. Sub-Group on Safety and Regulation of the Interdepartmental Committee on Biotechnology (ICB), 22/7/92
216. Hollebone, 21/8/92
217. ibid.
218. Winner, 1977, p.24
219. Rudy Platiel in *The Globe and Mail*, 30/12/91
220. see Cronon, Wm., *Changes in the Land – Indians, Colonists, and the Ecology of New England*, Hill & Wang, 1983
221. *Intellectual Property Rights in Biotechnology Worldwide*, S.A.Bent, R.S.Schwaab, D.G.Conlin, D.D. Jeffery, Stockton Press, 1987, pp. 129-142
222. Harding, Sandra, *The Science Question in Feminism*, Cornell, 1986, p. 16
223. Beversdorf, 24/3/92
224. Kloppenburg, Jack, in *Z Magazine*, Sept. 1990
225. Harding, 1991, p.12
226. Beversdorf, 24/3/92
227. Latour, Bruno, *Science in Action*, Harvard, 1987, p. 220
228. ibid., p.223
229. Rose, Steven, in Birke and Silvertown: *More than the Parts: Biology and Politics*, Pluto Press, 1984, pp 17-21
230. Rose, Steven, "Dialectical and Reductionist Biology" in *Rethinking Marxism*, Fall, 1989
231. see Goodman, D, Bernardo Sorj & John Wilkinson, *From Farming to Biotechnology*, Blackwell, 1987, for a discussion of substitutionism and appropriationism.
232. Hubbard, p.20
233. Anderson, p.4
234. Anderson, p.118
235. Winner, 1977, p.225
236. Harding, 1986, p.35
237. Winner, 1977, p.330
238. Bijker, W.B., T. Hughes, T. Pinch: *The Social Construction of Technological Systems*, MIT Press, 1989, p.27
240. Hubbard, p.51

241. Bijker, Hughes, & Pinch, p.44

242. *Science*, 24/8/90

243. Bijker, Hughes & Pinch, p.53

244. ibid., p.57

245. *US News & World Report*, 4/11/91

246. *New Scientist*, 7/12/91

247. Bijker, in Bijker, Hughes & Pinch, p.176

248. ibid., p.198

249. Constant in Bijker, Hughes & Pinch, p.231

250. Goldsmith, Edward, in *The Ecologist* (England, monthly), March/April 1990

251. Morrissey, Brian, at the University of Guelph, 5/10/92

252. ibid.

253. ibid.

254. *Scientific American*, June 1992

255. Duke, 18/9/92

256. ibid.

257. French Commission of Biomolecular Research, in *Circuits Europe*, Mai 1992

BIBLIOGRAPHY

Agriculture, Science and Technology

Anderson, Robert S., Edwin Levy, Barrie Morrison, *Rice Science and Development Politics - IRRI's Strategies and Asian Diversity 1950-1980*, Clarendon Press, Oxford, 1991

Belcher, Brian and Geoffrey Hawtin, *A Patent on Life - Ownership of Plant and Animal Research*, International Development Research Centre, Ottawa, 1991, 40pp.

Bent, Schwaab, Conlin, and Jeffery, *Intellectual Property Rights in Biotechnology Worldwide*, Stockton Press, 1987

Bijker, Wiebe E., Thomas Hughes, Trevor Pinch, *The Social Construction of Technological Systems*, MIT Press, 1989

Biotechnology's Bitter Harvest, A Report of the Biotechnology Working Group, 1990, 73pp.

Busch, Lawrence, W.B.Lacy, J.Burkhardt, L.R.Lacy, *Plants, Power, and Profit - Social, Economic, and Ethical Consequences of the New Biotechnologies*, Blackwell, 1991

Cronon, Wm., *Changes in the Land - Indians, Colonists, and the Ecology of New England*, Hill & Wang, 1983

Cronon, Wm., *Nature's Metropolis - Chicago and the Great West*, Norton, 1991

Fowler, Cary and Pat Mooney, *Shattering - Food, Politics, and the Loss of Genetic Diversity*, Univ. of Arizona Press, 1990

Goldsmith, Edward, "Evolution, Neo-Darwinism and the Paradigm of Science", pp. 67-73, *The Ecologist*, Vol. 20, No. 2, March/April 1990

Goodman, David, and Michael Redclift, eds., *The International Farm Crisis*, MacMillan, 1989

Goodman, David, Bernardo Sorj and John Wilkinson, *From Farming to Biotechnology*, Basil Blackwell, 1987

Harding, Sandra, *The Science Question in Feminism*, Cornell, 1986

Harding, Sandra, *Whose Science? Whose Knowledge?*, Cornell, 1991

Henderson, Kathryn, "Social Studies of Technical Work at the Crossroad" in *Science, Technology & Human Values*, Spring 1991

Hubbard, Ruth, *The Politics of Women's Biology*, Rutgers, 1990

Kloppenburg, J. R., *First the Seed - The Political Economy of Plant Biotechnology*, Cambridge Univ. Press, 1988

Latour, Bruno, *Science in Action*, Harvard, 1987

Levins, Richard, and Richard Lewontin, *The Dialectical Biologist*, Harvard University Press, 1985

Lewontin, R.C., Steven Rose and Leon Kamin, *Not In Our Genes - Biology, Ideology, and Human Nature*, Pantheon Books, 1984

Menzies, Heather, *Fast Forward and Out of Control*, MacMillan Canada, 1989,

Nabhan, Gary Paul, *Enduring Seeds - Native American Agriculture and Wild Plant Conservation*, North Point Press, 1989

Sachs, Wolfgang, ed., *The Development Dictionary - A guide to Knowledge as Power*, Zed, 1992

Winner, Langdon, *Autonomous Technology*, MIT Press, Cambridge, 1977

Winner, Langdon, *The Whale and the Reactor*, Chicago, 1986

Yoxen, Edward, *The Gene Business - Who Should Control Biology?* Harper and Row, New York, 1983

Rapeseed/Canola, Science Policy

Agriculture Canada: "Developing a Grains and Oilseeds Strategy, Part One", Ottawa, Aug. 1986

Agriculture Canada Research Branch, Saskatoon Research Station Research Highlights 1990

Bergh, Barbara, "The Canadian Oilseed Processing Sector, A Profile", Canadian Oilseed Processors Assoc., 1992, 10pp.

Campbell, Wayne, "Rise of a Prairie 'sun' flower", S/D 1975, 3pp.

Canbiocon Conference, 19/9/89, transcripts published 5/91

Canola Council of Canada, "Canada's Canola" 24pp, 1988

Canola Council of Canada, "Canola Digest", periodic

Canola Council of Canada, "Canola Oil - Properties and Performance", 1987, 50pp.

"Canola Marketing Task Force, Report of" - A report issued by the National Grains Bureau under the Grains 2000 program, Feb. 1991, 22pp.

CAST, "Herbicide-Resistant Crops" - Comments from CAST, Council for Agriculturtal Science and Technology (U.S), May 1991

CAST: "Past and Present Applications of Genetic Engineering to Agriculture" – Council for Agricultural Science and Technology, Report No. 110, Sept. 1986, in *Genetic Engineering in Food and Agriculture*

Craig, Burton, "Production and Utilization of Rapeseed in Canada", *Journal of the American Oil Chemists' Society*, Vol. 48 NO. 11, 1971

Department of Regional Industrial Expansion, Plant Products Division, "Canadian Oilseed Crushing Industry", Jan. 1986, 34pp.

Downey, K. & Robbelen, "Brassica Species" in Robbelen, Downey & Ashri, *Oil Crops of the World*, McGraw Hill, 1989

Guelph, University of, Department of Crop Science, Annual Reports 1989-1991

Health Protection Branch, Health & Welfare Canada: "Information Letter – Novel Foods and Novel Food Processes" IL 806, 5/8/92

International Development Research Centre (IDRC), Ottawa, *Project Summaries*, canola research in India and in China.

Jaeger, M., "Likely Effect on Ontario Soybean Producers of the Shift in Location of a Soybean Crushing Plant from Toronto to Windsor", Economics Branch, Ontario Ministry of Agriculture and Food, 1979

Knowles, P.F., "Genetics and Breeding of Oil Crops" in Robbelen, Downey & Ashri, *Oil Crops of the World*, McGraw Hill, 1989

Kramer, J.K.G, F.D. Saur, W.J. Pigden, W.J., eds., *High and Low Erucic Acid Rapeseed Oils*, Academic Press 1983

McAnsh, James, *The First Six Years – 1967-1973*, 48pp., Rapeseed Association of Canada, no date

McNamara, J.D., "A Review of the Canadian Oilseed Crushing Industry" Jan. 1987, 13pp.

National Biotechnology Advisory Committee, National Biotechnology Business Strategy, "Capturing Competitive Advantage for Canada", Fifth Report, 1991

National Research Council, "The National Research Council Biotechnology Program", Ottawa, no date

National Research Council, "Canola, the story of how one plant challenged two generations of prairie scientists", 1992 (manuscript)

"Potential for exports of Canadian canola to the United States" – A report issued by the National Grains Bureau under the Grains 2000 program, March 1990, 73pp.

Rapeseed in a Changing World, CGIRC, Saskatoon, July 1991, proceedings (7 vols.)

Rubin, Leon J., "Protein Supply in a Divided World", for the 20th International Society for Fat Research World Congress, Toronto, 5/92 (paper)

Rubin, Leon J., "Summary, Methanol-ammonia-hexane processing of canola and related oilseeds" 2/92 (paper)

Saskatchewan Wheat Pool, *The Story of Rapeseed in Western Canada*, 40pp., 1974

Science Council of Canada: "Seeds of Renewal: Biotechnology and Canada's Resource Industries", Report No. 38, Ottawa, 1985

Science Council of Canada Report: *Regulating the Regulators – Science, Values and Decisions*, Ottawa, 1982, 106pp.

NOTE: There is little literature on rapeseed/canola outside of brief specialized technical articles and research reports. In the computerized catalogue of the University of Guelph library there are 37 entries under "canola" and "rapeseed."

One document, written in the early 1980s and referred to as a corporate history of CSP Foods, seems to have disappeared altogether. Similarly, the corporate records of Canada Packers seem to have either disappeared or been destroyed in the takeover by Hillsdown Holdings.

INTERVIEWS

Arntfield, Sue, Food Science, Univ. of Manitoba, 26/9/90

Beare-Rogers, Joyce, Food and Drug Directorate, Health and Welfare Canada (ret.) 15/6/92

Beaussart, Mary, project officer, IDRC, Ottawa, 30/10/90, 15/6/92

Beversdorf, W.D., Department of Crop Science, Univ. of Guelph, 7/90, 20/8/91, 24/3/92, numerous phone conversations

Brandenburg, Fred, secretary-manager, Soybean Growers Marketing Board, Chatham, 15/7/92

Broeska, Robert, Executive Director, Canola Crushers of Western Canada, 27/9/90, 3/10/91, 21/7/92

Craig, Burton, Saskatoon, (ret.) 30/1/90

Daun, J.K., Head, Oilseeds Chemistry, Canadian Grain Commission, Winnipeg, 28/9/90

Diosady, Levent L., Prof. of Food Engineering, Univ. of Toronto, 25/5/92

Downey, Keith, Agriculture Canada Research Station, Saskatoon, 30/1/90, 19/7/90, 15/3/91

Glick, Harvey, research and product development director, the agriculture group, Monsanto, Winnipeg, 24/7/92

Grant, Ian, director, canola research, Allelix Crop Technologies/Pioneer Hi-Bred International, Georgetown, Ont., 24/10/90, 29/6/92

Hallock, Rick, CSP Foods, Winnipeg, 27/9/90

Hamill, E.C. (Ted), product development environmental assurance superintendent, Central Soya of Canada Ltd., Hamilton, 6/3/92

Hansen, David, manager, ICI Seeds, Winnipeg, 4/10/91, 24/7/92

Hayashi, Shigeo, manager, Grain and Provisions Division, C.Itoh, Vancouver, 29/11/90

Itoh, Shigeki, manager, Grains Department, Mitsubishi Canada, Vancouver, 29/11/90

Kemble, Roger, technology director, Allelix Crop Technologies, 22/4/92

Kennema, Kees, King Agro, Listowell, Ont., 19/11/90

Leask, William, executive vice-president, Canadian Seed Trade Association, 15/6/92

Magee, Bruce, Allelix Crop Technologies/Pioneer Hi-Bred International, Mississauga, Ont., 9/4/92

McHughen, Alan, plant ecology, Univ. of Saskatchewan, Saskatoon, 21/7/90

McVetty, Peter, plant science, University of Manitoba, 26/9/90, 24/7/92

More, Dwight, president, Canola Council of Canada, Winnipeg, 28/9/90, 3/10/91, 21/7/92

Pigden, Wallace J., Ottawa, 31/10/90

Rubin, Leon, Prof. of Food Engineering, Univ. of Toronto, 25/5/92

Stefansson, Baldur, Winnipeg, (ret.), 17/7/90

Scarth, Rachel, Plant Science, Univ. of Manitoba, 18/7/90

Scott-Pearse, Frank, Director of Research, King Agro, Chatham, 17/7/92, 5/10/92

Simpson, Graham, Plant Ecology, U. of Saskatchewan, Saskatoon, 19/7/90

Sippell, David, Allelix Crop Technologies/Pioneer Hi-Bred International, Mississauga, Ont., 9/4/92

Teasdale, B.F. (Bart), chemist, Canada Packers (ret.), 19/5/92

Voss, Joachim, director, sustainable production systems program, IDRC, Ottawa, 15/6/92

INDEX